SCAND

10663391

PHRASEBOOK

Scandinavian phrasebook
3rd edition – February 2001
First published – December 1992

Published by
Lonely Planet Publications Pty Ltd ABN 36 005 607 983
90 Maribyrnong St, Footscray, Victoria 3011, Australia

Lonely Planet Offices
Australia Locked Bag 1, Footscray, Victoria 3011
USA 150 Linden St, Oakland CA 94607
UK 10a Spring Place, London NW5 3BH
France 1 rue du Dahomey, 75011 Paris

Cover illustration
A horse is a horse, of course of course by Patrick Marris

ISBN 1 86450 225 8

text © Lonely Planet Publications 2001
cover illustration © Lonely Planet 2001

Printed by The Bookmaker International Ltd
Printed in China

All rights reserved. No part of this publication may be reproduced, stored in a retrieval system or transmitted in any form by any means, electronic, mechanical, photocopying, recording or otherwise, except brief extracts for the purpose of review, without the written permission of the publisher and copyright owner.

LONELY PLANET and the Lonely Planet logo are trademarks of Lonely Planet Publications Pty. Ltd.

439.5
Sca 6

About the Authors

Birgitte Hou Olsen updated the Danish chapter, based on a chapter by Peter A. Crozier.

Bergljót av Skardi wrote the Faroese chapter. She is 50 years old and teaches Faroese and English at the high school in her home town Tórshavn in the Faroe Islands.

Gerald Porter updated the Finnish chapter, based on an original chapter by Markus Lehtipuu. He's English but has lived in Finland for many years. He is at present lecturing in the English department at the University of Vaasa.

Icelandic was updated by Margrét Eggertsdóttir, based on a chapter by Ingibjörg Árnadóttir. Margrét was born in Reykjavik in 1960. At present she is a lecturer in Icelandic language and literature at the University of Copenhagen.

The Norwegian chapter was updated by Runa Eilertsen and Daniel Cash. Daniel is Australian but has lived in Norway. He currently works for a Melbourne-based newspaper. Runa is a native-born Norwegian who lives in Oslo. This chapter was developed from an original chapter by Doekes Lulofs.

Anna Herbst updated the Swedish chapter, based on an original chapter by Pär Sörme. Anna is Swedish but has lived in Australia since 1986. She has taught English and Swedish language and literature in secondary school, adult education and university in Sweden and Australia, and English and media subjects at university in China. She has also worked in broadcasting and once made a living as a folksinger.

From the Authors

Birgitte Hou Olsen wishes to thank Karin Vidstrup Monk from Lonely Planet for a creative and fruitful working relationship during the entire process.

Bergljót av Skardi wishes to thank her colleague Guðrun Gaard for passing the phrasebook job on to her. Also a big thank you to Hans Marius Johannessen for suggestions and advice.

Gerald Porter wants to record his thanks to Sirkku Aaltonen for love and constant guidance.

WEST BEND LIBRARY

Margrét Eggertsdóttir would like to thank Professor Robert Cook at the University of Iceland for his contribution to the chapter on body language, showing his clear insight into what characterises the Icelanders.

Runa Eilertsen would like to thank Daniel Cash.

Anna Herbst would like to thank Dino Bressan for being most helpful in allowing her to test the phonetic transcriptions on him.

From the Publisher

Thanks go to Christian Becker-Christensen and Jan Katlev for their invaluable linguistic advice and also to Wenche Eriksen and Natasha Sayer for their assistance on the Norwegian chapter.

Patrick Marris illustrated the book and the cover and still managed to find the time to help Yukiyoshi Kamimura lay out some of the chapters. Fabrice Rocher supervised layout. Karin Vidstrup Monk edited, proofed and oversaw the whole process. Emma Koch edited, Fleur Goding proofed and Natasha Velleley produced the map.

CONTENTS

INTRODUCTION 9

Map 10
Pronunciation Guide 13

DANISH 17

Pronunciation 18
Greetings & Civilities 19
Small Talk 20
Breaking the Language Barrier 25
Body Language 26
Paperwork 27
Getting Around 27
Accommodation 36
Around Town 41
Interests & Entertainment 44
In the Country 49
Food 50
At the Market 58
Shopping 60
Health 65
Time & Dates 69
Numbers & Amounts 71
Abbreviations 73
Emergencies 75

FAROESE 79

Pronunciation 79
Greetings & Civilities 81
Small Talk 83
Breaking the Language Barrier 88
Body Language 88
Paperwork 89
Getting Around 90
Accommodation 97
Around Town 101
Interests & Entertainment 104
In the Country 107
Food 109
Shopping 114
Health 119
Time & Dates 122
Numbers & Amounts 125
Abbreviations 126
Emergencies 127

FINNISH 131

Pronunciation 132
Greetings & Civilities 134
Small Talk 135
Breaking the Language Barrier ... 140
Body Language 141
Paperwork 142
Getting Around 143
Accommodation 151
Around Town 157
Interests & Entertainment 161
In the Country 164
Food 166
At the Market 174
Shopping 176
Health 183
Time & Dates 187
Numbers & Amounts ... 189
Abbreviations 191
Emergencies 192

ICELANDIC 197

Pronunciation 198
Greetings & Civilities .. 199
Small Talk 200
Breaking the Language Barrier ... 204
Body Language 205
Paperwork 206
Getting Around 206
Accommodation 211
Around Town 215
Interests & Entertainment 218
In the Country 221
Food 222
Shopping 228
Health 232
Time & Dates 235
Numbers & Amounts ... 237
Abbreviations 238
Emergencies 239

NORWEGIAN 243

Pronunciation 244
Greetings & Civilities .. 245
Small Talk 246
Breaking the Language Barrier ... 250
Body Language 252
Paperwork 252
Getting Around 253
Accommodation 261
Around Town 266

Interests & Entertainment 270
In the Country 273
Food 275
At the Market 286
Shopping 288
Health 294
Time & Dates 297
Numbers & Amounts 299
Abbreviations 301
Emergencies 302

SWEDISH 307

Pronunciation 308
Greetings & Civilities 310
Small Talk 311
Breaking the Language Barrier ... 316
Body Language 317
Paperwork 318
Getting Around 318
Accommodation 326
Around Town 331
Interests & Entertainment 334
In the Country 340
Food 341
Shopping 354
At the Market 356
Health 362
Time & Dates 366
Numbers & Amounts ... 368
Abbreviations 370
Emergencies 371

INTRODUCTION

Although it's not widely known outside Europe, the term 'Scandinavia' actually refers only to Denmark, Norway and Sweden while 'the Nordic countries' include Scandinavia plus Finland, Iceland and the Faroe Islands. This phrasebook covers all six languages and is thus really two in one: a Scandinavian phrasebook and a Nordic phrasebook!

To add to the confusion, five of the six languages – Danish, Swedish, Norwegian, Icelandic and Faroese – are referred to as the Scandinavian languages and they all form the northern branch of the Germanic languages tree. Finnish is the exception, being from a different family tree altogether. The Scandinavian languages have all descended from Old Norse, the language of the Vikings, while Finnish is related to Estonian and (more remotely) Hungarian.

However, luckily for English-speakers, these five languages are cousins of English and you'll be able to recognise quite a few words, eg, **dør/dör** for 'door' and **hus/hús** for 'house'. One big advantage of Danish, Swedish, Norwegian, Faroese and Icelandic being so closely related is that once you've got the hang of one language, the others should seem quite familiar.

This book provides the basics for you to get around while making the most of all the Nordic countries have to offer. English is spoken very widely (and very well!) throughout these countries but if you take the time to learn at least a few phrases in the local language you'll find that you're more than rewarded for your efforts.

SCANDINAVIAN & NORDIC

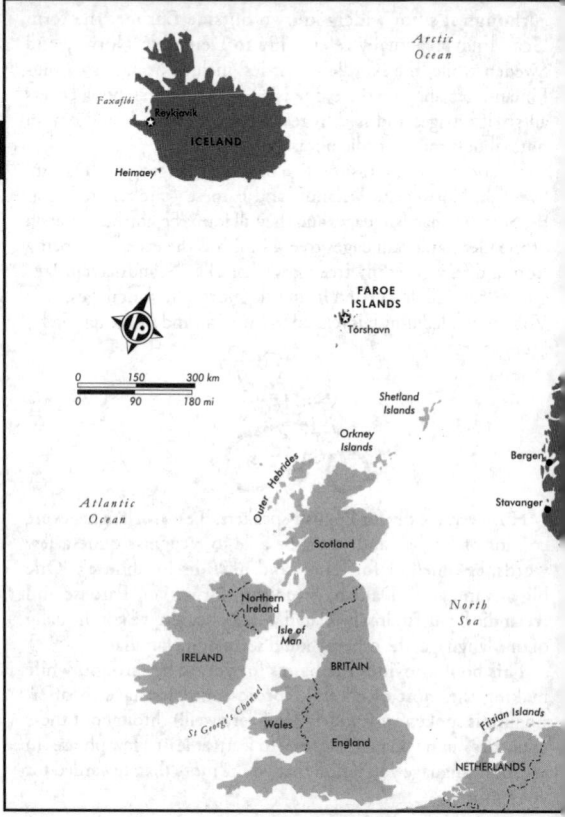

EUROPE

Barents Sea
Ladoga Lakes
Norwegian Sea
Oulu
FINLAND
Trondheim
SWEDEN
Gulf of Bothnia
Tampere
NORWAY
Turku
Helsinki
Oslo
Gulf of Finland
Åland
RUSSIAN FEDERATION
Stockholm
ESTONIA
Skagerrak
Gothenburg
Gulf of Riga
Gotland
Jutland
LATVIA
DENMARK
Öland
Helsingborg
Copenhagen
Malmö
Baltic Sea
LITHUANIA
Zealand
Fünen
Bornholm
RUSSIAN FEDERATION
BELARUS
GERMANY
POLAND

HOW TO USE THIS PHRASEBOOK

Transliterations

Simplified transliterations have been provided in blue throughout this book. Italic is used to indicate where to place stress in a word.

Polite Forms

When a language has polite and informal forms of the singular pronoun 'you', the polite form has been used in most cases. However, you'll come across the informal form of 'you' in some phrases, such as those for talking with children.

Arthur or Martha?

When there are both feminine and masculine forms of a word, it's indicated in either of two ways, with the feminine form always appearing first:

- with a slash separating the feminine form and masculine ending (which is added to the feminine form) of a word:

hot	**hait/-oor**	*heit/-ur* (f/m)

- when the distinction between masculine and feminine is more complex, each word is given in full, separated with a slash:

cold	**kerld/kuhld-oor**	*køld/kaldur* (f/m)

These distinctions occur mostly in Faroese and Icelandic, but you may see them pop up in the other languages from time to time.

Finally

Don't be concerned if you feel you can't memorise words. You'll find the most essential words and phrases in the Quick Reference section at the start of each chapter. You could also try tagging a few pages for other key phrases.

ABBREVIATIONS USED IN THIS BOOK

col	colloquial	n	neuter
f	feminine	pl	plural
inf	informal	pol	polite
m	masculine	sg	singular

PRONUNCIATION GUIDE

Below is a general pronunciation guide of the sounds that are common to the languages in this book, outlining in **blue** our representation of each sound, used in the simplified transliterations throughout the book. In addition, each language chapter contains a section about pronunciation particular to that language. It's a good idea to have a look at this as well, as it explains any sounds that might be slightly different in that language, or not found in any of the other languages.

Vowels

ah	as the 'a' in 'father'
uh	as the 'u' in 'cut'
a	as the 'a' in 'act'
eh	as the 'e' in 'bet'
ee	as the 'ee' in 'seethe'
i	as the 'i' in 'hit'
ü	a bit like the 'e' in British English 'dew' – try pursing your lips and saying 'ee'
o	a short 'o' as in 'pot'
oh	as the 'o' in 'note'
oo	a long 'oo' as in 'cool'
u	a short 'oo' as in 'foot'
ö	as the 'e' in 'summer'
or	as the 'or' in 'for', with less emphasis on the 'r'
er	as the 'er' in 'fern' but shorter, without the 'r'

Diphthongs

ae	as the 'ea' in 'bear'
ay	as the 'ay' in 'day'
ai	as the sound of 'eye'
oy	the 'oy' as in 'toy'
ow	as the 'ou' in 'out'

Semiconsonants

w	as in 'wet'
y	as in 'yet'

Consonants

g	always a hard 'g' as in 'get', never as in 'gentle'
s	always as in 'kiss', never as in 'treasure'
sh	as in 'ship'
ch	as in 'chew'
dj	as the 'j' in 'jaw'
th	as the 'th' in 'lather'
h	as the 'h' in 'horse'
ng	as in 'sing'
ngn	as the meeting of sounds in 'hang-nail'
rr	a trilled 'r'
rt	as the 'rt' in American English 'start'
rd	as the 'rd' in American English 'weird'
rn	as the 'rn' in American English 'earn'
rl	as the 'rl' in American English 'earl'
dn	as the 'dn' in 'hadn't'
dl	as the 'dl' in 'saddle'

All other consonants are pronounced as in English.

DANISH

QUICK REFERENCE

Hello.	hai/ghor-*da*	*Hej/Goddag.* (inf/pol)
Goodbye.	hai hai/fah-*vehl*	*Hej hej/Farvel.* (inf/pol)
Yes./No.	ya/nai	*Ja./Nej.*
Excuse me.	*ān*-sgül	*Undskyld.*
Sorry.	*ān*-sgül/bi-*kla*-ah	*Undskyld/Beklager.*
Thank you.	tahg	*Tak.*
That's fine.	di ehŕ ee *oŕ*-dehn.	*Det er i orden.*
You're welcome.	sehl tahg	*Selv tak.*
I'd like a ...	yai vi *gehŕ*-neh ha en ...	*Jeg vil gerne have en...*
one-way ticket	*ehng*-gild-bi-lehd	*enkeltbillet*
return ticket	ŕeh-*toor*-bi-lehd	*returbillet*

DANISH

I (don't) understand.
yai fo-*sdor* (ig) — *Jeg forstår (ikke).*

Do you speak English?
ta-lah dee *ehng*-ehlsg? — *Taler De engelsk?* (pol)

Where is ...?
vor ehŕ ...? — *Hvor er ...?*

Go straight ahead.
gä *li*-eh ooth — *Gå lige ud.*

Turn left/right.
dŕai ti *vehns*-dŕah/ *hoy*-yah. — *Drej til venstre/ højre.*

Do you have any rooms available?
hah ee *lith*-ee *vehŕl*-sah? — *Har I ledige værelser?*

I'm looking for a public toilet.
yai *li*-thah *ehŕ*-dah id *o*-fehnd-leed toy-*lehd* — *Jeg leder efter et offentligt toilet.*

1	in	*en*	6	sehgs	*seks*
2	tor	*to*	7	sü-w	*syv*
3	tŕeh	*tre*	8	*ä*-deh	*otte*
4	feeŕ	*fire*	9	nee	*ni*
5	fehm	*fem*	10	tee	*ti*

DANISH

Danish belongs to the North Germanic language group, together with Swedish, Norwegian, Icelandic and Faeroese.

Consequently, written Danish bears a strong resemblance to these languages. Spoken Danish, on the other hand, has evolved in a different direction, introducing sounds and pronunciation not found elsewhere.

Danish has a polite form of address, using the personal pronouns **De** and **Dem**. The words and phrases in this chapter are mostly in the familar form using **du** and **dig**, except where it's more appropriate to use the formal form. In general, use the formal form when speaking to senior citizens and officials, and the familiar form the rest of the time.

As Danish is not broadly spoken and few visitors take the time or effort to learn it, most Danes speak English. However, an effort to learn at least the basics is well received. It's a good idea to memorise the words for 'thank you', 'goodbye', 'hello' and 'I'm sorry'. This minimum effort will be appreciated, and with an increased command of the language you'll be rewarded by gaining a greater insight into Denmark and the Danes.

The pronunciation of each word and phrase in this chapter is transcribed using a simplified phonetic system, so with not too much effort it should be possible to grasp the basic sentence structure and begin creating your own sentences.

PRIMARY STRESS

In Danish the stress is usually placed on the first syllable, or on the first letter of the word.

PRONUNCIATION

Danish varies from island to island as well as from north to south, with each region having its distinct dialect. The translation and pronunciation presented here follows the form of Danish known as **Nudansk**, (literally 'Now Danish'). This is the form of Danish spoken in Copenhagen, and understood throughout the country.

Stressed syllables in multi-syllable words are printed here in italic type, and longer syllables have been split into more manageable lengths.

Danes do not necessarily pronounce what they write. The pronunciation of letters varies depending on the word, and written vowels and/or consonants will sometimes 'disappear' completely in the pronunciation. Unfortunately there are no hard and fast rules as to how any given letter is to be pronounced. In general, the best advice for good pronunciation is to listen and learn. Good luck!

Danish varies from the general pronunciation guide, given at the front of this book, in only two respects:

Vowels

DANISH	GUIDE	SOUNDS
u(n), *å*, *o*	ā	a long rounded 'a' as in 'walk'

Consonants

r	ŕ	rolled in the throat

PRONOUNS

SG			PL		
I	yai	*jeg*	we	vee	*vi*
you	doo	*du*	you (pl)	ee	*I*
he	han	*han*	they	dee	*de*
she	hoon	*hun*			
it	dehn (di)	*den (det)*			

GREETINGS & CIVILITIES

Useful Phrases

Hello.
hai/daow/ghor-*da* — *Hej/Dav/Goddag.* (inf/pol)

Goodbye.
hai hai/fah-*vehl* — *Hej hej/Farvel.* (inf/pol)

Yes./No.
ya/nai — *Ja./Nej.*

Excuse me.
***ān*-sgül** — *Undskyld.*

May I? Do you mind?
mā yai? *ti*-la-thah dee? — *Må jeg? Tillader De?* (pol)

Sorry. (excuse me, forgive me)
***ān*-sgül/bi-*kla*-ah** — *Undskyld/Beklager.*

Thank you.
tahg — *Tak.*

Many thanks.
***mahng*-eh tahg** — *Mange tak.*

That's fine. You're welcome.
di ehŕ ee *oŕ*-dehn. sehl tahg — *Det er i orden. Selv tak.*

Greetings

Good morning.
gor *morn* — *God morgen.*

Good afternoon.
gor *ehf*-dah-mi-da — *God eftermiddag.*

Good evening/night.
gor-*ahf*-dehn/go-*nad* — *Godaften./Godnat.*

How are you?
voŕ-*dan* gor di? — *Hvordan går det?*

Well, thanks.
god tahg — *Godt, tak.*

Forms of Address

Madam/Mrs	fŕoo	*fru*
Sir/Mr	hehŕ	*herr (hr.)*
Miss	*fŕer*-gehn	*frøken*
companion	kahm-ah-*ŕahd*	*kammerat*
friend	vehn	*ven*

SMALL TALK

Meeting People

What is your name?
va *hi*-thah doo/dee? — *Hvad hedder du/De?* (inf/pol)

My name is ...
mid naown ehŕ ... — *Mit navn er ...*

I'd like to introduce you to ...
yai vi *gehŕ*-neh pŕehsehn-*ti*-ah dai for ... — *Jeg vil gerne præsentere dig for ...*

I'm pleased to meet you.
di ehŕ *hüg*-lid ad *tŕah*-feh dehm/*mer*-theh dai — *Det er hyggeligt at træffe Dem/møde dig.* (pol/inf)

Nationalities

Where are you from?
vor *kom*-ah doo *frah*? — *Hvor kommer du fra?*

I'm from ...	yai ehŕ fŕah ...	*Jeg er fra ...*
Australia	aow-*sdŕahl*-yehn	*Australien*
Canada	*ka*-na-da	*Kanada*
Denmark	*dan*-mahg	*Danmark*
England	*ehng*-lan	*England*
Ireland	*eeŕ*-lan	*Irland*
New Zealand	nü *si*-lan	*New Zealand*
Scotland	*sgod*-lan	*Skotland*
the USA	oo ehs a	*USA*
Wales	*wa*-ehls	*Wales*

Age

How old are you?
vor *gah*-mehl ehŕ doo? *Hvor gammel er du?*

I'm ... years old.
yai ehŕ ... or *gah*-mehl *Jeg er ... år gammel.*

Occupations

What do you do?	va *la*-wah doo?	*Hvad laver du?*
I'm (a/an) ...;	yai ehŕ ...;	*Jeg er ...;*
I work as (a/an) ...	yai *ah*-bai-dah som ...	*Jeg arbejder som ...*
artist	*kānsd*-nah	*kunstner*
business person	fo-*ŕahd*-nings-dŕeeoo-neh	*forretnings-drivende*
doctor	*leh*-eh	*læge*
engineer	ing-shin-*yer*	*ingeniør*
farmer	*bā*-neh	*bonde*
journalist	shā-na-*lisd*	*journalist*
lawyer	ath-vor-*kad*	*advokat*
manual worker	*ah*-bai-dah	*arbejder*
mechanic	mi-*ka*-ni-gah	*mekaniker*
nurse	*sü*-eh-plai-yah-skeh	*sygeplejerske*
office worker	kon-*toor*-ah-bai-dah	*kontorarbejder*
scientist	*fors*-gah	*forsker*
student	sdoo-*di*-ah-neh	*studerende*
teacher	*lehŕ*-ah	*lærer*
waiter	*cheh*-nah	*tjener*
writer	fo-*fa*-dah	*forfatter*

PRETTY PLEASE

Note that there is no equivalent to the word 'please' in Danish. Politeness is most often expressed by tone of voice and/or by beginning the sentence with phrases such as 'May I ...' Må jeg ... or 'Could I ...' Kunne jeg ...

Religion

What is your religion?
vil-kehn ŕehlig-*yorn* *Hvilken religion*
til-her-ah doo? *tilhører du?*
I'm not religious.
yai ehŕ ig ŕehlig-*yers* *Jeg er ikke religiøs.*

I'm ...	yai ehŕ ...	*Jeg er ...*
Buddhist	boo-*deesd*	*buddist*
Catholic	kator-*leeg*	*katolik*
Christian	*kŕehs*-dehn	*kristen*
Hindu	*hin*-doo	*hindu*
Jewish	*yer*-theh	*jøde*
Muslim	moos-*leem*	*muslim*

DANISH

Family

Are you married?	ehŕ doo geefd?	*Er du gift?*
I'm ...	yai ehŕ ...	*Jeg er ...*
married	geefd	*gift*
single	*oo*-geefd	*ugift*

How many children do you have?
vor *mahng*-eh bern hah doo? *Hvor mange børn har du?*
I don't have any children.
yai hah *ing*-ehn bern *Jeg har ingen børn.*
I have a daughter/a son.
yai hah in *da*-dah/en sern *Jeg har en datter/en søn.*
How many brothers/
sisters do you have?
vor *mahng*-eh *brŕerth*-rah/ *Hvor mange brødre/*
sers-dŕah hah doo? *søstre har du?*
Is your husband/wife here?
ehŕ deen man/*kor*-ne hehŕ? *Er din mand/kone her?*
Do you have a boyfriend/girlfriend?
hah doo in *kehŕs*-deh? *Har du en kæreste?*

brother	bŕoŕ	*bror*
children	bern	*børn*
daughter	*da*-dah	*datter*
family	fa-*meel*-yeh	*familie*
father	fah	*far*
grandfather	*behs*-deh-fah	*bedstefar*
grandmother	*behs*-deh-mooŕ	*bedstemor*
grandparents (maternal)	*moŕ*-mooŕ o *moŕ*-fah	*mormor og morfar*
grandparents (paternal)	*fah*-mooŕ o *fah*-fah	*farmor og farfar*
husband	man	*mand*
mother	mooŕ	*mor*
sister	*sers*-dah	*søster*
son	sern	*søn*
wife	*kor*-ne	*kone*

Kids' Talk

How old are you?
vor *gah*-mehl ehŕ doo? *Hvor gammel er du?*

When's your birthday?
vo-*nor* hah doo *fer*-sehl-sda? *Hvornår har du fødselsdag?*

What do you do after school?
va *la*-wah doo *ehf*-dah *skor*-leh? *Hvad laver du efter skole?*

Do you have a pet at home?
hah doo id *keh*-leh-düŕ? *Har du et kæledyr?*

I have a ...	yai hah ...	*Jeg har ...*
bird	in fool	*en fugl*
budgerigar	in on-doo-*lad*	*en undulat*
canary	in ka-*nah*-yeh-fool	*en kanariefugl*
cat	in kad	*en kat*
dog	in hoon	*en hund*
frog	in fŕer	*en frø*
guinea pig	id *mah*-sveen	*et marsvin*

Feelings

I like ...	yai ka god lee ...	*Jeg kan godt lide ...*
I don't like ...	yai ka ig lee ...	*Jeg kan ikke lide ...*
I'm in a hurry.	yai hah tŕaowld	*Jeg har travlt.*
I'm well.	yai hah di god	*Jeg har det godt.*
I'm sorry.	di ger mai ān*d*	*Det gør mig ondt*
(condolence)	ad *her*-ah	*at høre.*
I'm grateful.	yai ehŕ	*Jeg er*
	tahg-*nehm*-lee	*taknemlig.*
I'm ...	yai ehŕ ...	*Jeg er ...*
angry	vŕehth	*vred*
happy	glath	*glad*
hungry	*sul*-dehn	*sulten*
sad	tŕeesd	*trist*
sleepy	*serv*-nee	*søvnig*
thirsty	*ters*-dee	*tørstig*
tired (fatigued)	tŕahd	*træt*
worried	be-*kerm*-ŕerth	*bekymret*
I'm cold/hot.	yai *frü*-sah/*svith*-ah	*Jeg fryser/sveder.*
You're right.	doo hah ŕahd	*Du har ret.*

Some Useful Phrases

Sure.	
seh-*fer*-lee/di ehŕ klahd	*Selvfølgelig./Det er klart.*
Just a minute.	
id *oy*-eh-*blig*	*Et øjeblik.*
It's (not) important.	
di ehŕ (ig) *vig*-deed	*Det er (ikke) vigtigt.*
It's (not) possible.	
di ehŕ (ig) *moo*-leed	*Det er (ikke) muligt.*
Wait!	
vehnd!	*Vent!*
Good luck!	
hehl o *ler*-geh!	*Held og lykke!*

BREAKING THE LANGUAGE BARRIER

Do you speak English? *ta*-lah dee *ehng*-ehlsg?	*Taler De engelsk?* (pol)
Does anyone speak English? ehŕ dah norn dah *ta*-lah *ehng*-ehlsg?	*Er der nogen der* *taler engelsk?*
I speak a little ... yai *ta*-lah in *smoo*-leh ...	*Jeg taler en smule ...*
I don't speak ... yai *ta*-lah ig ...	*Jeg taler ikke ...*
I (don't) understand. yai fo-*sdor* (ig)	*Jeġ forstår (ikke).*

Could you repeat that? *koo*-neh dee *gehn*-ta *di*?	*Kunne De gentage det?* (pol)
Could you speak more slowly please? *koo*-neh dee *ta*-leh *lahng*-som-ah?	*Kunne De tale* *langsommere?* (pol)
How do you say ...? vor-*dan see*-ah man ...?	*Hvordan siger man ...?*
What does ... mean? va bi-*tüth*-ah ...?	*Hvad betyder ...?*

I speak ...	yai *ta*-lah ...	*Jeg taler ...*
English	*ehng*-ehlsg	*engelsk*
French	ffahnsg	*fransk*
German	tüsg	*tysk*
Italian	ee-tal-*yehnsg*	*italiensk*
Spanish	sbansg	*spansk*

BODY LANGUAGE

The good old handshake is the go in Denmark! The older generation has always used it, and still do, the younger seemed to drop it for a number of years but have reintroduced it. This applies not only to men but also women.

Never shake someone's hand with the other hand in your pocket as this is considered impolite. A single kiss on the cheek (just one) – often accompanied by a hug – is used for closer friends and relatives. And don't forget that men hug in Denmark too!

To express the affirmative, Danes will sometimes pull in air abruptly while making a 'hah' sound accompanied by a slight backward tilt of the head, and a 'no' can be expressed by the usual shaking of the head.

When Danes raise their glasses to toast they will seek brief eye contact with everyone at the table before and after drinking and say Skål!. You shouldn't start eating a meal until everybody is ready and the host(ess) nods to everyone and says Værsgo (please start).

Danes have a tradition of thanking their hosts after a meal or any type of get-together by either ringing up specifically to do so or by saying Tak for sidst (lit. thanks for last) next time they meet.

SIGNS

FORBUDT	PROHIBITED
GRATIS ADGANG	FREE ADMISSION
INDGANG	ENTRANCE
INFORMATION	INFORMATION
INGEN ADGANG	NO ENTRY
NØDUDGANG	EMERGENCY EXIT
RESERVERET	RESERVED
RYGNING FORBUDT	NO SMOKING
TELEFON	TELEPHONE
TOILET	TOILET
UDGANG	EXIT
VARM/KOLD	HOT/COLD
ÅBEN/LUKKET	OPEN/CLOSED

PAPERWORK

address	a-*dŕah*-seh	*adresse*
age	*al*-ah	*alder*
birth certificate	*fer-sels*-a-tehsd/ *dābs*-a-tehsd	*fødselsattest/ dåbsattest*
border	*gŕahn*-seh	*grænse*
car registration	*in*-ŕeh-gee-sdŕeh-ŕing (s-a-tehsd)	*indregistre-ring (sattest)*
customs	tol	*told*
date of birth	*fer*-sehls-da-tor	*fødselsdato*
driver's licence	*ker*-koŕd	*kørekort*
identification	li-gee-tee-ma-*shorn*	*legitimation*
immigration	i-mee-gŕah-*shorn*	*immigration*
marital status	see-*veel*-sdan	*civilstand*
name	naown	*navn*
nationality	na-shor-na-lee-*tid*	*nationalitet*
passport	*pas*	*pas*
passport number	*pas*-nām-mah	*pasnummer*
place of birth	*fer*-theh-*sdehth*	*fødested*
profession	pŕor-feh-*shorn*	*profession*
reason for travel	*foŕ*-māl meh *ŕai*-sehn	*formål med rejsen*
religion	ŕeh-leeg-*yorn*	*religion*
sex	kern	*køn*
visa	*vee*-sām	*visum*

GETTING AROUND

What time does the ... leave/arrive?	vo-*nor* gor/ *an*-kom-ah ...	*Hvornår går/ ankommer ...*
(air)plane	*flü*-ehth	*flyet*
boat	*bā*-thehn	*båden*
bus	*boo*-sehn/ *ŕoo*-deh-bee-lehn	*bussen/ rutebilen*
train	*tā*-wehth	*toget*

Directions

Where is ...?	
vor ehŕ ...?	*Hvor er ...?*
How do I get to ...?	
vo-*dan kom*-ah yai ti ...?	*Hvordan kommer jeg til ...?*
Is it far from here?	
ehŕ di lahngd *hiŕ-fŕah*?	*Er det langt herfra?*
Is it near here?	
ehŕ di ee *nehŕ*-hi-thehn?	*Er det i nærheden?*
Can I walk there?	
ka yai *gā* dah-*hehn*?	*Kan jeg gå derhen?*
Can you show me (on the map)?	
koo-neh dee/doo vee-seh mai di (pā *koŕd*-ehth)?	*Kunne De/du vise mig det (på kortet)?* (pol/inf)
Are there other means of getting there?	
ehŕ dehŕ *ahn*-dŕah *māth*-ah ad *kom*-eh dehŕ-*hehn* pā?	*Er der andre måder at komme derhen på?*
I want to go to ...	
yai vi *gehŕ*-neh ti ...	*Jeg vil gerne til ...*
Go straight ahead.	
gā *li*-eh ooth	*Gå lige ud.*
It's two streets down.	
di ehŕ tor *gath*-ah *lehng*-ah *ni*-theh	*Det er to gader længere nede.*

DANISH

HYGGE!

Hygge is a concept close to Danish hearts. It describes many things, like being cosy and comfortable in a warm bed, or sitting in front of the fireplace with a cup of hot cocoa, or a surprise visitor with whom you stay up all night chatting. So if you're experiencing what you think is hygge, you could always try saying: Det er hyggeligt! and watch the reaction...

Turn left/ right ...	dŕai ti *vehns*-dŕah/ *hoy*-yah ...	*Drej til venstre/ højre ...*
at the next corner	vi *nehs*-deh *yer*-neh	*ved næste hjørne*
at the traffic lights	vi tŕah-*feeg*-lü-sehth	*ved trafiklyset*

behind	ba	*bag*
far	fyehŕn	*fjern*
near	nehŕ	*nær*
in front of	*foŕ*-an	*foran*
opposite	pā dehn *morth*-sa-deh *see*-theh a	*på den* *modsatte* *side af*

Booking Tickets

Where can I buy a ticket? vor ka yai *ker*-beh in bi-*lehd?*	*Hvor kan jeg købe en billet?*
I want to go to ... yai vi *gehŕ*-neh ti ...	*Jeg vil gerne til ...*
Do I need to book? ehŕ di nerth-*vehn*-deed ad bi-sdi-leh plas?	*Er det nødvendigt at bestille plads?*
I'd like to book a seat to ... yai vi *gehŕ*-neh bi-sdi-leh plas ti ...	*Jeg vil gerne bestille plads til ...*
It's full. di ehŕ *ful*-d *book*-ehth	*Det er fuldt booket.*
Are there no seats available at all? ehŕ dah slehd *ing*-ehn *le*-thee plas-ah?	*Er der slet ingen ledige pladser?*
Can I get a stand-by ticket? ka yai mās-gi *ker*-beh in stan-*bai* bi-*lehd?*	*Kan jeg måske købe en stand-by billet?*

I'd like ...	yai vi *gehŕ*-neh ha ...	*Jeg vil gerne have ...*
a one-way ticket	en *ehng*-gild-bi-lehd	*en enkeltbillet*
a return ticket	en ŕeh-*tooŕ*-bi-lehd	*en returbillet*
two tickets	tor bi-*lehd*-ah	*to billetter*
tickets for all of us	bi-*lehd*-ah ti os *al*-eh	*billetter til os alle*
a student discount	sdoo-*dehn*-dah-ŕah-bad	*studenterrabat*
a child's fare	in *ber*-neh-bi-lehd	*en børnebillet*
a pensioner's fare	in pahng-sho-*neesd*-bi-lehd	*en pensionist-billet*
1st class	*fers*-deh *klas*-eh	*første klasse*
2nd class	*an*-ehn *klas*-eh	*anden klasse*

Air

Is there a flight to ...?	
ehŕ dehŕ id flü ti ...?	*Er der et fly til ...?*
When is the next flight to ...?	
vo-*nor* gor *nehs*-deh flü ti ...?	*Hvornår går næste fly til ...?*
How long does the flight take?	
vor lahng tith tah *flüu*-too-ahn?	*Hvor lang tid tager flyveturen?*
What is the flight number?	
va ehŕ *flaid*-nām-mahth?	*Hvad er flight-nummeret?*
You must check in at ... (time)	
doo sga cheh-geh *in klog*-gehn ...	*Du skal checke ind klokken ...*

airport tax	*lâfd*-haown-sgad	*lufthavnsskat*
boarding pass	*boŕ*-ding-koŕd	*boardingkort*
customs	tol	*told*

SIGNS	
BAGAGE(AFHENTNING)	LUGGAGE PICKUP
BAGAGE(SKRANKE)	BAGGAGE COUNTER
CHECK IN/ INDCHEKNING	CHECKING IN
CHECK-IN (SKRANKE)	CHECK-IN COUNTER
REGISTRERING	REGISTRATION
TOLD	CUSTOMS

Bus

Where is the bus stop?	
vor ehf *boos*-stop-peh-stehth-ehd?	*Hvor er busstoppestedet?*
Which bus goes to ...?	
vil-gehn boos gor ti ...?	*Hvilken bus går til ...?*
Does this bus go to ...?	
gor *dehn*-neh *boos* ti ...?	*Går denne bus til ...?*
How often do buses pass by?	
vor *of*-deh *gor boos*-sen?	*Hvor ofte går bussen?*
Could you let me know when we get to ...?	
koo-neh dee/doo *see*-eh *ti* nor vee *kom*-ah ti ...?	*Kunne De/du sige til når vi kommer til ...?* (pol/inf)

I want to get off!	yai vi a!	*Jeg vil af!*
What time is the ... bus?	vo-*nor* gor dehn ... boos?	*Hvornår går den ... bus?*
next	*nehs*-deh	*næste*
first	*fers*-deh	*første*
last	*sees*-deh	*sidste*

Metro

The first phase of the Copenhagen metro is operational from 2002, the second from 2003.
(See the Train section, page 32)

Train

Which line takes me to ...?	
vil-gehth tāw gor ti ...?	*Hvilket tog går til ...?*
What is the next station?	
va ehŕ *nehs*-deh sda-*shorn*?	*Hvad er næste station?*
Is this the right platform for ...?	
ehŕ *di*-deh dehn *ŕig*-dee pa-*ŕong* nor yai sga meh *tā*-wehth ti ...?	*Er dette den rigtige perron når jeg skal med toget til ...?*
The train leaves from platform ...	
tā-wehth gor fŕah pa-*ŕong* ...	*Toget går fra perron ...*
Passengers must change trains/platforms.	
pa-sa-*shi*-ah-neh sga *sgeef*-deh *tāw*/pa-*ŕong*	*Passagererne skal skifte tog/perron.*

dining car	*sbee*-seh-vown	*spisevogn*
express	ehgs-*pŕahs*	*ekspres*
local	lor-*kal*	*lokal*
sleeping car	*sow*-eh-vown	*sovevogn*

DANISH

SIGNS

AFGANG	DEPARTURES
ANKOMST	ARRIVALS
BILLETKONTOR	TICKET OFFICE
BUSSTOPPESTED	BUS STOP
HOVEDBANEGÅRD	CENTRAL STATION
KØREPLAN	TIMETABLE
MINIMETRO	SUBWAY
PERRONNUMMER	PLATFORM NO.
STATION	STATION
TOGSTATION	TRAIN STATION
UDGANG	WAY OUT
VEKSEL	CHANGE (for coins)

Taxi

Can you take me to ...?
ka dee/doo ker mai ti ...? — *Kan De/du køre mig til ...?* (pol/inf)

How much does it cost to go to ...?
vor *mah*-eth *kos*-dah di ad ker ti ...? — *Hvor meget koster det at køre til ...?*

Here is fine, thank you.
sdob hehŕ tahg — *Stop her, tak.*

The next corner, please.
vi *nehs*-deh *yer*-neh tahg — *Ved næste hjørne, tak.*

The next street to the left/right.
nehs-deh *gath*-eh ti *vehns*-dŕah/*hoy*-yah — *Næste gade til venstre/højre.*

Please slow down.
vehŕ so *vehn*-lee ad ker *lahng*-som-ah — *Vær så venlig at køre langsommere.*

Continue! *foŕd*-sehd! — *Fortsæt!*
Stop here! sdob hehŕ! — *Stop her!*
Please wait here. vehnd *vehn*-leesd hehŕ — *Vent venligst her.*

Some Useful Phrases

The train is delayed/cancelled.
tāw-ehth ehŕ fo-*sing*-gehth/*aw*-lüsd — *Toget er forsinket/aflyst.*

How long will it be delayed?
vor *mah*-ehth ehŕ *tāw*-ehth fo-*sing*-gehth? — *Hvor meget er toget forsinket?*

Can I reserve a place?
ehŕ di *moo*-lid ad ŕeh-sehŕ-*vi*-ah plas? — *Er det muligt at reservere plads?*

How long does the trip take?
vor lahng teeth tah *too*-ahn? — *Hvor lang tid tager turen?*

Is it a direct route?
ehŕ di in *dee*-ŕaig-deh fo-*bin*-ehl-seh? — *Er det en direkte forbindelse?*

Is that seat taken?
ehŕ dehn plas *ob*-ta-ehth? — *Er den plads optaget?*

I want to get off at ...
yai vi *gehŕ*-neh a vi ... — *Jeg vil gerne af ved ...*

Where can I hire a bicycle?
vor ka yai *lai*-eh in *sü*-gehl? — *Hvor kan jeg leje en cykel?*

Car

Where can I rent a car?
vor ka yai *lai*-eh in beel? — *Hvor kan jeg leje en bil?*

How much is it daily/weekly?
vor *mah*-eth *kos*-dah di pehŕ da/pehŕ *oo*-eh? — *Hvor meget koster det per dag/per uge?*

Does that include insurance/mileage?
ing-kloo-*di*-ah di fo-*sig*-ŕing/*oo*-bi-gŕahn-seh-theh kee-lor-*mi*-dah? — *Inkluderer det forsikring/ubegrænsede kilometer?*

Where's the next petrol station?
vor ehŕ *nehs*-deh bin-*seen*-sda-*shorn*? — *Hvor er næste benzinstation?*

How long can I park here?
vor *lehng*-eh mä yai pah-*ki*-ah hiŕ? — *Hvor længe må jeg parkere her?*

Does this road lead to ...?
fer-ah *dehn*-neh vai ti ...? — *Fører denne vej til ...?*

I need a mechanic.
yai hah bŕoo for in mi-*ka*-ni-gah — *Jeg har brug for en mekaniker.*

What make is it?
vil-gehth *mehŕ*-geh ehŕ di? — *Hvilket mærke er det?*

The battery is flat.
ba-dah-*ŕee*-ehth ehŕ derd — *Batteriet er dødt.*

The radiator is leaking.
ker-lahn ehŕ *oo*-tehd — *Køleren er utæt.*

I have a flat tyre.
yai ehŕ pāng-*ti*-ahth — *Jeg er punkteret.*

It's overheating. (engine)
mor-toŕ-ahn *kā*-wah *ow*-ah — *Motoren koger over.*

It's not working.
dehn *veeŕ*-gah ig — *Den virker ikke.*

air (for tyres)	lāfd	*luft*
battery	ba-dah-*ŕee*	*batteri*
brakes	*bŕahm*-sah	*bremser*
clutch	*kob*-ling	*kobling*
driver's licence	*ker*-kord	*kørekort*
engine	*mor*-toŕ	*motor*
lights	lüs	*lys*
oil	*orl*-yeh	*olie*
radiator	*ker*-lah	*køler*
road map	*vai*-koŕd	*vejkort*
tyres	dehg	*dæk*
windscreen	for-*ŕoo*-theh	*forrude*

SIGNS

BLYFRI	UNLEADED
ENSRETTET	ONE WAY
GARAGE/AUTOVÆRKSTED	GARAGE
INDKØRSEL FORBUDT	NO ENTRY
MEKANIKER	MECHANIC
MOTORVEJ	FREEWAY
OKTAN	OCTANE
OMKØRSEL	DETOUR
PARKERING FORBUDT	NO PARKING
SELVBETJENING	SELF SERVICE
VEJARBEJDE	ROADWORKS
VIGEPLIGT	GIVE WAY

ACCOMMODATION

Where is a ...?	vor ehŕ dah id ...?	*Hvor er der et ...?*
cheap hotel	*bee*-leed hor-*tehl*	*billigt hotel*
good hotel	god hor-*tehl*	*godt hotel*
nearby hotel	hor-*tehl* ee *nehŕ*-hith-ehn	*hotel i nærheden*

What's the address?
va ehŕ a-*dŕah*-sehn? *Hvad er adressen?*

Could you write the address, please?
koo-neh dee *sgŕee*-w a-*dŕah*-sehn nith? *Kunne De skrive adressen ned?* (pol)

DANISH

At the Hotel

Do you have any rooms available?
hah ee *lith*-ee *vehŕl*-sah? *Har I ledige værelser?*

I'd like ...	yai vi *gehŕ*-neh ha ...	*Jeg vil gerne have ...*
a single room	id *ehng*-gild-vehŕl-seh	*et enkeltværelse*
a double room	id *dob*-ehld-vehŕl-seh	*et dobbeltværelse*
to share a dorm	plas ee in *sow*-sahl	*plads i en sovesal*
a bed	in sehng	*en seng*

I want a room with a ...	yai vi *gehŕ*-neh ha id *vehŕl*-seh meh ...	*Jeg vil gerne have et værelse med ...*
bathroom	bath	*bad*
double bed	*do*-behld-sehng	*dobbeltseng*
shower	*bŕoo*-seh-bath	*brusebad*
TV	ti vi	*TV*
window	*vin*-doo	*vindue*

I'm going to stay for ...	yai bleeŕ ...	*Jeg bliver ...*
one day	in nad	*en nat*
two days	tor *nehd*-ah	*to nætter*
one week	in *oo*-eh	*en uge*

Do you have identification?
hah dee/doo li-gee-tee-ma-*shorn*? — *Har De/du legitimation?* (pol/inf)

Your (pl) membership card, please.
yehŕs *mehth*-lehms-kord tahg — *Jeres medlemskort, tak.*

Sorry, we're full.
bi-*kla*-ah ald ehŕ *ob*-ta-ehth — *Beklager, alt er optaget.*

How long will you (pl) be staying?
vor *lehng*-eh bleeŕ ee? — *Hvor længe bliver I?*

How many nights?
vor *mahng*-eh *neh*-dah? — *Hvor mange nætter?*

It's ... per day/per person.
di *kos*-dah ... pehŕ da/ pehŕ pehŕ-*sorn* — *Det koster ... per dag/ per person.*

How much is it per night/ per person?
vor *mah*-eth *kos*-dah di pehŕ nad/pehŕ pehŕ-*sorn*? — *Hvor meget koster det per nat/per person?*

Can I see it?
mä yai si *vehŕl*-sehth? — *Må jeg se værelset?*

Are there any others?
ehŕ dehŕ *ahn*-dŕah *vehŕl*-sah? — *Er der andre værelser?*

Are there any cheaper rooms?
***fin*-ehs dehŕ *bee*-lee-ah *vehŕl*-sah?** — *Findes der billigere værelser?*

Can I see the bathroom?
mä yai si *ba*-theh-vehŕl-sehth? — *Må jeg se badeværelset?*

Is there a reduction for students/children?
ehŕ dehŕ sdoo-*dehn*-dah-ŕah-bad/ *ber*-neh-ŕah-bad? — *Er der studenterrabat/ børnerabat?*

Does it include breakfast?
ehŕ *morn*-math ing-kloo-*di*-ahth? — *Er morgenmad inkluderet?*

It's fine, I'll take it.
di ehŕ feend yai tah di — *Det er fint, jeg tager det.*

I'm not sure how long I'm staying.
yai vith ig vo *lehng*-eh yai bleeŕ — *Jeg ved ikke hvor længe jeg bliver.*

Where is the bathroom?
vor ehŕ toy-*lehd*-ehth? — *Hvor er toilettet?*

Is there somewhere to wash clothes?
ehŕ dehŕ id sdehth yai ka vas-geh toy? — *Er der et sted jeg kan vaske tøj?*

Is there a lift?
ehŕ dehŕ i-leh-*va*-tor? — *Er der elevator?*

Can I use the kitchen?
mä yai bŕoo *kerg*-nehth? — *Må jeg bruge køkkenet?*

Can I use the telephone?
mä yai bi-*ner*-deh ti-leh-*for*-nehn? — *Må jeg benytte telefonen?*

SIGNS

CAMPINGPLADS	CAMPING GROUND
HOTEL	HOTEL
KRO	INN
MOTEL	MOTEL
PENSIONAT/HOTELPENSION	GUEST HOUSE
VANDREHJEM	YOUTH HOSTEL

Requests & Complaints

Please wake me up at ...
koo-neh dee *veh*-geh
mai *klog*-gehn ...?
Kunne De vække mig klokken ...? (pol)

The room needs to be cleaned.
vehŕl-sehth *tŕaing*-ah ti
ad blee gyooŕd ŕehnd
Værelset trænger til at blive gjort rent.

Please change the sheets.
vi dee *vehn*-leesd *sgeef*-deh
sehng-eh-toy-yehth?
Vil De venligst skifte sengetøjet? (pol)

I can't open/close the window.
yai ka ig *āb*-neh/
lā-geh *vin*-doo-ehth
Jeg kan ikke åbne/ lukke vinduet.

I've locked myself out of my room.
yai hah lāsd mai *oo*-theh
a *vehŕl*-sehth
Jeg har låst mig ude af værelset.

The toilet won't flush.
toy-*lehd*-dehth *sger*-lah ig
Toilettet skyller ikke.

I don't like this room.
yai süns ig om *di*-deh
vehŕl-seh
Jeg synes ikke om dette værelse.

It's (too) ...	di ehŕ (fo) ...	*Det er (for) ...*
small	*lee*-leh	*lille*
noisy	*sdoy*-yeh-neh	*støjende*
dark	mergd	*mørkt*
expensive	düŕd	*dyrt*

Some Useful Words & Phrases

I'm/We're leaving now/tomorrow.
yai/vee *ŕai*-sah noo/i morn
Jeg/Vi rejser nu/i morgen.

I'd like to pay the bill.
yai vi *gehŕ*-neh bi-*ta*-leh
ŕai-ning-ehn
Jeg vil gerne betale regningen.

name	naown	*navn*
surname	*ehf*-dah-naown	*efternavn*
address	a-*dŕah*-seh	*adresse*
room number	*vehŕl*-sehs-nām-mah	*værelsesnummer*
air-conditioning	*ehŕ*-kon-dee-shon	*aircondition*
balcony	bal-*kong*/al-*tan*	*balkon/altan*
bed	sehng	*seng*
bill	*ŕai*-ning	*regning*
blanket	*teh*-beh	*tæppe*
chair	sdorl	*stol*
clean	ŕehn	*ren*
dirty	*snaow*-sehth	*snavset*
doona	dü-neh	*dyne*
electricity	i-lehg-tŕee-see-*tid*	*elektricitet*
excluded	*ehgs*-kloo-siw	*ekslusive*
included	ing-kloo-*di*-ahth	*inkluderet*
key	*noy*-leh	*nøgle*
lift (elevator)	i-leh-*va*-tor	*elevator*
light bulb	i-*lehg*-tŕeesg pehŕ	*elektrisk pære*
lock	lās	*lås*
mattress	ma-*dŕahs*	*madras*
mirror	sbail	*spejl*
padlock	*hehng*-eh-lās	*hængelås*
pillow	*hor*-wehth-poo-theh	*hovedpude*
quiet	*sdil*-eh	*stille*
sheet	*la*-yehn	*lagen*
soap	*seh*-beh	*sæbe*
suitcase	*kāf*-ahd	*kuffert*
swimming pool	*sver*-meh-ba-sehng	*svømmebassin*
table	booŕ	*bord*
toilet	toy-*lehd*	*toilet*
toilet paper	toy-*lehd*-pah-peeŕ	*toiletpapir*
towel	*hon*-kleh-theh	*håndklæde*
water	van	*vand*
hot/cold water	vahmd/kold van	*varmt/koldt vand*

AROUND TOWN

I'm looking for ...	yai *li*-thah *ehf*-dah ...	*Jeg leder efter ...*
the art gallery	*kānsd*-moo-sehth	*kunstmuseet*
a bank	in bang-g	*en bank*
the church	*keeŕ*-gehn	*kirken*
the city centre	*sehn*-tŕām	*centrum*
the ...	dehn ...	*den ...*
embassy	ahm-ba-*sa*-theh	*ambassade*
my hotel	meed hor-*tehl*	*mit hotel*
a market	id *mah*-gehth	*et marked*
the museum	moo-*sehth*	*museet*
the police	por-lee-*tee*-ehth	*politiet*
the post office	*posd*-kon-toŕ-ehth	*postkontoret*
a public toilet	id *o*-fehnd-leed toy-*lehd*	*et offentligt toilet*
a telephone centre	in ti-leh-*forn*	*en telefon*
the tourist information office	too-*ŕeesd*-in-for-ma-shor-nehn	*turist-informationen*

What time does it open/close?
vo-*nor āb*-nah/*lā*-gah di? — *Hvornår åbner/lukker det?*

What street/suburb is this?
vil-gehn *ga*-theh/ *for*-sdath ehŕ *di*-deh? — *Hvilken gade/ forstad er dette?*

For directions, see the Getting Around section, page 28.

At the Post Office

I'd like to send ...	yai vi *gehŕ*-neh sehn-eh ...	*Jeg vil gerne sende ...*
a letter	id *bŕeh*-w	*et brev*
a postcard	id *posd*-kord	*et postkort*
a parcel	in *pah*-geh	*en pakke*
a telegram	id ti-leh-*gŕahm*	*et telegram*

I'd like some stamps.
yai vi *gehŕ*-neh ha *nor*-leh *fŕee*-mehŕ-gah — *Jeg vil gerne have nogle frimærker.*

How much is the postage?
vor *mah*-eth ehŕ *poŕ*-tor-ehn? — *Hvor meget er portoen?*

How much does it cost to send this to ...?
vor *mah*-ehth *kos*-dah di ad *sehn*-eh *di*-deh ti ...? — *Hvor meget koster det at sende dette til ...?*

an aerogram	id eh-for-*gŕahm*	*et aerogram*
air mail	*lāfd*-posd	*luftpost*
envelope	kon-vor-*lood*	*konvolut*
mailbox	*posd*-ka-seh	*postkasse*
parcel	*pah*-geh	*pakke*
registered mail	*ŕeh*-kom-man-di-ahth	*rekommanderet*
surface mail	*ow*-ah-fla-theh-posd	*overfladepost*

Telephone & Internet

I want to ring ...
yai vi *gehŕ*-neh *ŕehng*-eh ti ... — *Jeg vil gerne ringe til ...*

The number is ...
nām-mahth ehŕ ... — *Nummeret er ...*

I want to speak for three minutes.
yai vi *gehŕ*-neh *ta*-leh tŕeh mee-*noo*-dah — *Jeg vil gerne tale tre minutter.*

How much does a three-minute call cost?
vo *mah*-ehth *kos*-dah di fo tŕeh mee-*noo*-dah? — *Hvor meget koster det for tre minutter?*

How much does each extra minute cost?
vo *mah*-ehth *kos*-dah vehŕd mee-*nood ehgs*-dŕah?
Hvor meget koster hvert minut ekstra?

I'd like to speak to (Mr Pedersen).
yai vi *gehŕ*-neh *ta*-leh meh (hehŕ *pih*-dah-sehn)
Jeg vil gerne tale med (Hr. Pedersen).

It's engaged.
dah ehŕ *ob*-ta-ehth
Der er optaget.

I want to make a reverse-charges phone call.
yai *erns*-gah ad *morth*-ta-ahn sga bi-*ta*-leh
Jeg ønsker at modtageren skal betale.

I've been cut off.
yai bli *aow*-bŕood
Jeg blev afbrudt.

Where can I get Internet access?
vor ka yai for *in*-tuh-neht *ath*-guhng?
Hvor kan jeg få Internet adgang?

I'd like to send an email.
yai vil *gehŕ*-neh *sehn*-neh ehn *ee*-mayl
Jeg vil gerne sende en email.

At the Bank

I want to exchange some money/travellers cheques.
yai vi *gehŕ*-neh *vehgs*-leh *nor*-leh *pehng*-eh/ *ŕai*-seh-shehgs
Jeg vil gerne veksle nogle penge/ rejsechecks.

What is the exchange rate?
va ehŕ *kooŕ*-sehn?
Hvad er kursen?

How many kroner per dollar?
vo *mahng*-eh *kŕor*-nah pehŕ *dol*-ah?
Hvor mange kroner per dollar?

Can I have money transferred here from my bank?
ka yai fä *pehng*-eh *ow*-ah-ferd hehŕ-*til* ffah meen *bahng*-g?
Kan jeg få penge overført hertil fra min bank?

How long will it take to arrive?
vo lahng teeth vi di *ta* **fer dee** *kom*-**ah?** — *Hvor lang tid vil det tage før de kommer?*

Has my money arrived yet?
ehŕ *meen*-**eh** *pehng*-**eh** *kom*-**ehth?** — *Er mine penge kommet?*

bank draft	*bahng*-g-an-vees-ning	*bankanvisning*
bank notes	*sehth*-lah	*sedler*
cashier	ka-*si*-ah	*kasserer*
coins	*mern*-dah	*mønter*
credit card	kŕeh-*deed*-kord	*kreditkort*
to exchange	at *vehg*-sleh	*at veksle*
loose change	*smo*-pehng-eh	*småpenge*
signature	*ān*-ah-sgŕehfd	*underskrift*

DANISH

INTERESTS & ENTERTAINMENT

Sightseeing

Do you (pl) have a guidebook/ local map?
hah ee in *ŕai*-**seh-hon-bāw/ id lor-***kal*-**kord?** — *Har I en rejsehåndbog/ et lokalkort?*

What are the main attractions?
va ehŕ *hor*-**wehth-a-tŕahg-shorn-ah-neh?** — *Hvad er hovedattraktionerne?*

What is that?
va ehŕ di? — *Hvad er det?*

How old is it?
vo *gah*-**mehl ehŕ dehn/di?** — *Hvor gammel er den/det?*

Can I take photographs?
mā yai ta *bil*-**thah?** — *Må jeg tage billeder?*

What time does it open/close?
vo-*nor āb*-**nah/ lāg-ah di?** — *Hvornår åbner/ lukker det?*

ancient	*gah*-mehl/ hee-*stor*-ŕeesg	*gammel/ historisk*
archaeological	ah-keh-or-*lor*-isg	*arkæologisk*
beach	sdŕahn	*strand*
building	*büg*-ning	*bygning*
castle	slod	*slot*
cathedral	ka-deh-*dŕahl/ dom*-keeŕ-geh	*katedral/ domkirke*
church	*keeŕ*-geh	*kirke*
concert hall	kon-*sehŕd*-sal	*koncertsal*
library	beeb-lee-or-*tig*	*bibliotek*
main square	*hor*-wehth-toŕw	*hovedtorv*
market	*mah*-gehth	*marked*
monastery	*klos*-dah	*kloster*
monument	mor-noo-*mehnd*	*monument*
mosque	mor-*sgi*	*moské*
the old city	dehn *gahm*-leh *bü*-dil	*den gamle bydel*
opera house	*or*-pi-ŕah-hoos	*operahus*
palace	pa-*las*	*palads*
ruins	ŕoo-*een*-ah	*ruiner*
stadium	*sdad*-yon	*stadion*
statues	*sda*-too-ah	*statuer*
synagogue	sü-na-*gor*	*synagoge*
temple	*tehm*-behl	*tempel*
university	oo-nee-vehŕ-see-*tid*	*universitet*

Going Out

What's there to do in the evenings?

va ehŕ dah o *la*-w om *ahfd*-nehn?	*Hvad er der at lave om aftenen?*

Are there any discos?

ehŕ dah dees-gor-*ti*-gah?	*Er der diskoteker?*

Are there places where you can hear local folk music?

fin-ehs dah *sdeh*-thah vor man ka *her*-ah *lor*-kal *fol*-geh-moo-seeg?	*Findes der steder hvor man kan høre lokal folkemusik?*

How much does it cost to get in?	vo *mah*-eth *kos*-dah di ad *kom*-eh in?	*Hvor meget koster det at komme ind?*
cinema	bi-or-*gŕahf*	*biograf*
concert	kon-*sehŕd*	*koncert*
discotheque	dees-gor-*tig*	*diskotek*
theatre	ti-*a*-dah	*teater*

Sports & Interests

What do you do in your spare time?

va *la*-wah doo ee deen *fŕee*-teeth?	*Hvad laver du i din fritid?* (inf)

What sport do you play?

vil-gehn spord *düŕ*-gah doo?	*Hvilken sport dyrker du?* (inf)

art	kānsd	*kunst*
basketball	*bah*-sgehd-borl	*basketball*
boxing	*bogs*-ning	*boksning*
cooking	math-la-w-ning	*madlavning*
fishing	fis-gah-*ŕee*	*fiskeri*
going out	gor ee *bü*-ehn	*gå i byen*
going to the cinema	gor ee bee-or-*gŕahf*-ehn	*gå i biografen*
music	moo-*seeg*	*musik*
photography	for-tor-gŕah-*fi*-ŕing	*fotografering*
reading	*leh*-seh	*læse*
rugby	*ŕog*-bee	*rugby*
shopping	*han*-leh	*handle*
soccer	*forth*-bold	*fodbold*
sport	sbord	*sport*
the theatre	ti-*a*-dahth	*teatret*
travelling	*ŕai*-seh	*rejse*
writing	*sgŕee*-weh	*skrive*

Festivals

In Denmark the main Christmas celebration takes place on the evening of 24 December, **juleaften**. The Christmas tree, **juletræ**, is normally decorated with home-made paper hearts and tinsel. After dinner, which traditionally consists of duck, **and** and/or roast pork, **flæskesteg**, followed by **ris a l'amande**, the family join hands and 'dance' around the tree singing **julesalmer** (Christmas carols). If you want to exchange Christmas greetings with a Dane, the phrase is **god/glædelig jul** (merry Christmas).

Fastelavn (Shrovetide) celebrations take place seven weeks before Easter. Children get **fastelavnsris**, birch rods decorated with sweets and paper cats. During the day they dress up in fancy costumes and walk from door to door singing, for which they receive sweets. A traditional Shrovetide game involves a barrel (**fastelavnstønde**) full of sweets hanging from a rope, which children take turns to try to break with a bat. During Shrovetide people eat **fastelavnsboller** (Shrovetide buns).

Påske (Easter) goes from Maundy Thursday (**skærtorsdag**), including Good Friday (**langfredag**), until the Monday after Easter Sunday. Traditionally, children look for **påskeæg** (Easter eggs) hidden by **påskeharen** (the Easter bunny) on Easter Sunday (**påskesøndag**), or they paint their own Easter eggs. The Easter greeting in Denmark is **god påske** (happy Easter).

Pinse (Whitsun) is a Christian holiday on the seventh Sunday after Easter which includes **pinsedag** (Whit Sunday) and **anden pinsedag** (Whit Monday). People greet each other with **god pinse** (Happy Whitsun).

Music festivals play a big role in weekend outdoor entertainment during the Danish summer.

Probably the biggest international music event in Denmark, **Roskilde Festival** takes place near the town of Roskilde. It attracts as many as 70,000 visitors from all over Europe and spans a huge variety of music, including rock, pop, folk and ethnic music.

Midtfynsfestival, on the island of Funen, is a smaller version of Roskilde, focusing on rock and pop.

Langelandsfestival is a family festival that takes place on the island of Langeland, with a focus on rock, folk and popular music, and lots of fun for kids.

Copenhagen Jazz Festival runs for several weeks over summer. It attracts many brilliant (primarily Danish but also international) jazz, folk and blues artists.

MAD MEAL!

After a meal you should always say **Tak for mad** (thanks for the meal) before getting up.

IN THE COUNTRY

Weather

What's the weather like?
vo-*dan* ehŕ *vehŕ*-ehth? *Hvordan er vejret?*

It's ... today.	di ehŕ ... ee da	*Det er ... i dag.*
Will it be ...	bleer di ...	*Bliver det ...*
tomorrow?	ee morn?	*i morgen?*
cloudy	*ow*-ah-sgü-ehth	*overskyet*
cold	kold	*koldt*
foggy	*tā*-wehth	*tåget*
frosty	*fŕosd*-vehŕ	*frostvejr*
hot	vahmd	*varmt*
raining	*ŕain*-vehŕ	*regnvejr*
snowing	sni-vehŕ	*snevejr*
sunny	*sorl*-sgins-vehŕ	*solskinsvejr*
windy	*bleh*-seh-vehŕ	*blæsevejr*

Camping

Am I allowed to camp here?
mā yai kahm-*pi*-ah hehŕ? *Må jeg campere her?*

Is there a campsite nearby?
fin-ehs dah in *kahm*-ping-plas ee *nehŕ*-hith-ehn? *Findes der en campingplads i nærheden?*

backpack	*ŕerg*-sehg	*rygsæk*
can opener	*dā*-seh-*āb*-nah	*dåseåbner*
compass	kom-*pas*	*kompas*
crampons	*klad*-ŕah-yehŕn	*klatrejern*
firewood	*bŕahn*-eh	*brænde*
gas cartridge	*gas*-bi-hol-ah	*gasbeholder*
hammock	*hehng*-eh-koy-yeh	*hængekøje*
ice axe	*ees*-erg-seh	*isøkse*
mattress	ma-*dŕahs*	*madras*
penknife	*lom*-eh-knee-w	*lommekniv*
rope	tow	*tov*
sleeping bag	*sow*-eh-por-seh	*sovepose*

stove	*kahm*-ping-vown	*campingovn*
tent	tehld	*telt*
tent pegs	*tehld*-peh-leh	*teltpæle*
torch (flashlight)	*lom*-eh-lerg-deh	*lommelygte*
water bottle	*fehld*-flas-geh	*feltflaske*

FOOD

Traditional Danish cooking is dominated by, although not to the same extent as the other Scandinavian countries, smoked, cured, pickled or otherwise preserved food, due to the short growing season and long winters. Regional variations are not strong, although proximity to the ocean flavours menus with seafood.

breakfast	*morn*-math	*morgenmad*
lunch	*fŕā*-kosd	*frokost*
dinner	*mi*-da/*ahf*-dehns-math	*middag/aftensmad*

Table for ..., please.
id booŕ ti ... tahg — *Et bord til ..., tak.*

Can I see the menu please?
mā yai si mi-*nü*-ehn? — *Må jeg se menuen?*

I'd like the set menu, please.
yai tah *dah*-ehns ŕahd tahg — *Jeg tager dagens ret, tak.*

What does it include?
va ing-kloo-*di*-ah dehn? — *Hvad inkluderer den?*

Not too spicy please.
ig fo *kŕerth*-ŕahth tahg — *Ikke for krydret, tak.*

Vegetarian Meals

I'm a vegetarian.
yai ehŕ veh-geh-*tah* — *Jeg er vegetar.*

I don't eat meat.
yai *sbees*-ah ig kerth — *Jeg spiser ikke kød.*

I don't eat chicken, or fish, or pork.
yai *sbees*-ah ig *kü*-ling eh-lah fisg eh-lah *svee*-neh-kerth — *Jeg spiser ikke kylling eller fisk eller svinekød.*

ashtray	*as*-geh-beh-ah	*askebæger*
the bill	*ŕai*-ning-ehn	*regningen*
a cup	in kob	*en kop*
dessert	di-*sehŕd*	*dessert*
a drink	in *dŕing*-g	*en drink* (always alcoholic)
a fork	in *gahf*-ehl	*en gaffel*
fresh	fehŕsg/fŕehsg	*ferskfrisk*
a glass	id glas	*et glas*
a knife	in knee-w	*en kniv*
a plate	in ta-*lehŕ*-gehn	*en tallerken*
spicy	*kŕerth*-ŕahth	*krydret*
a spoon	in sgi	*en ske*
stale	*gah*-mehl/*dor*-lee	*gammel/dårlig*
sweet	serth	*sød*
a teaspoon	in *ti*-sgi	*en teske*
toothpicks	*tan*-sdi-gah	*tandstikker*

Staple Foods & Condiments

beef	*og*-seh-kerth	*oksekød*
bread	bŕerth	*brød*
butter	smer	*smør*
cucumber	a-*goorg*	*agurk*
garlic	*vith*-loy	*hvidløg*
meat	kerth	*kød*
mustard	*seh*-nob	*sennep*
mutton	lahm	*lam*
oil	*orl*-yeh	*olie*
pasta	*pas*-da	*pasta*
pepper	*pi*-wah	*peber*
pork	*svee*-neh-kerth	*svinekød*
potatoes	kah-*tof*-lah	*kartofler*
rice	ŕees	*ris*
salt	sald	*salt*
sugar	*sā*-gah	*sukker*
veal	*kal*-veh-kerth	*kalvekød*
vegetables	*gŕern*-sa-ah	*grønsager*
vinegar	*ith*-geh	*eddike*

MENU DECODER

Breakfast Menu

cheese	äsd	*ost*
coffee	*kaf*-eh	*kaffe*
corn flakes	*koorń*-flehgs	*cornflakes*
fried egg (always sunny side up)	*spaił*-ehg	*spejlæg*
fruit	frägd	*frugt*
hardboiled egg	*hor*-kogd ehg	*hårdkogt æg*
jam	*sül*-deh-toy	*syltetøj*
milk	mehlg	*mælk*
oatmeal	*hah*-wah-gŕün	*havregryn*
porridge	*hah*-wah-gŕerth	*havregrød*
scrambled eggs	*ŕehŕ*-ehg	*røræg*
softboiled egg	*blerth*-kogd ehg	*blødkogt æg*
tea	ti	*te*
toast	*ŕis*-dehth bŕerth/ täwsd	*ristet brød/ toast*
yoghurt	*yoo*-goord	*yoghurt*

Sandwiches

bøftartar — *berf*-ta-tah
beef tartar – raw ground beef topped with a raw egg yolk, onion and capers

dyrlægens natmad — *dür*-leh-ehns *nad*-math
'the veterinarian's midnight snack' – liver paté topped with a thin slice of salt beef, raw onions and beef jelly

gravad laks — *gŕah*-wath lahgs
cured salmon

leverpostej — *li*-wah-por-sdai
liver paté

marineret sild — mah-ee-*ni*-ath seel
pickled herring; served with raw onions

ostemad — äs-deh-math
cheese – Denmark is famous for its cheeses, and produces an enormous variety

rejemad — *ŕai*-yeh-mahth
small shrimp served with mayonnaise and lemon slices

røget laks *roy*-yehth lahgs
smoked salmon, served with scrambled eggs
røget sild *roy*-yehth seel
smoked herring on rye bread with chives and a raw egg yolk
røget ål *roy*-yehth ăl
smoked eel, a delicacy

baguette	*frahns*-brerth	*franskbrød*
bread	brerth	*brød*
crusty roll	*rän*-sder-geh	*rundstykke*
Danish pastry	*vee*-nah-brerth	*wienerbrød*
rye bread	*roo*-brerth	*rugbrød*
soft roll	*bol*-eh	*bolle*

Danish Delights
Danish open rye bread sandwiches are ornate and tasty – a feast for the eye and a delight to the palate!

øllebrød *er*-leh-brerth
a smooth beer and bread dish, a bit like porridge, served hot with milk or whipped cream

Soup
fiskesuppe *fis*-geh-sä-beh
fish soup, usually creamy
grønsagssuppe *grern*-sas-sä-beh
vegetable soup
gule ærter *goo*-leh *ehr*-dah
split pea soup served with pork
hønsekødssuppe *hern*-seh-kerth-sä-beh
chicken soup

Meat
bankekød *bahng*-geh-kerth
similar to Wienerschnitzel
boller i karry bol-ah ee kah-ee
meat balls in a curry sauce, served with rice or potatoes
bøf med løg berf meh loy
hamburger served with fried onions, potatoes and brown gravy

flæskeæggekage (*flehs*-geh)-eh-geh-ka-eh
egg dish with bacon (a bit like an omelette, but made with flour)

flæskesteg *flehs*-geh-sdai
pork roast with crispy crackling, served with potatoes, brown gravy and pickled cucumbers

frikadeller fri-ga-*dehl*-ah
meat patties made of pork, veal and onion served with potatoes, brown gravy, and pickled cucumbers

fyldt füld

hvidkålshoved *veeth*-käls-hor-wehth
cabbage leaves wrapped around ground beef

medisterpølse mi-*dees*-dah-*perl*-seh
large fried sausage served with potatoes, brown gravy and pickled cucumbers

spaghetti med kødsovs sba-*gehd*-dee meh *kerth*-sows
spaghetti with ground beef in a tomato sauce

stegt flæsk med persillesovs sdehgd flehsg meh pehr-*sil*-eh-sows
thick slices of fried bacon with potatoes and a white parsley sauce

chicken	*kül*-ing	*kylling*
duck	an	*and*
hamburger	*hag*-eh-berf	*hakkebøf*
meat chops	ko-deh-*leh*-dah	*koteletter*
roast beef	*og*-seh-sdai	*oksesteg*
roast lamb	*lahm*-meh-sdai	*lammesteg*
roast pork	*flehs*-geh-sdai	*flæsksteg*
sausage	*perl*-seh	*pølse*
sirloin	*mer*-bŕah	*mørbrad*
steak	*ehng*-ehlsg berf	*engelsk bøf*
turkey	kal-*koon*	*kalkun*

Denmark is a major meat exporter, and is best known for its pork, ham and bacon.

Seafood

kogt torsk kogd torsg
poached cod in a mustard sauce served with boiled potatoes

stegt sild sdehgd seel
fried herring served with potatoes and a white parsley sauce

stegt ål med sdehgd äl meh

stuvede kartofler *sdoo*-weh-theh kah-*tof*-lah
fried eel with boiled potatoes in a white sauce

cod	torsk	*torsk*
fish	*fis*-g	*fisk*
haddock	*kool*-ah	*kuller*
halibut	*hehl*-eh-flün-ah	*helleflynder*
herring	seel	*sild*
plaice	*ŕerth*-sbeh-deh	*rødspætte*
salmon	lahgs	*laks*
shrimp	*ŕai*-yah	*rejer*
sole	*ser*-täng-eh	*søtunge*
trout	for-*ŕahl*	*forel*

Vegetables

asparagus	a-*sbahs*	*asparges*
beets (usually served pickled)	ŕerth-*bi*-thah	*rødbeder*
broccoli	*bŕo*-kor-lee	*broccoli*
cabbage	käl	*kål*
carrots	*goo*-leh-ŕerth-ah	*gulerødder*
cauliflower	*blom*-käl	*blomkål*
celery	*blath*-si-lah-ŕee	*bladselleri*
cucumber	a-*goorg*	*agurk*
lettuce	gŕern sa-*lad*	*grøn salat*
mushrooms	*shahm*-pin-yong-ah	*champignoner*
onions	loy	*løg*
peas	*ehŕ*-dah	*ærter*
pickled cucumbers	sooŕd/ *sül*-dehth a-*goor*-gah	*surt/ syltede agurker*
potato	kah-*tof*-ehl	*kartoffel*
rice	ŕees	*ris*
string beans	*snee*-deh-bern-ah	*snittebønner*
tomatoes	tor-*ma*-dah	*tomater*

Fruit

apple	*eh*-bleh	æble
banana	ba-*nayn*	*banan*
grapes	*vin*-droo-ah	*vindruver*
lemon	sit-*ŕorn*	*citron*
orange	ah-behl-*seen*	*appelsin*
pear	*peh*-ŕah	pære
strawberry	*yoŕ*-behŕ	*jordbær*

Desserts

budding *boo*-thing
a kind of pudding flavoured with, for example, rum or almonds, served warm

chokoladeis/ shor-gor-*la*-theh-ees/
vanilleis va-*neel*-yeh-ees
chocolate ice cream/vanilla ice cream

fromage fŕor-*ma*-sheh
a kind of mousse served cold flavoured with, for example, lemon

jordbær *yoŕ*-behŕ
med fløde meh *fler*-theh
strawberries with cream

kage *ka*-eh
cake

konditorkager kon-*dee*-dah-ka-ah
French pastries

rødgrød *ŕerth*-gŕerth
med fløde meh *fler*-theh
fruit pudding (red currant, raspberry, strawberry) served with cream

pandekager *pa*-neh-ka-ah
crepes rolled around a jam, sugar, or ice cream filling

Non-Alcoholic Drinks

apple juice	*eh*-bleh-djoos	*æblejuice*
cordial	*sahf*-deh-van	*saftevand*
coffee (with cream)	*kah*-feh (meh *fler*-theh)	*kaffe (med fløde)*
orange juice	ah-behl-*seen*-djoos	*appelsinjuice*
skim milk	*sgã*-mehth-mehlg	*skummetmælk*
soft drink/ carbonated water	*sor*-da-van/ *dansg*-van	*sodavand/ danskvand*
tea	ti	*te*
water/ice water	van/*ees*-van	*vand/isvand*
full cream milk	*serth*-mehlg	*sødmælk*

Alcoholic Drinks

øl	erl	beer/lager
hvidvin	*veeth*-veen	white wine
rødvin	*ŕerth*-veen	red wine

bajer *bay*-yah
beer – specifically means a darker beer more like ale, but is used colloquially to mean any beer

snaps/akvavit snahbs/ak-va-*veed*
various kinds of clear grain alcohol flavoured with different herbs, often with caraway. Traditionally consumed with pickled herring.

bitter *bi*-dah
a darker variant of snaps flavoured with different herbs. The most popular kinds are Jägermeister and Gammel Dansk. Believed to help settle an uneasy stomach and consumed either at breakfast or with beer.

SKÅL OR SKULL?

When Danes raise their glasses to you and say Skål! it means 'Cheers!', not to be confused with the Australian concept 'to skull', meaning emptying your drink in one go! Also, be prepared to say Skål! a lot more than once during a meal.

AT THE MARKET

Basics

bread	bŕerth	*brød*
butter	smer	*smør*
cheese	äsd	*ost*
chocolate	sho-koh-la-theh	*chokolade*
eggs	ehg	*æg*
flour	meh-l	*mel*
jam	*sül*-deh-toy	*syltetøj*
margarine	mah-gah-*ree*-neh	*margarine*
marmalade	mah-meh-*la*-theh	*marmelade*
milk	mehlg	*mælk*
oil	*orl*-yeh	*olie*
pasta	*pas*-da	*pasta*
rice	ŕees	*ris*
sugar	*sä*-gah	*sukker*
carbonated water	*dansg*-van	*danskvand*
water	van	*vand*
yoghurt	*yoo*-gooŕd	*yoghurt*

Meat & Poultry

beef	*og*-seh-kerth	*oksekød*
chicken	*kül*-ing	*kylling*
duck	an	*and*
ham	skin-keh	*skinke*
meat	kerth	*kød*
mutton	lahm	*lam*
pork	*svee*-neh-kerth	*svinekød*
sausage	*perl*-seh	*pølse*
veal	*kal*-veh-kerth	*kalvekød*

Vegetables

beets	ŕerth-*bí*-thah	*rødbeder*
broccoli	*bŕo*-kor-lee	*broccoli*
cabbage	käl	*kål*

AT THE MARKET

carrots	*goo*-leh-*ŕ*erth-ah	*gulerødder*
cauliflower	*blom*-käl	*blomkål*
celery	*blath*-si-lah-*ŕ*ee	*bladselleri*
cucumber	a-*goo*ŕ*g*	*agurk*
lettuce	gŕern sa-*lad*	*grøn salat*
mushrooms	*shahm*-pin-yong-ah	*champignoner*
onions	loy	*løg*
peas	*eh*ŕ-dah	*ærter*
pickled cucumbers	soo*ŕ*d/ *sül*-dehth a-*goo*ŕ-gah	*surt/ syltede agurker*
potato	kah-*tof*-ehl	*kartoffel*
string beans	*snee*-deh-bern-ah	*snittebønner*
tomatoes	tor-*ma*-dah	*tomater*
vegetables	*gŕern*-sa-ah	*grønsager*

Seafood

cod	torsk	*torsk*
fish	*fis*-g	*fisk*
herring	seel	*sild*
salmon	lahgs	*laks*
shrimp	*ŕai*-yah	*rejer*
sole	*ser*-täng-eh	*søtunge*
trout	for-*ŕahl*	*forel*

Fruit

apple	*eh*-bleh	*æble*
banana	ba-*nayn*	*banan*
fruit	frägd	*frugt*
grapes	*vin*-droo-ah	*vindruver*
lemon	sit-*ŕorn*	*citron*
orange	ah-behl-*seen*	*appelsin*
pear	*peh*-ŕah	*pære*
strawberry	*yo*ŕ-behŕ	*jordbær*

SHOPPING

bookshop	*bāw*-han-ehl	*boghandel*
camera shop	*for*-tor-han-ehl	*fotohandel*
clothing store	*toy*-boo-teeg	*tøjbutik*
delicatessen	de-lee-ka-*teh*-seh-fo-ŕahd-ning	*delikatesseforretning*
general store/shop	boo-*teeg*	*butik*
laundry	vas-gah-*ŕee*	*vaskeri*
market	*mah*-gehth	*marked*
newsagency	a-*vees*-kee-yosg	*aviskiosk*
pharmacy	ah-por-*tig*	*apotek*
shoeshop	*sgor*-toys-fo-ŕahd-ning	*skotøjsforretning*
souvenir shop	soo-veh-*neeŕ*-boo-teeg	*souvenirbutik*
stationers	pah-*peeŕ*-han-ehl	*papirhandel*
supermarket	*soo*-bah-mah-gehth	*supermarked*
vegetable shop	*gŕernd*-han-lah	*grønthandler*

DANISH

I'd like to buy ...
yai vi *gehŕ*-neh ha ... — *Jeg vil gerne have ...*

How much is it?
vo *mah*-ehth *kos*-dah di? — *Hvor meget koster det?*

Do you (inf) have others?
hah doo *an*-ehth? — *Har du andet?*

I don't like it.
dehn/di ka yai ig li — *Den/Det kan jeg ikke lide.*

Can I look at it?
mā yai si dehn/di? — *Må jeg se den/det?*

I'm just looking.
yai *kee*-gah bah — *Jeg kikker bare.*

Can you write down the price?
ka doo *sgŕee*-w *pŕee*-sehn nith? — *Kan du skrive prisen ned?*

Do you accept credit cards?
tah ee kŕeh-*deed*-kord? — *Tager I kreditkort?*

Can I help you?
ka yai *yehl*-beh dehm? — *Kan jeg hjælpe Dem?* (pol)

Will that be all?
ehŕ di di *hi*-leh? — *Er det det hele?*

Would you like it wrapped?
ern-sgah dee di *pah*-gehth in? — *Ønsker De det pakket ind?* (pol)

Sorry, this is the only one.
dis-*vehŕ di*-deh ehŕ dehn *i*-nehs-deh — *Desværre, dette er den eneste.*

How much/many do you want?
vo *mah*-ehth/*mahng*-eh *ern*-sgah dee? — *Hvor meget/mange ønsker De?* (pol)

Essential Groceries

bread	bŕerth	*brød*
butter	smer	*smør*
milk	mehlg	*mælk*
rice	ŕees	*ris*
salt	sald	*salt*
shampoo	*sham*-por	*shampoo*
sugar	*sā*-gah	*sukker*
toilet paper	toy-*lehd*-pah-peeŕ	*toiletpapir*
toothpaste	*tan*-pas-da	*tandpasta*
vegetables	*gŕern*-sa-ah	*grønsager*

Souvenirs

earrings	*er*-ŕing-eh	*øreringe*
handicraft	*kānsd*-hon-vehŕg	*kunsthåndværk*
necklace	*hals*-keh-theh	*halskæde*
pottery	ki-ah-*meeg*	*keramik*
ring	ŕing	*ring*
rug	*teh*-beh	*tæppe*

Clothing

clothing	toy	*tøj*
coat	*fŕah*-geh	*frakke*
dress	*kyor*-leh	*kjole*
jacket	*yah*-geh	*jakke*
jumper (sweater)	*sweh*-dah	*sweater*
shirt	*sgyoŕ*-deh	*skjorte*
shoes	sgor	*sko*
skirt	*nith*-ah-dil	*nederdel*
trousers	*bāg*-sah	*bukser*
It doesn't fit.	dehn *pas*-ah ig	*Den passer ikke.*
It's too ...	dehn ehŕ fo ...	*Den er for ...*
big	sdooŕ	*stor*
small	*lee*-leh	*lille*
short	koŕd	*kort*
long	lahng	*lang*
tight	sdŕahm	*stram*
loose	lers	*løs*

Materials

cotton	*bom*-ool	*bomuld*
handmade	*hon*-la-wehth	*håndlavet*
leather	*lehth*-ah	*læder*
brass	*mehs*-sing	*messing*
gold	gool	*guld*
silver	serl	*sølv*
silk	*sil*-geh	*silke*
wool	ool	*uld*

Colours

black	soŕd	*sort*
blue	blā	*blå*
brown	bŕoon	*brun*
green	gŕern	*grøn*

orange	or-*ŕang*-sheh	*orange*
pink	*ŕor*-sa	*rosa*
purple	*li*-la	*lilla*
red	ŕerth	*rød*
white	veeth	*hvid*
yellow	gool	*gul*

Toiletries

comb	kahm	*kam*
condoms	kon-*dorm*-ah	*kondomer*
deodorant	di-or-dor-*ŕahnd*	*deodorant*
hairbrush	*hor*-bers-deh	*hårbørste*
moisturising cream	*fäg*-dee-hiths-kŕehm	*fugtighedscreme*
razor	bah-*biŕ*-knee-w	*barberkniv*
sanitary napkins	bin	*bind*
shampoo	shahm-poo	*shampoo*
shaving cream	bah-*biŕ*-kŕehm	*barbercreme*
soap	*seh*-beh	*sæbe*
sunblock cream	*sorl*-kŕehm	*solcreme*
tampons	tahm-*pong*-ah	*tamponer*
tissues	*ŕahn*-seh-sehŕ-vee-ehd	*renseserviet*
toilet paper	toy-*lehd*-pah-peeŕ	*toiletpapir*
toothbrush	*tan*-bers-deh	*tandbørste*
toothpaste	*tan*-pas-da	*tandpasta*

Stationery & Publications

map	koŕd	*kort*
newspaper	a-*vees*	*avis*
newspaper in English	a-*vees* på *ehng*-ehlsg	*avis på engelsk*
novels in English	ŕo-*man*-ah	*romaner*
	på *ehng*-ehlsg	*på engelsk*
paper	pa-*peeŕ*	*papir*
pen (ballpoint)	*koo*-leh-pehn	*kuglepen*
scissors	sahgs	*saks*

Photography

How much is it to process this film?
vo *mah*-ehth *kos*-dah
di ad *ŕahm*-ka-leh
dehn-neh feelm?

Hvor meget koster det at fremkalde denne film?

When will it be ready?
vo-*nor* ehŕ dehn *fehŕ*-dee?

Hvornår er den færdig?

I'd like a film for this camera.
yai vi *geŕh*-neh ha in feelm
ti *deh*-deh *ka*-meh-ŕah

Jeg vil gerne have en film til dette kamera.

B&W (film)	*soŕd*-veeth	*sort-hvid*
camera	*ka*-meh-ŕah	*kamera*
colour (film)	*fah*-weh	*farve*
film	feelm	*film*
flash	bleeds	*blitz*
lens	ob-yehg-*tee*-w	*objektiv*
light meter	*lüs*-mä-lah	*lysmåler*

Smoking

A packet of cigarettes, please.
in *pah*-geh
see-gah-*ŕah*-dah tahg

En pakke cigaretter, tak.

Are these cigarettes strong/mild?
ehŕ *dees*-eh see-gah-*ŕah*-dah
sdehŕ-geh/*meel*-eh?

Er disse cigaretter stærke/milde?

Do you have a light?
hah doo il?

Har du ild? (inf)

cigarette papers	see-gah-*ŕahd*-pah-peeŕ	*cigaretpapir*
cigarettes	see-gah-*ŕah*-dah	*cigaretter*
filtered	meh *feel*-dah	*med filter*
lighter	*lai*-dah	*lighter*
matches	*tehn*-sdig-ah	*tændstikker*
menthol	mehn-*torl*	*mentol*
pipe	*pee*-beh	*pibe*
tobacco (pipe)	*pee*-be-tor-bahg	*pibetobak*

Sizes & Comparisons

small	*lee*-leh	*lille*
big	*sdooŕ*	*stor*
heavy	tāng	*tung*
light	lehd	*let*
more	*mi*-ah	*mere*
less	*min*-dŕah	*mindre*
too much/many	fo *mah*-ehth/ *mahng*-eh	*for meget/ mange*
many	*mahng*-eh	*mange*
enough	nog	*nok*
also	*os*-eh	*også*
a little bit	in *lee*-leh *smoo*-leh	*en lille smule*

HEALTH

Where is the ...?	voŕ ehŕ ...?	*Hvor er ...?*
hospital	hors-bi-*ta*-lehth	*hospitalet*
chemist	ah-por-*tig*-ehth	*apoteket*
the casualty ward	sga-theh-sdoo-ehn	*skadestuen*
Where is a ...?	voŕ ehŕ dehŕ in ...?	*Hvor er der en ...?*
doctor	*leh*-eh	*læge*
dentist	*tan*-leh-eh	*tandlæge*

I'm sick.
yai ehŕ sü — *Jeg er syg.*

My friend is sick.
meen vehn ehŕ sü — *Min ven er syg.*

Could I see a female doctor?
mā yai fā in *kvin*-lee *leh*-eh? — *Må jeg få en kvindelig læge?*

What's the matter?
va ehŕ dah ee *vai*-yehn? — *Hvad er der i vejen?*

Where does it hurt?
voŕ ger di ānd? *Hvor gør det ondt?*
It hurts here.
di ger ānd heeŕ *Det gør ondt her.*
My ... hurts.
meen/meed ... ger ānd *Min/mit ... gør ondt.*

Parts of the Body

ankle	*ahng*-gehl	*ankel*
arm	ahm	*arm*
back	ŕerg	*ryg*
chest	bŕersd	*bryst*
ear	*er*-ah	*øre*
eye	*oy*-yeh	*øje*
finger	*fing*-ah	*finger*
foot	forth	*fod*
hand	hon	*hånd*
head	*hor*-wehth	*hoved*
heart	*yehŕ*-deh	*hjerte*
leg	bin	*ben*
mouth	mān	*mund*
ribs	*ŕee*-bin	*ribben*
skin	hooth	*hud*
stomach	*ma*-weh	*mave*
teeth	*tehn*-ah	*tænder*
throat	hals	*hals*

Ailments

I have (a/an) ...	yai hah ...	*Jeg har ...*
allergy	a-lah-*gee*	*allergi*
anaemia	a-neh-*mee*	*anæmi*
blister	in *va*-behl	*en vabel*
burn	id *bŕahn*-sor	*et brandsår*
cold	in fo-*kerl*-seh	*en forkølelse*
constipation	fo-*sdob*-ehl-seh	*forstoppelse*
cough	*hors*-deh	*hoste*
diarrhoea	dee-a-*ŕeh*	*diarré*
fever	*fi*-bah	*feber*
headache	*hor*-wehth-pee-neh	*hovedpine*
hepatitis	hi-pa-*tee*-tees	*hepatitis*
indigestion	*ma*-weh-bi-svehŕ	*mavebesvær*
infection	in in-fehg-*shorn*	*en infektion*
influenza	in-floo-*ehn*-sa	*influenza*
lice	loos	*lus*
low/high	*la*-wd/hoyd	*lavt/højt*
blood pressure	*blorth*-tŕerg	*blodtryk*
sore throat	ānd ee *hal*-sehn	*ondt i halsen*
sprain	in fo-*sdoo*-ning	*en forstuvning*
stomachache	ānd ee *ma*-wehn	*ondt i maven*
temperature	*fi*-bah	*feber*
venereal disease	in *kerns*-sü-dom	*en kønssygdom*
worms	ooŕm	*orm*

Some Useful Words & Phrases

I'm ...	yai hah ...	*Jeg har ...*
asthmatic	*asd*-ma	*astma*
diabetic	dee-a-*bi*-tehs	*diabetes*
epileptic	eh-pee-lehb-*see*	*epilepsi*

I'm allergic to antibiotics/penicillin.	
yai ehŕ a-*lehŕ*-geesg *ow*-ah fo an-tee-bee-*or*-tee-ka/ pin-ee-see-*leen*	*Jeg er allergisk over for antibiotika/ penicillin.*

I'm pregnant.
yai ehŕ gŕah-*veeth* — *Jeg er gravid.*

I'm on the pill.
yai *bŕoo*-ah *pi*-pil-lah — *Jeg bruger p-piller.*

I haven't had my period for ... months.
yai hah ig hahfd mins-dŕoo-ah-*shorn* ee ... mā-neh-thah — *Jeg har ikke haft menstruation i ... måneder.*

I have been vaccinated.
yai ehŕ *bli*-wehth vahg-see-*ni*-ahth — *Jeg er blevet vaccineret.*

I have my own syringe.
yai hah meen *ai*-yehn ka-*nü*-leh — *Jeg har min egen kanyle.*

I feel better/worse.
yai hah di *behth*-ah/*vehŕ*-ah — *Jeg har det bedre/værre.*

DANISH

At the Chemist

I need medication for ...
yai sga *bŕoo*-eh *nā*-ehth mi-dee-*seen* morth ... — *Jeg skal bruge noget medicin mod ...*

I have a prescription.
yai hah in ŕeh-*sehbd* — *Jeg har en recept.*

At the Dentist

I have a toothache.
yai hah *tan*-pee-neh — *Jeg har tandpine.*

I've lost a filling.
yai hah tahbd en *plām*-beh — *Jeg har tabt en plombe.*

I've broken a tooth.
yai hah *kneh*-gehth in tan — *Jeg har knækket en tand.*

My gums hurt.
meed *tan*-kerth ger ānd — *Mit tandkød gør ondt.*

I don't want it extracted.
yai vi ig ha dehn *tŕā*-gehth ooth — *Jeg vil ikke have den trukket ud.*

Please give me an anaesthetic.
yai vi *gehŕ*-neh bi-*der*-wehs — *Jeg vil gerne bedøves.*

Some Useful Words

accident	*oo*-ler-geh	*ulykke*
addiction	ahw-*hehng*-ee-hith	*afhængighed*
aspirin	as-bee-*ŕeen*	*aspirin*
a bandage	in ban-*da*-sheh	*en bandage*
blood test	*blorth*-pŕer-veh	*blodprøve*
contraception	pŕeh-vehn-*shorn*	*prævention*
medicine	mi-dee-*seen*	*medicin*
menstruation	mins-dŕo-oah-*shorn*	*menstruation*
nausea	*kval*-meh	*kvalme*
oxygen	og-sü-*gin*/eeld	*oxygen/ilt*
vitamins	vee-ta-*meen*-ah	*vitaminer*

TIME & DATES

What date is it today?	
vil-gehn *da*-tor ehŕ di ee da?	*Hvilken dato er det i dag?*
What time is it?	
va ehŕ *klog*-gehn?	*Hvad er klokken?*
It's ... am/pm.	
klog-gehn ehŕ ...	*Klokken er ...*
om *moŕn*-n/*ahfd*-nehn	*om morgenen/aftenen.*

in the morning	om *moŕ*-n	*om morgenen*
in the afternoon	om *ehf*-dah-mi-da-ehn	*om eftermiddagen*
in the evening	om *ahfd*-nehn	*om aftenen*

Days of the Week

Monday	*man*-da	*mandag*
Tuesday	*teeŕs*-da	*tirsdag*
Wednesday	*āns*-da	*onsdag*
Thursday	*toŕs*-da	*torsdag*
Friday	*fŕeh*-da	*fredag*
Saturday	*ler*-da	*lørdag*
Sunday	*sern*-da	*søndag*

Months

January	*yan*-oo-ah	*januar*
February	*feb*-foo-ah	*februar*
March	mahds	*marts*
April	a-*pŕeel*	*april*
May	mai	*maj*
June	*yoo*-nee	*juni*
July	*yoo*-lee	*juli*
August	ahw-*gāsd*	*august*
September	sib-*tehm*-bah	*september*
October	org-*tor*-bah	*oktober*
November	nor-*vehm*-bah	*november*
December	di-*sehm*-bah	*december*

Seasons

summer	*som*-ah	*sommer*
autumn	*ehf*-dah-or	*efterår*
winter	*vin*-dah	*vinter*
spring	*for*-or	*forår*

Present

today	ee da	*i dag*
this morning	ee moŕ-seh	*i morges*
tonight	ee nad	*i nat*
this week	*dehn*-neh *oo*-eh	*denne uge*
this year	ee or	*i år*
now	noo	*nu*

Past

yesterday	ee gor	*i går*
day before yesterday	ee *for*-gors	*i forgårs*
yesterday morning	ee gor mor-seh	*i går morges*
last night	ee (gor) nad;	*i (går) nat;*
	ee (gor) *ahf*-dehs	*i (går) aftes*
last week	*for*-ee *oo*-eh	*forrige uge*
last year	*sees*-deh or	*sidste år*

Future

tomorrow	ee morn	*i morgen*
day after tomorrow	ee *ow*-ah-morn	*i overmorgen*
tomorrow morning	ee morn *teeth*-lee	*i morgen tidlig*
tomorrow afternoon/ evening	ee morn *ehf*-dah-mi-da/ *ahf*-dehn	*i morgen eftermiddag/ aften*
next week	*nehs*-deh *oo*-eh	*næste uge*
next year	*nehs*-deh or	*næste år*

During the Day

afternoon	*ehf*-dah-mi-da	*eftermiddag*
dawn	*daow*-gŕü	*daggry*
day	da	*dag*
early	*teeth*-lee	*tidlig*
midnight	*meeth*-nad	*midnat*
morning	morn	*morgen*
night	nad	*nat*
noon	*mi*-das-teeth	*middagstid*
sundown	*sorl*-nith-gahng	*solnedgang*
sunrise	*sorl*-ob-gahng	*solopgang*

NUMBERS & AMOUNTS

0	nāl	*nul*
1	in	*en*
2	tor	*to*
3	tŕeh	*tre*
4	feeŕ	*fire*
5	feh	*fem*
6	sehgs	*seks*
7	sü-w	*syv*
8	*ā*-deh	*otte*
9	nee	*ni*
10	tee	*ti*
11	*ehl*-veh	*elve*

12	tol	*tolv*
13	*tŕah*-dehn	*tretten*
14	*fyor*-dehn	*fjorten*
15	*fehm*-dehn	*femten*
16	*sais*-dehn	*seksten*
17	*ser*-dehn	*sytten*
18	*a*-dehn	*atten*
19	*ni*-dehn	*nitten*
20	*tü*-weh	*tyve*
21	*in*-o-tü-weh	*enogtyve*
30	*tŕahth*-veh	*tredive*
40	*feŕ*-eh	*fyrre*
50	hal-*tŕehs*	*halvtreds*
60	tŕehs	*tres*
70	hal-*fyehŕs*	*halvfjerds*
80	feeŕs	*firs*
90	hal-*fehms*	*halvfems*
100	*hoon*-ahth	*hundrede*
1000	*too*-sehn	*tusind*
one million	in mee-lee-*orn*	*en million*

1st	*fers*-deh	*første*
2nd	*an*-ehn	*anden*
3rd	*tŕehth*-yeh	*tredje*
1/4	in *fyi*-ah-dil	*en fjerdedel*
1/3	in *tŕehth*-yeh-dil	*en tredjedel*
1/2	in hal	*en halv*
3/4	tŕeh *fyi*-ah-di-leh	*tre fjerdedele*

Some Useful Words

a little (amount)	en *lee*-leh *smoo*-leh	*en lille smule*
double	*dob*-ehld	*dobbelt*
a dozen	id doo-*seen*	*et dusin*
enough	nog	*nok*
few	fã	*fã*
less	*min*-dfah	*mindre*
many	*mahng*-eh	*mange*
more	*mi*-ah	*mere*
once	*in* gahng	*en gang*
a pair	id pah	*et par*
percent	pfor-*sehnd*	*procent*
some	*nor*-leh	*nogle*
too much	fo *mah*-ehth	*for meget*
twice	tor *gahng*-eh	*to gange*

ABBREVIATIONS

0800/2000	am/pm
a/s – aktieselskab	Ltd/Inc.
BZ – besættere	squatters
DSB – de Danske Statsbaner	the Danish National Railways
DUH – de Danske Ungdomsherberger	Danish Youth Hostel Association
DVH – de Danske Vandrehjem	Danish Youth Hostel Association
dagl. – dagligt	daily (Monday to Saturday)
EF – det Europæiske Fællesmarked	EEC, the Common Market
ekskl. – eksklusive	excluded, except
EU – den Europæiske Union	the European Union
FN – de Forenede Nationer	UN
f.kr/e.kr.	BC/AD
frk. – frøken	Miss
fr – fredag	Friday
fru	Mrs
Gd/V	St/Rd

hel. – hellig	holy (as in holiday)
hlp. – holdeplads	bus stop
Hr. – herr	Mr/Sir
inkl. – inklusive	including
jb – jernbane	railway
jrbst – jernbanestation	station/railway station
Kbh – København	Copenhagen
KDAK	the Royal Danish Automobile Association
kgl. – kongelig	royal
kl. – klasse	class (on trains and aeroplanes)
kl. – klokken	o'clock
km/t – kilometer i timen	kilometres per hour
kr – krone	crown (Danish monetary unit)
lø – lørdag	Saturday
m. – med	with
ma – mandag	Monday
moms	VAT, sales tax (included in the price on all goods and services)
ndf. – nedenfor	below (used in notices, timetables, etc)
Ndr. – nordre	to the north (pertaining to place names)
on – onsdag	Wednesday
SAS	Scandinavian Airline System
Sdr. – søndre	to the south (pertaining to place names)
sø – søndag	Sunday
t.h. – til højre	to the right (used in addresses)
ti – tirsdag	Tuesday
tlf. – telefon	telephone
to – torsdag	Thursday
t.v. – til venstre	to the left (used in addresses)

EMERGENCIES

Go away!	fo-*svin*!	*Forsvind!*
Help!	yehlb!	*Hjælp!*
Thief!	tüw!	*Tyv!*

SIGNS

POLITI
POLICE

POLITISTATION
POLICE STATION

It's an emergency!
deh-deh ehŕ en *nerth*-si-too-a-shorn! — *Dette er en nødsituation!*

There's been an accident!
dah ehŕ skid in *oo*-ler-geh! — *Der er sket en ulykke!*

Call a doctor!
ŕing *ehf*-dah in *leh*-eh! — *Ring efter en læge!*

Call an ambulance!
ŕing *ehf*-dah in ahm-boo-*lahng*-seh! — *Ring efter en ambulance!*

I've been raped.
yai ehŕ *bli*-wehth *vol*-ta-ehth — *Jeg er blevet voldtaget.*

I've been robbed.
yai ehŕ *bli*-wehth bi-*sdyā*-lehth! — *Jeg er blevet bestjålet!*

Call the police!
ŕing ehf-dah por-li-*tee*-ehth! — *Ring efter politiet!*

Where is the police station?
vor ehŕ por-li-*tee*-sda-shor-nehn? — *Hvor er politistationen?*

I'll call the police!
yai *ŕing*-ah ti por-li-*tee*-ehth! — *Jeg ringer til politiet!*

I'm/My friend is ill.
yai ehr/meen vehn ehŕ sü — *Jeg er/Min ven er syg.*

I'm lost.
yai ehŕ *fah*-ehth vil — *Jeg er faret vild.*

Where are the toilets?
vor ehŕ toy-*lehd*-dah-neh? — *Hvor er toiletterne?*

Could you help me please?
ka dee *yehl*-beh mai? — *Kan De hjælpe mig?* (pol)

Could I please use the telephone?
mā yai *lā*-neh ti-leh-*for*-nehn? — *Må jeg låne telefonen?*

I'm sorry. I apologise. bi-*kla*-ah. *ān*-sgül	*Beklager. Undskyld.*
I didn't realise I was doing anything wrong. yai *vis*-deh *ig* ad yai gyoŕ *nā*-ehth gald	*Jeg vidste ikke at jeg gjorde noget galt.*
I didn't do it. di vah ig *mai* dah *gyoŕ* di	*Det var ikke mig der gjorde det.*
I wish to contact my embassy/consulate. yai vi *gehŕ*-neh kon-*tahg*-deh meen ah-mba-*sa*-theh/ meed kon-soo-*lad*	*Jeg vil gerne kontakte min ambassade/ mit konsulat.*
I speak English. yai *ta*-lah *ehng*-elhsg	*Jeg taler engelsk.*
I have medical insurance. yai hah *sü*-ėh-fo-sig-ŕing	*Jeg har sygeforsikring.*
My possessions are insured. mee-neh *ai*-ehn-*di*-leh ehŕ fo-*sig*-ŕahth	*Mine ejendele er forsikret.*

My ... was stolen.	meed/meen ... ehŕ *bli*-wehth *sdyā*-lehth	*Mit/min... er blevet stjålet.*
I've lost my...	yai hah *mis*-dehth ...	*Jeg har mistet ...*
bags	meen ba-*ga*-sheh	*min bagage*
handbag	meen *hon*-tas-geh	*min håndtaske*
money	*mee*-neh *pehng*-eh	*mine penge*
passport	meed pas	*mit pas*
travellers cheques	*mee*-neh *ŕai*-seh-shehgs	*mine rejsechecks*

FAROESE

QUICK REFERENCE

Hello.	huh-lloh!/huhy!	*Halló!/Hey!*
Goodbye.	for-vael	*Farvæl.*
Yes./No.	yae/nai	*Ja./Nei.*
Excuse me.	or-sae-kuh!	*Orsaka!*
Sorry.	um-shil-duh/ or-saek-i-meh	*Umskylda/ Orsakið meg.*
Please.	djehr-i so vael	*Gerið so væl.*
Thank you.	tuhk	*Takk.*
That's fine./ You're welcome.	on-chi uh tuhk-kuh fi-ri	*Onki at takka fyri.*
I'd like ...	kun-di ehg fin-dji ...	*Kundi eg fingið ...*
a one-way ticket	ain-veh-yis fehr-uh-seh-yil	*einvegis ferðaseðil*
a return ticket	fehr-uh-seh-yil uht-tur o fruhm	*ferðaseðil aftur og fram*

I (don't) understand.
eh shil-yi (ich-i) — *Eg skilji (ikki).*

Do you speak English?
du-vir too ain-gilst? — *Dugir tú eingilskt?*

Where is ...?
kvaer ehr ...? — *Hvar er ...?*

Go straight ahead.
faer baint fruhm — *Far beint fram.*

Turn left/right.
faer teel vin-stru/herg-ru. — *Fær til vinstru/høgru.*

Do you have any rooms available?
ehr-u nerk-ur luhys kerm-ur? — *Eru nøkur leys kømur?*

I'm looking for a public toilet.
eh lait-eh eht-tir uhl-mehn-nun vehs-eh — *Eg leiti eftir almennum vesi.*

1	aitt	*eitt*	6	sehks	*seks*
2	tvuhy	*tvey*	7	shuhy	*sjey*
3	trooi	*trý*	8	ot-tuh	*átta*
4	fooir-uh	*fíra*	9	nooi-djeh	*níggju*
5	fim	*fimm*	10	tooi-djeh	*tíggju*

FAROESE

Faroese (often spelled Faeroese) is a twig of the North Germanic branch of the Indo-European tree, which includes Icelandic, Danish, Norwegian and Swedish.

The population of the Faroe Islands, or Faroes, is about 46,000, which means that Faroese is the mother tongue of only a very small number of people.

The Norwegian settlers (about 900 AD) brought their own language to the places they colonised, among them the Faroes, and over the centuries a distinct language developed in the Faroe Islands. The most important factor in the preservation of the language was the oral literature, particularly the **kvæði**, long epic ballads dealing with ancient legendary characters and events, which are a unique cultural heritage.

Historically the Faroe Islands have been under Norwegian and Danish rule. For several centuries Danish was the dominating language in all administration and in public institutions like schools and the church, and Faroese was degraded to the privacy of the home. In 1846 a Faroese scholar set out to recreate a written norm for Faroese. Today books and newspapers are in Faroese, as are church services and school lessons.

Modern Faroese is under the constant influence of the surrounding world, particularly through the mass media, and there is an ongoing struggle to promote and nourish Faroese in the face of the massive influence of Danish and American English.

PRONUNCIATION

The written norm, created in 1846 and still in use, is based on etymology and thus reflects an older stage of Faroese than does the pronunciation.

STRESS

Stress is normally on the first syllable of the word.

Pronunciation is given in the pronunciation guide at the front of this book, with the following exceptions:

Vowels

In front of two or more consonants, vowels are short and have a more open quality than their long equivalents.

Semivowels

FAROESE	GUIDE	SOUND
á long	wah	as the 'oi' in French *moi*
í, ý long	ooi	as in Spanish *muy*

Consonants

FAROESE	GUIDE	SOUND
ð		silent in a final position; otherwise taking on the value of surrounding vowels
ðr	gr	as the 'gr' in 'grab'
dj, ge, gi, gy, gey, gj, ggj	dj	as the 'j' in 'jaw'
ft	tt	as the 'tt' in 'bitter'
g		silent in a final position; otherwise taking on the value of surrounding vowels
hj	y	as the 'y' in 'yet'
ke, ki, ky, key, kj	ch	as the 'ch' 'chew'
r	r	as the 'r' in 'grab'
rn	dn	as the 'dn' in 'hadn't'
ll	dl	as the 'dl' in 'saddle'
sj, sk, ske, ski, sky, skey, skj	sh	as in 'ship'

GREETINGS & CIVILITIES

Top Useful Phrases

Hello.	huh-lloh!/huhy!	*Halló!/Hey!*
How do you do?	goh-uhn dae(-yin)	*Góðan dag(in).*
Goodbye.	for-vael	*Farvæl.*
See you later.	veet sooi-djuhst	*Vit síggjast.*
Yes/No.	yae/nai	*Ja./Nei.*
Excuse me.	or-sae-kuh!	*Orsaka!*
Maybe.	kuhn-skuh	*Kanska.*
Please.	djehr-i so vael	*Gerið so væl.*
Thank you.	tuhk	*Takk.*

May I? Do you mind?
kuhn eh? slehp-pi eh? — *Kann eg? Sleppi eg?*

Sorry. (excuse me, forgive me)
um-shil-duh/or-saek-i-meh — *Umskylda/Orsakið meg.*

Many thanks.
too-sun tuhk — *Túsund takk.* (lit. thousand thanks)

You too!
sholv/-ur tuhk! — *Sjálv/-ur takk!* (f/m) (lit. self thanks)

That's fine. You're welcome.
on-chi uh tuhk-kuh fi-ri — *Onki at takka fyri.*

That's all right.
tae ehr ooi lae-yee — *Tað er í lagi.*

THANKS FOR THE MEMORIES

Takk fyri seinast. tuhk fi-ri sain-uhst
Thanks for the last time I saw you – used when you meet someone again after a party or a social event

Manga takk! muhn-guh tuhk!
Many thanks – used to your hostess after a meal

Væl gagnist! vael guhg-nist
May the food do you good – answer to the above

Greetings

Good morning.	goh-uhn mor-gun	*Góðan morgun.*
Good afternoon.	goh-uhn dae(-yin)	*Góðan dag(in).*
Good evening.	gott kverld	*Gott kvøld.*
Good night.	goh-uh nott	*Góa nátt.*
How are you?	kvus-seh heh-vur too tae?	*Hvussu hevur tú tað?*
Well, thanks.	gott tuhk	*Gott takk.*

Forms of Address

Madam/Mrs	froo	*frú*
Sir/Mr	huhr-ruh	*harra*
Miss	frer-kun	*frøkun*
companion/friend	vin-kon-uh/vee-nur	*vinkona/vinur* (f/m)

PRONOUNS		
SG		
I	eh	*eg*
you	too	*tú*
she/he/it	hon/huhn/tae	*hon/hann/tað*
PL		
we	veed	*vit*
you (pl)	teed	*tit*
they	taer/tair/tuhy	*tær/teir/tey (f/m/n)*

SMALL TALK

Meeting People

What is your name?	kvus-seh ai-tuh ti-yun?	*Hvussu eita tygum?*
My name is ...	eh ai-ti ...	*Eg eiti ...*

I'd like to introduce you to ...
chehn-nir too ...? — *Kennir tú ...?* (lit. know you ...?)

I'm pleased to meet you.
stutt-litt aet hitt-uh teh — *Stuttligt at hitta teg.*

Nationalities

Where are you from?
kvae-uhn-i ehr-u tiy-un? — *Hvaðani eru tygum?*

I'm from ...	eh ehr-i oor ...	*Eg eri úr ...*
Australia	uhu-strah-li-uh	*Avstralia*
Canada	kah-nuh-duh	*Kanada*
Denmark	duhm-muhrsk	*Danmark*
England	ong-luhn-di	*Onglandi*
Iceland	ooish-luhn-di	*Íslandi*
Ireland	ur-luhn-di	*Írlandi*
New Zealand	nooi-sae-luhn-di	*Ný Sælandi*
Norway	nor-ruh	*Noregi*
Scotland	sgot-luhn-di	*Skotlandi*
Sweden	sverr-ooi-chi	*Svoríki*
the USA	uh-mehr-i-kuh/ u-ehs-ah	*Amerika/ USA*

Age

How old are you?
kvus-seh go-mul/ gae-muhl ehrs-too? — *Hvussu gomul/ gamal ert tú?* (f/m)

I'm ... years old.
eh ehr-i ... wah-ruh go-mul/ gae-muhl — *Eg eri ... ára gomul/ gamal.* (f/m)

Occupations

What do you do?

kvaet djeh-ruh ti-yun? *Hvat gera tygum?* (pol)

I work as ...	eh uhr-buh-yi sum ...	*Eg arbeiði sum ...*
artist	lis-tuh-ferlk	*listafólk*
business person	huhn-dils-kvin-nuh/ huhn-dil-mae-vur	*handilskvinna/ handilsmaður* (f/m)
doctor	luhk-ni/dok-tuhr-i	*læknl/doktari*
engineer	muh-sheen-mai-stuhr-i	*maskinmeistari*
farmer	bern-di	*bóndi*
journalist	tooin-duh-ferlk	*tíðindafólk*
lawyer	saek-ferr-uhr-i	*sakførari*
manual worker	uhr-bais-kvin-nuh/ uhr-bais-mae-vur	*arbeiðskvinna/ arbeiðsmaður* (f/m)
mechanic	meh-kahn-i-kuhr-i	*mekanikari*
nurse	shook-ruh-sis-tir	*sjúkrasystir*
office worker	skriv-sto-vu-ferlk	*skrivstovufólk*
sailor/seaman	shoh-mae-vur	*sjómaður*
scientist	voois-in-duh-ferlk	*vísindafólk*
student	stu-dehn-tur	*studentur*
teacher	lae-ruhr-i	*lærari*
waiter	tae-nuhr-i	*tænari*
writer	rit-her-vun-dur	*rithøvundur*

Religion

What is your religion?

kverr-yuh trigv heh-vur too? *Hvørja trúgv hevur tú?*

I'm not religious.

eh ehr-i ich-i reh-li-gi-ers/-ur *Eg eri ikki religiøs/-ur.* (f/m)

I'm (a) ...	eh ehr-i ...	*Eg eri ...*
Buddhist	budd-is-tur	*buddistur*
Catholic	kuh-to-lik-kur	*katolikkur*
Christian	kris-tin	*kristin*
Hindu	hin-du	*hindu*
Jewish	yer-di	*jødi*
Muslim	mus-lee-mur	*muslimur*

Family

Are you married?	ehrs-too djift/-ur	*Ert tú gift/-ur?* (f/m)
I'm ...	eh ehr-i ...	*Eg eri ...*
single	oh-djift/-ur	*ógift/-ur* (f/m)
married	djift/-ur	*gift/-ur* (f/m)
divorced	shild/-ur	*skild/-ur* (f/m)
a widow/er	ain-chuh/ ain-chu-mae-vur	*einkja/ einkjumaður* (f/m)
available	luhys/-ur	*leys/-ur* (f/m)

How many children do you have?
kvus-su nehgv berdn heh-vur too? *Hvussu nógv børn hevur tú?*

I don't have any children.
eh hae-vi on-dji berdn *Eg havi ongi børn.*

I have a daughter/a son.
eh hae-vi ain-uh der-ttur/ ain son *Eg havi eina dóttur/ ein son.*

How many brothers/ sisters do you have?
kvus-su nehgv sish-in heh-vur too? *Hvussu nógv systkin hevur tüu?*

Do you have a boyfriend/girlfriend?
Heh-vur too shaik/dah-mu? *Hevur tú sjeik/damu?*

brother	brohir/bai-dji	*bróðir/beiggi*
children	berdn	*børn*
daughter	der-ttir	*dóttir*
family	fuhm-il-yuh/shil-ferlk	*familja/skyldfólk*
father	fae-yir/pwah-pi	*faðir/pápi*
grandfather	uhb-i	*abbi*
grandmother	om-uh	*omma*
husband	mae-vur	*maður*
mother	moh-ir/muhm-uh	*móðir/mamma*
sister	sis-tir	*systir*
son	son-ur	*sonur*
wife	ko-nuh	*kona*

Kids' Talk

How old are you?
kvu-su nehgv wahr ehrs-too? *Hvussu nógv ár ert tú?*

When's your birthday?
naer fidl-ir too? *Nær fyllir tú?*

What do you do after school?
kvaet gehrs-too ehtt-ir skoo-luh-tooi? *Hvat gert tú eftir skúlatíð?*

Do you have a pet at home?
Heh-vur too nae-kuh chehl-i-dooir? *Hevur tú nakað kelidýr?*

I have/own a ...	eh hae-vi/ai-yi ...	*eg havi/eigi ...*
bird	ain fugl	*ein fugl*
budgerigar	un-du-laht	*undulat*
canary	kuhn-ahr-i-u-fugl	*kanariufugl*
cat	cheht-u	*kettu*
dog	hund	*hund*

Feelings

I (don't) like ...
maer dwah-muhr (ich-i) ... *Mær dámar (ikki)...*

I love/hate ..
eh ehl-shi/hae-ti ... *Eg elski/hati ...*

I'm in a hurry.
eh mwah skund-uh maer *Eg má skunda mær.* (lit. I must hurry me)

I'm well.
eh hae-vi tae got *Eg havi tað gott.*

I'm sorry. (condolence)
tae vaer sind ooi taer/ tik-un *Tað var synd í tær/ tykkum.* (sg/pl)

I'm grateful.
eh si-yi stohr-uh tuhk *Eg sigi stóra takk.* (lit. I say great thank-you)

You're right.	too heh-vur ruhtt	*Tú hevur rætt.*
I'm ...	eh ehr-i ...	*Eg eri ...*
angry	idl/-ur	*ill/-ur* (f/m)
cold	kerld/kuhld-ur	*køld/kaldur* (f/m)
full/satisfied	mehtt/-ur	*mett/-ur* (f/m)
happy	glae/-vur	*glað/-vur* (f/m)
hot	hait/-ur	*heit/-ur* (f/m)
hungry	svong/svehng-ur	*svong/svangur* (f/m)
sad	chehdd/-ur	*kedd/-ur* (f/m)
thirsty	tist/-ur	*tyst/-ur* (f/m)
tired (fatigued)	moh/-ur	*móð/-ur* (f/m)
worried	stoor-in	*stúrin*

Some Useful Phrases

Just a minute.	
booi-yuh aitt sin-dur	*Bíða eitt sindur.*
It's (not) important.	
tae ehr (ich-i) um-rwahn-di	*Tað er (ikki) umráðandi.*
It's (not) possible.	
tae ehr (ich-i) mer-vi-litt	*Tað er (ikki) møguligt.*
Wait!	
booi-yuh!/booi-yi!	*Bíða!/Bíðið!* (sg/pol & pl)
Good luck!	
goh-uh ehd-nu!	*Góða eydnu!*

BODY LANGUAGE

The Faroese are rather shy or wary when it comes to expressing their feelings, be it in words or in physical manifestation.

Shaking hands is the usual form of greeting when you meet someone for the first time. Friends and family who meet after having been apart for some time may hug each other, and good friends also kiss each other. Women tend to hug and kiss more than men, who mostly prefer to slap each other's back. When you meet people who you see often, you don't shake hands every time, nor do you shake hands every time you leave.

Gesticulation is not a characteristic of the Faroese, more typically they keep their hands and arms still, and some – particularly men – keep one or both hands in their pockets.

BREAKING THE LANGUAGE BARRIER

Do you speak English?	
du-vir too ain-gilst?	*Dugir tú eingilskt?*
Does anyone speak English?	
du-vir nae-gar ain-gilst?	*Dugir nakar eingilskt?*
I speak a little ...	
eh du-vi aitt sin-dur ...	*Eg dugi eitt sindur ...*
I don't speak ...	
eh du-vi ich-i ...	*Eg dugi ikki ...*
I (don't) understand.	
eh shil-yi (ich-i)	*Eg skilji (ikki).*
Could you repeat that?	
kuhnst too tae-kuh huhtt-uh up-uhtt-ur?	*Kanst tú taka hatta uppaftur?*
Could you speak more slowly please?	
kuhns-too djehr-uh so vael uht tos-uh saint?	*Kanst tú gera so væl at tosa seint?*
How do you say ...?	
kvus-u si-yuh teet ...?	*Hvussu siga tit ...?*

I speak ...	eh du-vi ...	*Eg dugi ...*
English	ain-gilst	*eingilskt*
French	fruhnkst	*franskt*
German	tooikst	*týskt*
Italian	i-tuhlst	*italskt*
Spanish	spuhnkst	*spanskt*

PAPERWORK

address	boos-tae-vur	*bústaður*
age	uhld-ur	*aldur*
birth certificate	fer-yi-braev	*fødibrøv*
car owner's title	beel-skrwah-seht-ing-uhr-vott-uhn	*bilskrásetingarváttan*
car registration	vot-tuhn	*váttan*
customs	to-dlur	*tollur*
date of birth	fer-ying-uhr-dae-vur	*fødingardagur*
driver's licence	koy-ri-korst	*koyrikort*
identification	suhm-lai-kuh-prehgv	*samleikaprógv*
immigration	in-fleet-ing	*innflyting*
marital status	choon-uh-ster-vuh	*hjúnastøða*
name	nuhun	*navn*
nationality	choh-skae-pur	*tjóðskapur*
passport (number)	puhs(-num-uhr)	*pass(nummar)*
place of birth	fer-ying-uhr-stae-vur	*fødingarstaður*
profession	uhr-bai-yi	*arbeiði*
reason for travel	ehn-duh-mwahl vee fehr-in-i	*endamál við ferðini*
religion	trigv	*trúgv*
sex	cheen	*kyn*
visa	vee-suh	*visa*

PREPOSITIONS

English 'at' corresponds to a number of Faroese prepositions (*í* ooi, *á* wah, *við* vee).

GETTING AROUND

What time does the ... leave/arrive?	naer fehr/ chehm-ur ...?	*Nær fer/ kemur ...?*
(air)plane	flog-faer-i	*flogfarið*
boat	bwaht-ur-in	*báturin*
bus (city)	(booi)bus-ur-in	*(bý)bussurin*
bus (intercity)	bus-ur-in	*bussurin*
car ferry	beel-fehr-yuhn	*bilferjan*

Directions

Where is ...?	
kvaer ehr ...?	*Hvar er ...?*
How do I get to ...?	
kvus-seh slehp-i eh teel ...?	*Hvussu sleppi eg til ...?*
Is it far from here?	
ehr tae lehnkt hee-yuhn-i?	*Er tað langt hiðani?*
Can I walk there?	
kuhn eh faer-uh til gong-u hae-uhr?	*Kann eg fara til gongu hagar?*
Can you show me (on the map)?	
kun-nu tiy-um vooi-suh maer (wah korst-in-um)?	*Kunnu tygum vísa mær (á kortinum)?*
Are there other means of getting there?	
kvus-seh kuhn ain uhn-uhrs faer-uh hae-uhr?	*Hvussu kann ein annars fara hagar?*
I want to go to ...	
ehg uht-li maer uht faer-uh teel ...	*Eg ætli mær at fara til ...*
Go straight ahead.	
faer baint fruhm	*Far beint fram.*
It's two streets down.	
tae ehr tvaer gert-ur o-muhn-ehtt-ir	*Tað er tvær gøtur omaneftir.*

Turn left/ right at the ...	faer teel vin-stru/ herg-ru ...	*Fær til vinstru/ høgru ...*
next corner	wah nuhst-uh hod-ni	*á næsta horni*
traffic lights	vee fehrs-leh-lyohs-in-i	*við ferðsluljósini*
behind	uht-tuhn-feer-i	*aftanfyri*
far	lehnkt	*langt*
in front of	fruhm-muhn-feer-i	*frammanfyri*
near	naer	*nær*
opposite	ee-vir-aev	*yvirav*

SIGNS

ATGONGD BANNAÐ/ EINGIN ATGONGD	ENTRANCE PROHIBITED
BUSSUR	BUS
EINVEGIS	ONE WAY
FARSTØÐIN	TERMINAL
FERÐASEÐLAR	TICKETS
FLOGVØLLUR	AIRPORT
FRÁFERÐ	DEPARTURE
HÝRUVOGNUR	TAXI
KOMA	ARRIVAL
NEYÐÚTGONGD	EMERGENCY EXIT
ROYKING BANNAÐ	NO SMOKING
TOLLUR	CUSTOMS
UPPLÝSINGAR	INFORMATION

Booking Tickets

Where can I buy a ticket?	
kvaer fwah-yi ehg chuhypt fehr-uh-seh-yil?	*Hvar fái eg keypt ferðaseðil?*
I want to go to ...	
eh veel feh-yin faer-uh teel ...	*Eg vil fegin fara til ...*
Do I need to book?	
mwah eh booi-leh-djuh?	*Má eg bíleggja?*
I'd like to book a seat to ...	
eh sgael bi-yuh um aitt plos teel ...	*Eg skal biðja um eitt pláss til ...*
Is it completely full?	
ehr tae hailt ootsehlt?	*Er tað heilt útselt?*
Can I get a stand-by ticket?	
kuhn eh fwah ain fehr-uh-seh-yil ooi sooist-u lert-u?/kuhn eh slehp-uh wah booi-yeh-list-uh?	*Kann eg fái ein ferðaseðil í síðstu løtu?/Kann eg sleppa á bíðilista?*

I'd like ...	**kun-di ehg fin-dji ...**	*Kundi eg fingið ...*
a one-way ticket	**ain-veh-yis**	*einvegis*
	fehr-uh-seh-yil	*ferðaseðil*
a return ticket	**fehr-uh-seh-yil**	*ferðaseðil*
	uht-tur o fruhm	*aftur og fram* (lit. ticket back and forth)
two tickets	**tvair fehr-uh-sehl-uhr**	*tveir ferðaseðlar*
a student's fare	**ain fehr-uh-seh-yil teel leh-suhn-di**	*ein ferðaseðil til lesandi*
a child's fare	**ain buhd-nuh-fehr-uh-seh-yil**	*ein barnaferðaseðil*
a pensioner's fare	**fehr-uh-seh-yil teel pehn-sion-ist**	*ein ferðaseðil til pensionist*
1st class	**fis-ti kluhs-si**	*fyrsti klassi*
2nd class	**uhn-nuhr kluhs-si**	*annar klassi*

Air

Is there a flight to ...?
ehr naek-uh flo-faer teel ...? *Er nakað flogfar til ...?*
How long does the flight take?
kvus-seh long ehr *Hvussu long er*
flig-vi tooi-yin? *flúgvitíðin?*

airport tax	flo-vuhdl-uhr-skuht-tur	*flogvallarskattur*
boarding pass	bor-ding puhs	*boarding pass*

Bus

Where is the bus stop?
kvaer ehr bus-steh-dji-plos-si? *Hvar er bussteðgiplássið?*
Which bus goes to ...?
kverr bus-sur fehr teel ...? *Hvør bussur fer til ...?*
Could you let me know
when we get to ...?
kun-nuh ti-yun si-yuh maer *Kunna tygum siga mær*
frwah twah ooi veet *frá tá ið vit*
ko-muh teel ...? *koma til ...?*
I want to get off!
eh veel slehp-puh aev! *Eg vil sleppa av!*
Must I change buses?
sgael eh shif-tuh bus? *Skal eg skifta buss?*

What time is the ... bus?	naer fehr ... bus-sur-in?	*Nær fer ... bussurin?*
next	nuhs-ti	*næsti*
first	fis-ti	*fyrsti*
last	sain-uhs-ti	*seinasti*

DID YOU KNOW ... There are no trains in the Faroe Islands.

Boat

Which harbour is next?
kverr ehr nuhs-tuh huhvn? *Hvør er næsta havn?*
Is this the ferry for ...?
ehr heht-tuh fehr-yuhn teel ...? *Er hetta ferjan til ...?*

cafeteria	kuhff-eh-teh-ri-uh	*kafeteria*
car deck	beel-dehk	*bildekk*
smoking saloon	roy-chi-suh-long	*roykisalon*
sun deck	sohl-dehk	*sóldekk*
ticket including a bunk	koy-dju-plos	*koyggjupláss*

Taxi

Can you take me to ...?
kun-nuh ty-djun koy-ruh meh teel ...? *Kunna tygum koyra meg til ...?*
How much does it cost to go to ...?
kvus-seh nehgv kos-tuhr tae teel ...? *Hvussu nógv kostar tað til ...?*
Here is fine, thank you.
hehr ehr fooint tuhk *Her er fint, takk.*
Continue!
koyr long-ur! *Koyr longur!*
The next street to the left/right.
nuhs-tuh ger-tuh teel vin-stru/herg-ru *Næsta gøta til vinstru/høgru.*
Stop here!
stehg-guh hehr! *Steðga her!*
Please slow down.
djehr-i so vael uht min-kuh fehr-in-uh *Gerið so væl at minka ferðina.*
Please wait here.
djehr-i so vael uht booi-yuh hehr! *Gerið so væl at bíða her!*

Some Useful Phrases

The ... is delayed/cancelled. **... ehr sain-kuh-vur/ aev-loois-tur**	*... er seinkaður/ avlýstur.*
How long will it be delayed? **kvus-seh nehgv ehr huhn sain-kuh-vur?**	*Hvussu nógv er hann seinkaður?*
There is a delay of ... hours. **sain-chin-djin ehr ... tooi-muhr**	*Seinkingin er ... tímar.*
Can I reserve a place? **kuhn eh booi-leh-djuh plos?**	*Kann eg bíleggja pláss?*

How long does the trip take? **kvus-su lehng-uh tooi tehk-ur toor-ur-in?**	*Hvussu langa tíð tekur túrurin?*
Is it a direct route? **ehr tae ain bain-lai-yis rut-uh?**	*Er tað ein beinleiðis ruta?*
Is that seat taken? **ehr huht-tuh plos-si up-teech-i?**	*Er hatta plássið upptikið?*
I want to get off at ... **eh sgael aev ooi ...**	*Eg skal av í ...*
Where can I hire a bicycle? **kvaer fwah-yi eh lai-yuh ain-uh sük-klu?**	*Hvar fái eg leigað eina súkklu?*

Car

Where can I rent a car?
kvaer fwah-yi eh lai-yuh ain beel? — *Hvar fái eg leigað ein bil?*

How much is it daily/weekly?
kvus-seh nehgv kos-tuhr huhn um dae-yin/vee-ku-nuh? — *Hvussu nógv kostar hann um dagin/vikuna?*

Does that include insurance/mileage?
ehr tri-djing/keel-o-meh-truh-tael rok-nuh up-ooi? — *Er trygging/kilometratal roknað uppí?*

Where's the next petrol station?
kvaer ehr nuhst-uh behns-een-ster? — *Hvar er næsta bensinstað?*

How long can I park here?
kvus-su lain-dji ehr lov aet puhr-kehr-uh hehr? — *Hvussu leingi er lov at parkera her?*

Does this road lead to ...?
ehr heht-tuh veh-vur-in teel ...? — *Er hetta vegurin til ...?*

air (for tyres)	luft (teel dehk)	*luft (til dekk)*
battery	uhk-ku-mo-lah-tor-ur	*akkumolatorur*
brakes	brehm-sir	*bremsur*
clutch	kob-ling	*kobling*
driver's licence	koy-ri-korst	*koyrikort*
engine	mo-tor-ur	*motorur*
lights	lyohs	*ljós*
oil	ol-yuh	*olja*
puncture	punk-tehr-ing	*punktering*
radiator	ker-luhr-i	*kølari*
road map	veh-korst	*vegkort*
tyres	dehk	*dekk*
windscreen	fruhm-roo-tur	*framrútur*

I need a mechanic.
eh haev-i brook fir-i ain-un meh-kahn-i-kuhr-uh — *Eg havi brúk fyri einum mekanikara.*

The battery is flat.
buht-tuhr-ooi-yi er fluhtt — *Battaríið er flatt.*

The radiator is leaking.
kerl-uhr-in lehk-ur — *Kølarin lekur.*

I have a flat tyre.
ehg ehr-i punk-tehr-uh-vur — *Eg eri punkteraður.*

It's overheating. (engine)
huhn gong-ur hait-ur — *Hann gongur heitur.*

It's not working.
huhn rig-guhr i-chi — *Hann riggar ikki.*

ACCOMMODATION

Where is a ...?	kvaer ehr aitt ...?	*Hvar er eitt ...?*
cheap hotel	booil-itt ho-tehll	*bíligt hotell*
good hotel	gott ho-tehll	*gott hotell*
nearby hotel	ho-tehll ooi nond	*hotell í nánd*

What is the address?
kvus-seh ait-ur gert-uhn? — *Hvussu eitur gøtan?*

Could you write the address, please?
kun-nu ti-yun djehr-uh so vael aet sgree-vuh ger-tu-nuhv-ni? — *Kunnu tygum gera so væl at skriva gøtunavnið?* (pol)

SIGNS

GISTINGARHÚS	GUESTHOUSE
HOTELL	HOTEL
VALLARAHEIM	YOUTH HOSTEL

At the Hotel

Do you have any rooms available?
ehr-u nerk-ur luhys kerm-ur? *Eru nøkur leys kømur?*

Sorry, we're full.
tooi-vehr-ri hehr ehr fult *Tíverri, her er fult.*

How many nights?
kvus-seh nehg-vuhr naet-ur? *Hvussu nógvar nætur?*

It's ... per day/per person.
tae kos-tuhr ... *Tað kostar ...*
um dae-yin fyr-i kvern *um dagin fyri hvønn.*

How much is it per night/per person?
kvus-seh nehgv kos-tuhr *Hvussu nógv kostar tað*
tae fir-i kvern ain-uh nott? *fyri hvønn eina nátt?*

I'd like ...	ehg veel feh-yin haev-uh ...	*Eg vil fegin hava ...*
a single room	aitt ain-kult-kaem-uhr	*eitt einkultkamar*
a double room	aitt du-bult-kaem-uhr	*eitt dupultkamar*
to share a dorm	aitt feh-luhks-kaem-uhr	*eitt felagskamar*
a bed	ain-uh song	*eina song*
I want a room with a ...	eh veel haev-uh aitt kaem-uhr vee ...	*Eg vil hava eitt kamar við ...*
bathroom	bae	*bað*
shower	broos-u	*brúsu*
TV	shohn-vuhrs-pi	*sjónvarpi*
window	vin-dae	*vindeyga*
I'm going to stay for ...	eh steh-dji ooi ...	*Eg steðgi í ...*
one day	ain dae	*ein dag*
two days	tvair dehahr	*tveir dagar*
one week	ain-uh veek-u	*eina viku*

Requests & Complaints

Can I see it?
kuhn eh slehp-puh aet sooi-djuh tae? *Kann eg sleppa at síggja tað?*

Are there any other/cheaper rooms?
ehr-u nerk-ur on-nur/ booi-li-yuhr-i kerm-ur? *Eru nøkur onnur/ bíligari kømur?*

Is there a reduction for students/children?
ehr aev-slot-tur fir-i stu-dehnt-uhr/berdn? *Er avsláttur fyri studentar/børn?*

Does it include breakfast?
ehr mor-gun-maet-ur up-pi ooi? *Er morgunmatur uppi í?*

It's fine, I'll take it.
tae ehr fooint eh tae-chi tae *Tað er fint, eg taki tað.*

I'm not sure how long I'm staying.
eh vait i-chi kvus-seh lain-dji eh steh-dji *Eg veit ikki hvussu leingi eg steðgi.*

Where is the bathroom?
kvaer ehr bae-yi-room-i? *Hvar er baðirúmið?*

Is there somewhere to wash clothes?
behr teel aet vuhs-kuh klae-yi? *Ber til at vaska klæði?*

Can I use the kitchen?
kuhn eh broo-kuh ker-chin? *Kann eg brúka køkin?*

Can I use the telephone?
kuhn eh broo-kuh tehl-eh-fon-in-uh? *Kann eg brúka telefonina?*

Some Useful Words & Phrases

I'm/We're leaving now/tomorrow.
eh faer-i/veet faer-uh noo/ ooi mor-djin *Eg fari/Vit fara nú/ í morgin.*

I'd like to pay the bill.
kuhn eh fwah rok-nin-djin-uh? *Kann eg fáa rokningina?*

name	nuhun	*navn*
surname	eht-tir-nuhun	*eftirnavn*
address	boo-stae-vur	*bústaður*
room number	kaem-uhr-num-muhr	*kamarnummar*
bathroom	bae-yi-room	*baðirúm*
bed	song	*song*
blanket	tehp-peh	*teppi*
chair	sdohl-ur	*stólur*
clean	raint	*reint*
dirty	shee-ti	*skitið*
double bed	dub-ilt-song	*dupultsong*
electricity	ruhu-muhgn	*ravmagn*
excluded	i-chi ooi-rok-nuh	*ikki íroknа*
included	ooi-rok-nuh	*íroknað*
key	lee-chil	*lykil*
lift (elevator)	lif-tuh	*lyfta*
light bulb	lyohs-pehr-uh	*ljóspera*
a lock	lwahs	*lás*
mattress	muh-druhs-suh	*madrassa*
mirror	spehgl	*spegl*
padlock	hon-dji-lwahs	*heingilás*
pillow	kod-di	*koddi*
room (in hotel)	kaem-uhr	*kamar*
quiet	free-yuhr-litt	*friðarligt*
sheet	laek	*lak*
shower	broos-uh	*brúsa*
soap	swahb-uh	*sápa*
suitcase	kuf-fehrst	*kuffert*
swimming pool	svim-yeh-heel-ur	*svimjihylur*
table	bor	*borð*
toilet (paper)	veh-seh(-puhp-pooir)	*vesi(pappír)*
towel	huhn-klae	*handklæði*
(hot/cold) water	(haitt/kuhlt) vuhtn	*(heitt/kalt) vatn*
window	vin-dae	*vindeyga*

AROUND TOWN

I'm looking	eh lait-eh	*Eg leiti*
for the/a ...	eht-tir ...	*eftir ...*
art gallery	list-uh-suhun-in-un	*listasavninum*
bank	ain-un buhn-kuh	*einum banka*
church	ain-uhr-eh chir-cheh	*einari kirkju*
city centre	mib-booi-nun	*miðbýnum*
... embassy	... uhm-buhs-sah-dun-eh	*... ambassaduni*
hotel	ain-un ho-tehll-i	*einum hotelli*
market street	huhn-dils-gert-ehn-eh	*handilsgøtuni*
museum	fon-min-ni-su-hun-in-un	*fornminnis-savninum*
police	lerg-rehg-lun-eh	*løgregluni*
post office	post-hoos-in-un	*posthúsinum*
public toilet	uhl-mehn-nun vehs-eh	*almennum vesi*
telephone centre	teh-leh-fon-ster-yin-eh	*telefonstøðini*
tourist information office	fehr-uh-skreev-sto-vun-eh/ tu-rist-kon-tohr-in-un	*ferða-skrivstovuni/ turistkontórinum*

What time does it open/close?
naer klok-kuhn leht-ur tae up/uht-tur? — *Nær klokkan letur tað upp/aftur?*

What ... is this?	kvus-seh ait-ur ...?	*hvussu eitur ...?*
street	hehn-duh gert-uhn	*henda gøtan*
suburb	hehs-in booi-uhr-puhrs-tur-in	*hesin býarparturin*

For directions, see the Getting Around section, page 90.

At the Post Office

I'd like to send ...	eh sgael sehn-duh ...	*Eg skal senda ...*
a letter	aitt braev	*eitt bræv*
a postcard	aitt post-korst	*eitt postkort*
a parcel	ain puhk-kuh	*ein pakka*
a telegram	aitt teh-leh-gruhm	*eitt telegramm*

I'd like some stamps.	
kuhn eh fwah nerg-ur frooi-mehr-cheh?	*Kann eg fáa nøkur frímerki?*
How much does it cost to send this to ...?	
kvus-seh nehgv kos-tuhr tae aet sehn-duh heht-tuh teel ...?	*Hvussu nógv kostar tað at senda hetta til ...?*

FAROESE

an aerogram	aitt luft-braev	*eitt luftbræv*
air mail	luft-post-ur	*luftpostur*
e-mail	tehl-deh-post-ur	*teldupostur*
envelope	braev-bdjolv-eh/ kon-vo-lut-tur	*brævbjálvi/ konvoluttur*
mailbox	post-kuhs-seh	*postkassi*
registered mail	in-sgree-vuh braev	*innskrivað bræv*
surface mail	ships-post-ur	*skipspostur* (lit. ship post)

Telephone & Internet

I want to ring ...
eh sgael rin-djuh teel ...
Eg skal ringja til ...

The number is ...
num-muhr-eh ehr ...
Nummarið er ...

How much does a three-minute call cost?
kvus-seh nehgv kos-tuhr aet tos-uh ooi trooi-djuhr min-ut-tir?
Hvussu nógv kostar at tosa í tríggjar minuttir?

How much does each extra minute cost?
kvus-seh nehgv kos-tuhr kverr uhy-kuh min-ut-tur?
Hvussu nógv kostar hvør eyka minuttur?

I'd like to speak to (Mr Pedersen).
kuhn eh slehp-puh aet tos-uh vee (huhr-ruh peh-dehr-sehn)?
Kann eg sleppa at tosa við (harra Pedersen)?

It's engaged.
tae ehr bun-deh
Tað er bundið.

I want to make a reverse-charges phone call.
eh sgael rin-djuh moh-tae-kuhr-in beh-tae-lir
Eg skal ringja móttakarin betalir.

I've been cut off.
eh bluhyv aev-brot-in
Eg bleiv avbrotin.

Where can I get Internet access?
kvaer fwah-yeh eh brookt in-tehr-neh-ti?
Hvar fái eg brúkt internetið?

I'd like to send an email.
eh veel feh-yin sehn-duh ain ee-mayl
Eg vil fegin senda ein e-mail.

At the Bank

I want to exchange some money/ travellers cheques.
eh sgael vehk-sluh aitt sin-dur aev pehng-um/fehr-uh-chehk-kum — *Eg skal veksla eitt sindur av pengum/ferðakekkum.*

What is the exchange rate?
kvaet ehr kurs-ur-in? — *Hvat er kursurin?*

How many kroner per dollar?
kvus-seh nehg-vuhr krohn-ur fir-i doll-uhr-uhn? — *Hvussu nógvar krónur fyri dollaran?*

bank draft	pehng-uh-wah-vooi-sing	*pengaávísing*
bank notes	pehng-uh-sehl-uhr	*pengaseðlar*
cashier	kuhs-suh-dahm-uhn	*kassadaman*
coins	min-tir	*myntir*
credit card	kreh-ditt-korst	*kredittkort*
exchange	vehk-sling	*veksling*
loose change	smwah-pehng-uhr	*smápengar*
signature	un-dir-skrift	*undirskrift*

INTERESTS & ENTERTAINMENT

Sightseeing

Do you have a guidebook/local map?
haev-uh tee-yun naek-ruh fehr-uh-huhnd-bohk/ naek-uh korst? — *Hava tygum nakra ferðahandbók/ nakað kort?* (pol)

What are the main attractions?
kvaet ehr vehrst aet sooi-djuh? — *Hvat er vert at síggja?* (lit. what is worth to see?)

What is that?
kvaet ehr huht-tuh? — *Hvat er hatta?*

How old is it?
kvus-seh gaem-uhlt ehr tae? — *Hvussu gamalt er tað?*

Can I take photographs?
kuhn eh taek-uh min-dir — *Kann eg taka myndir?*

What time does it open/close?
naer leht-ur tae up/uhtt-ur? *Nær letur tað upp/aftur?*

ancient	fod-nur	*fornur*
archaeological	fon-frer-yi-lee-yur	*fornfrøðiligur*
beach	suhn-dur/strond	*sandur/strond*
building	big-ning-ur	*bygningur*
castle	slott	*slott*
cathedral	dohm-chir-chuh	*dómkirkja*
church	chir-chuh	*kirkja*
concert hall	kon-sehrt-herdl	*konserthøll*
library	boh-kuhs-uhun	*bókasavn*
main square	mib-booi-yur	*miðbýur*
market	huhn-dils-chuhd-neh	*handilskjarni*
monastery	klos-tur	*klostur*
monument	min-nis-vaer-eh	*minnisvarði*
old city	gaem-uhl booi-uhr-puhrst-ur	*gamal býarpartur*
opera house	op-ehr-uh-hoos	*opera hús*
palace	kongs-borg	*kongsborg*
ruins	hoos-uh-laiv-dir	*húsaleivdir*
stadium	ooi-trot-uhr-verdl-ur	*ítróttarvøllur*
statues	stuhnd-min-dir	*standmyndir*
temple	tehm-pil	*tempul*
university	froh-sgae-buhr-seh-dur	*fróðskaparsetur*

Going Out

What's there to do in the evenings?
kvaet kuhn muhn djehr-uh um kverl-deh? *Hvat kann mann gera um kvøldið?*

Are there places where you can hear local folk music?
behr teel uh hoy-ruh ferr-is-guhn tohn-laig? *Ber til at hoyra føroyskan tónleik?*

Can one see Faroese dancing anywhere?
behr teel uh sooi-djuh ferr-is-guhn duhns nae-gruh-staen-i? *Ber til at síggja føroyskan dans nakra staðni?*

How much does it cost to get in?
kvus-seh nehgv kos-tuhr tae uh slehp-puh in? *Hvussu nógv kostar tað at sleppa inn?*

cinema	bi-o-gruhf-ur	*biografur*
concert	kon-sehrst	*konsert*
discotheque	dis-ko-tehk	*diskotek*
theatre	shohn-laig-uhr-hoos	*sjónleikarhús*

UNDER AGE?

aldursmark	uhl-durs-muhrsk	age limit

Sports & Interests

What do you do in your spare time?
kvaet djehr-stoo ooi frooi-tooi-yin-eh? *Hvat gert tú í frítíðini?*
What sport do you play?
kvern ooi-trott ooik-kuhr too? *Hvønn ítrótt íðkar tüu?*

art	list	*list*
basketball	kurv-uh-berlt	*kurvabólt*
boxing	bok-sing	*boksing*
cooking	muh-djehr	*matgerð*
fishing trout	uh fis-kuh sooil	*at fiska sil*
football/soccer	foht-berlt	*fótbólt*
going/out	uh faer-uh/ooi booi-yin	*at fara/í bytin*
to the cinema	ooi bi-o-gruhf	*í biograf*
music	tohn-laig	*tónleik*
photography	fo-to-gruh-fehr-ing	*fotografering*
reading	leh-sing	*lesing*
shopping	uh faer-uh teel huhn-dils	*at fara til handils*
sport	ooi-trott	*ítrótt*
the theatre	shohn-laig	*sjónleik*
travelling	uh fehr-uhst	*at ferðast*
writing	uh sgreev-uh	*at skriva*

Festivals

During the summer months, June and July, almost every weekend offers a village festival. The first one is **Norðoyastehvna** in Klaksvík, and the last one is **Ólavsøka** in Tórshavn. There are sports events, music and dancing, and many people wear their national costume. The traditional rowing competition features the ancient Faroese rowing boat – a descendant from the Viking ship. Participants are boys and girls from the competing villages.

Grækarismessa 12 March – celebrated as the arrival day of the national bird **tjaldur**. Boy- and girlscouts march in procession and speeches are delivered.

Flag Day 25 April – celebrated in memory of the sanctioning of the Faroese flag by the British during WWII.

Ólavsøka 29 July – celebration in the capital Tórshavn lasting at least two days. In ancient times the celebration was for the Holy King Olav of Norway who died in 1030 AD.

A relatively new custom is having a bonfire on the small beach in Tórshavn on the shortest night of the year, 21 June.

IN THE COUNTRY

Weather

What's the weather like?

kvus-seh ehr vehg-reh?	*Hvussu er veðrið?*

It's ... today.

vehg-reh ehr ... ooi dae	*Veðrið er ... í dag.*

Will it be ...	**Vehr-ur tae ...**	*Verður tað ...*
tomorrow?	**ooi mor-djin?**	*í morgin?*
cloudy	**sgooi-djuh**	*skýggjað*
cold	**kuhlt**	*kalt*
foggy	**myerr-cheh**	*mjørki*
frosty	**frost**	*frost*
hot	**haitt**	*heitt*
raining	**rehgn**	*regn*
snowing	**kaev-eh**	*kavi*
sunny	**serl-shin**	*sólskin*
windy	**vin-dur**	*vindur*

Camping

Am I allowed to camp here?
ehr loyft uh chuhl-duh hehr? *Er loyvt at tjalda her?*
Is there a campsite nearby?
ehr naeg-uh chuhld-plos ooi nond? *Er nakað tjaldpláss í nánd?*

backpack	**rigg-sehk-kur**	*ryggsekkur*
can opener	**dohs-uh-op-nuhr-eh**	*dósaopnari*
compass	**kum-puhs**	*kumpass*
firewood	**brehn-neh**	*brenni*
gas cartridge	**guhs-puh-trohn**	*gass patrón*
mattress	**muh-druhs-suh**	*madrassa*
penknife	**fehd-leh-knooi-vur**	*felliknívur*
rope	**buhnd**	*band*
sleeping bag	**so-veh-pos-eh**	*soviposi*
stove	**ohn-ur**	*ovnur*
tent (pegs)	**chuhld (hael-ir)**	*tjald (hælir)*
torch/flashlight	**ligt**	*lykt*
water bottle	**vuhn-flers-guh**	*vatnfløska*

SIGNS

TJÁLDPLASS CAMPING GROUND

FOOD

Traditional Faroese food includes fish, mutton, whalemeat and birds from the steep cliffs. Not many vegetables are cultivated in the Faroes, but potatoes and rhubarb are popular.

A Faroese specialty is skerpikjøt, mutton which has been wind dried, eaten mostly with bread. Another dish is ræst kjøt, the same meat only half dried and then cooked or roasted. The same drying methods are used with fish and whalemeat.

Some Useful Words & Phrases

breakfast	mor-gun-drehk-kuh	*morgundrekka*
lunch	mor-gun-maet-ur	*morgunmatur*
dinner	derv-reh	*døgurði*

Table for ..., please. bor teel ... tuhk *Borð til ... takk.*

Can I see the menu please?
kuhn eh fwah maet-seh-yil-in? *Kann eg fáa matseðilin?*
What does it include?
kvaet hoy-rir teel? *Hvat hoyrir til?*

ashtray	ers-keh-beek-uhr	*øskubikar*
the bill	rok-nin-djin	*rokningin*
a cup	ain kop-pur	*ein koppur*
dessert	deh-sehrst/ o-muhn-wah	*dessert/ omaná*
a drink	ok-kurst uh drehk-kuh	*okkurt at drekka*
a fork	ain guhf-fil	*ein gaffil*
fresh	nooi-djur/fehs-kur	*nýggjur/feskur*
a glass	aitt glaes	*eitt glas*
a knife	ain knooi-vur	*ein knívur*
a plate	ain bor-isk-ur	*ein borðiskur*
spicy	krid-duh	*kryddað*
a spoon	ain sgai	*ein skeið*
stale	sbil-tur	*spiltur*
sweet	sert-ur	*søtur*
a teaspoon	ain teh-sgai	*ein teskeið*
toothpicks	tuhn-nuhs-tuhy-tuhr-uhr	*tannasteytarar*

Vegetarian Meals

I'm a vegetarian.

eh eht-i baer-uh grern-meht-eh;	*Eg eti bara grønmeti;*
eh ehr-eh veh-geh-tuhr-ur	*Eg eri vegetarur.*

I don't eat meat.

eh eht-i i-chi chert	*Eg eti ikki kjøt.*

I don't eat chicken, or fish, or pork.

eh eht-i ich-i hers-nuhr-ung-uh	*Eg eti ikki høsnarunga*
edl-uh fisk edl-uh grwees-uh-chert	*ella fisk ella grísakjøt.*

Staple Foods & Condiments

bread	bruhy	*breyð*
butter	smerr	*smør*
garlic	kvooit-luhy-gur	*hvítleykur*
meat	chert	*kjøt*
mustard	sin-nop-pur	*sinoppur*
oil	ol-yuh	*olja*
pepper	pee-puhr	*pipar*
pickled cucumbers	sült-uh-yuhr	*súltaðar*
	uh-gursk-ir	*agurkir*
rice	roois	*rís*
salt	suhlt	*salt*
string beans	bern-ir	*bønir*
sugar	suk-ur	*sukur*
vinegar	eh-dik-kur	*edikur*

Vegetables

beets	ruhy-rert-ur	*reyðrøtur*
(usually served pickled)		
cabbage	kwahl	*kál*
carrots	gu-luh-rert-ur	*gularøtur*
cauliflower	blom-kwahl	*blomkál*
celery	sehl-luh-rooi	*sellarí*
cucumber	uh-gursk	*agurk*
mashed potatoes	eh-pluh-morl	*eplamorl*
mushrooms	hun-duh-luhnd	*hundaland*
onions	luhy-kur	*leykur*
peas	ehrs-truhr	*ertrar*
pickled cucumbers	sült-uh-yuhr	*súltaðar*
	uh-gursk-ir	*agurkir*
potato	eh-pli	*epli*
(boiled/baked)	(kohg-uh/baeg-uh)	*(kókað/bakað)*
rice	roois	*rís*
string beans	bern-ir	*bønir*

Fruit

apple	süur-eh-pleh	*súrepli*
banana	buh-nahn	*banan*
grapes	vooin-drüu-vir	*víndrúvur*
lemon	si-trohn	*sitrón*
orange	uh-pil-seen	*appilsin*
pear	peh-ruh	*pera*
strawberry	jar-ber	*jarðber*

MENU DECODER

Breakfast Menu

toast	rist-uh bruhy	*ristað breyð*
bacon	buhy-kon	*bacon*
cheese	ost-ur	*ostur*
eggs	ehgg	*egg*
jam	sül-teh-toy	*súltutoy*
milk	myerlk	*mjólk*
rye bread	rub-bruhy	*rugbreyð*
white bread	fruhns-bruhy	*fransbreyð*

Main Meals

chicken	hers-nuhr-un-djeh	*høsnarungi*
lamb chops	luhms-chert	*lambskjøt*
roast beef	nuhy-tuh-staik	*neytasteik*
roast lamb	luhms-staik	*lambssteik*
roast pork	groois-uh-staik	*grísasteik*
sausage	pil-suh	*pylsa*
steak	büf-fur	*búffur*
whale meat with blubber	grind o speek	*grind og spik*
wind-dried meat (boiled or roasted)	ruhst chert	*ræst kjøt*
wind-dried meat	turt chert/ shehr-peh-chert	*turt kjøt/ skerpikjøt*
wind-dried fish (boiled)	ruhst-ur fis-kur	*ræstur fiskur*
wind-dried fish	tur-rur fis-kur	*turrur fiskur*

Seafood

fish	fis-kur	*fiskur*
haddock	hoois-uh	*hýsa*
halibut	kuhlv-i	*kalvi*
herring	sild	*sild*
plaice	rehs-prerk-uh	*reyðsprøka*
salmon	luhk-sur	*laksur*
shrimp	raech-ur	*rækjur*
sole	tung-uh	*tunga*
trout	sooil	*sil*

Soups

fesk súpan fehsk soop-uhn
broth from boiled meat with vegetables
røst súpan rerst soop-uhn
broth from boiled *ræst kjøt* with vegetables and rice
breyðsúpan bruhy-soop-uhn
soup made from bread, sugar and non-alcoholic beer

fiskasúpan	fis-kuh-soop-uhn	fish soup
asparssúpan	uhs-puhrs-soop-uhn	asparagus soup
blábersúpan	blwah-behr-soop-uhn	blueberry soup

Desserts

ice cream	oois-ur	*ísur*
cake	kaek-uh	*kaka*
rhubarb cake	ruh-buhr-beh-kaek-uh	*rabarbukaka*
rhubarb jelly	ruh-buhr-beh-gruhyt-ur	*rabarbugreytur*
pancakes	puhn-neh-kaek-ur	*pannukakur*

Drinks

coffee(with cream)	kuhf-fi (vee roh-muh)	*kaffi (við róma)*
orange juice	uhp-pil-seen-djoos	*appelsindjús*
skim/ full cream milk	skoo-muh/ vuhn-li myerlk	*skúmað/ vanlig mjólk*
soft drink, carbonated water	suhft, so-duh-vuhtn	*saft,sodavatn*
tea	teh	*te*
(ice) water	(oois-)vuhtn	*(ís)vatn*

snapsur snuhp-sur
small glass 2-4 cl of (particularly) akvavit
flúgvari flig-vuhr-i
mixture of coke and akvavit (lit. flyer)
svartideyð svuhr-steh-duhy-yeh
Icelandic brand of alcohol (lit. the black death)
durasnapsur dur-uh-snuhp-sur
snaps offered at the door as you enter (lit. door *snaps*)
bjóða ein lítlan byoh-uh ain looitl-uhn
also *snaps* (lit. offer a 'small one')

SHOPPING

How much is it?
kvus-seh nehgv kos-tuhr tae? *Hvussu nógv kostar tað?*

bookshop	bohk-huhnd-il	*bókhandil*
camera shop	foto huhnd-il	*foto handil*
clothing store	kluhd-nuh-huhnd-il	*klædnahandil*
general store/shop	huhnd-il	*handil*
laundry	vuhs-kuhr-ooi	*vaskarí*
market	muhrk-nuh-vur	*marknaður*
newsagency	ki-osk	*kiosk*
pharmacy	uh-po-tehk	*apotek*
shoeshop	skoh-huhnd-il	*skóhandil*
souvenir shop	su-vehn-eer huhnd-il	*souvenir handil*
stationers	puhp-pooirs-huhnd-il	*pappírshandil*
supermarket	sholvt-erk-eh-huhnd-il	*sjálvtøkuhandil*
vegetable shop	grern-meht-is-huhnd-il	*grønmetishandil*

FAROESE

I'd like to buy ...
eh sgael chuhy-puh ... *Eg skal keypa ...*
Do you have others?
haev-uh teet aer-uhr? *Hava tit aðrar?* (inf)
I don't like it.
maer dwahm-uhr haen-uh/ huhn/tae i-chi *Mær dámar hana/ hann/tað ikki.* (f/m/n)
Can I look at it?
kuhn eh sooi-djuh haen-uh/ huhn/tae? *Kann eg síggja hana/ hann/tað?* (f/m/n)
I'm just looking.
eh baer-uh hi-djeh *Eg bara hyggi.*
Can you write down the price?
kuhns-too sgreev-uh proois-in nee-yur? *Kannst tú skriva prísin niður?*

Do you accept credit cards?
taek-uh teet kreh-ditt-korst? *Taka tit kredittkort?*
Can I help you?
fwah-yeh eh yolt tee-yuhn? *Fái eg hjálpt tygum?* (pol)
Will that be all?
naeg-uh uhn-nuh? *Nakað annað?*

Essential Groceries

bread	**bruhy**	*breyð*
butter	**smerr**	*smør*
milk	**myerlk**	*mjólk*
rice	**roois**	*ris*
salt	**suhlt**	*salt*
shampoo	**shuhm-po**	*shampo*
sugar	**suk-ur**	*sukur*
toilet paper	**veh-seh-puhp-pooir**	*vesipappír*
toothbrush	**tuhn-bust**	*tannbust*
vegetables	**grern-meht-i**	*grønmeti*

Souvenirs

earrings	**oyr-nuhr-ing-uhr**	*oyrnaringar*
handicraft	**hond-uhr-bai-yeh**	*handarbeiði*
necklace	**hols-buhnd**	*hálsband*
pottery	**stain-toy**	*steintoy*
ring	**ring-ur**	*ringur*
rug	**tehp-pi**	*teppi*

Clothing

coat	**fruh-chi**	*frakki*
dress	**chohl-eh**	*kjóli*
jacket	**yuh-cheh**	*jakki*
jumper (sweater)	**troy-djuh**	*troyggja*
shirt	**shür-tuh**	*skjúrta*
shoes	**skehg-vuhr**	*skógvar*
skirt	**shürt**	*skjúrt*
trousers	**buk-sir**	*buksur*

It doesn't fit.
tae puhs-suhr i-chi *Tað passar ikki.*

It's too ...	tae ehr o ...	*Tað er ov ...*
big	sterrst	*stórt*
small	looit-i	*lítið*
short	stutt	*stutt*
long	lehnkt	*langt*
tight	tronkt	*trongt*
loose	vooit	*vítt*

Materials

cotton	bum-udl	*bumull*
handmade	hond-djerrt	*hondgjørt*
leather	leh-vur	*leður*
brass	mehs-sing	*messing*
gold	gudl	*gull*
silver	sil-vur	*silvur*
silk	sil-chi	*silki*
wool	udl	*ull*
of wool	ud-lint	*ullint*

Colours

black	svuhrt	*svart*
blue	blott	*blátt*
brown	brünt	*brúnt*
green	grernt	*grønt*
orange	uhp-pil-seen-gult	*appelsingult*
pink	lyohs-uh-rehtt	*ljósareytt*
purple	lil-luh	*lilla*
red	rehtt	*reytt*
white	kvooitt	*hvítt*
yellow	gult	*gult*

Toiletries

comb	kuhm-bur	*kambur*
condoms	hooit-ir	*hítir*
deodorant	deh-o-do-ruhnt	*deodorant*
hairbrush	ho-uhr-bust	*hárbust*
moisturising cream	vae-teh-krehm	*vætukrem*
razor	rae-cheh-muh-sheen-uh	*rakimaskina*
sanitary napkins	(duh-meh)bind	*(damu)bind*
shampoo	shuhm-po	*shampo*
shaving cream	rae-cheh-swah-puh	*rakisápa*
soap	swah-puh	*sápa*
sunblock cream	sohl-krehm	*sólkrem*
tampons	tuhm-pon-djir	*tampongir*
tissues	sehr-vi-eht-tuhr	*serviettar*
toilet paper	veh-seh-puhp-pooir	*vesipappír*
toothpaste	tuhn-krehm	*tannkrem*

Stationery & Publications

map	korst	*kort*
newspaper	(ain-gilst)	*(eingilskt)*
(in English)	duhg-blae	*dagblað*
novels in English	ain-gils-guhr	*eingilskar*
	skuhld-ser-vur	*skaldsøgur*
paper	puhp-pooir	*pappír*
pen (ballpoint)	koo-lu-pehn-nur	*kúlupennur*
scissors	suhk-sur	*saksur*

Photography

How much is it to process this film?

kvus-seh nehgv kos-tuhr duh uh fruhm-kuhd-luh hehn-duh film-in? *Hvussu nógv kostar tað at framkalla henda filmin?*

When will it be ready?

naer vehr-ur huhn li-yu-vur? *Nær verður hann liðugur?*

I'd like a film for this camera.

eh sgael haev-uh ain film teel heht-tuh fo-to-toh-leh *Eg skal hava ein film til hetta fototólið.*

B&W (film)	**svuhrt kvooit-ur film-ur**	*svart hvítur filmur*
camera	**fo-to-tohl**	*fototól*
colour (film)	**leet-film-ur**	*litfilmur*
film	**fil-mur**	*filmur*
flash	**blits**	*blits*
lens	**lin-suh**	*linsa*
light meter	**lyohs-mwah-tuhr-eh**	*ljósmátari*

Smoking

A packet of cigarettes, please.

ain si-guh-rehtt-puhk-kuh tuhk *Ein sigarettpakka, takk.*

Are these cigarettes strong/mild?

ehr-u hehs-uhr si-guh-rehtt-ir-nuhr stehr-kuhr/mil-duhr? *Eru hesar sigarettirnar sterkar/mildar?*

Do you have a light?

heh-vur too ehld? *Hevur tú eld?*

cigarette papers	**si-guh-rehtt-puhp-pooir**	*sigarettpappír*
cigarettes	**si-guh-reht-tir**	*sigarettir*
filtered	**vee fil-tri**	*við filtri*
lighter	**tehn-druh-ri**	*tendrari*
matches	**svwah-vul-pin-nuhr**	*svávulpinnar*
menthol	**mehn-tol**	*mentol*
pipe	**pooi-puh**	*pípa*
tobacco (pipe)	**tub-buhk**	*tubbakk*

Sizes & Comparisons

big	sterrt	*stórt*
small	looiti	*lítið*
heavy	tunkt	*tungt*
light	luhtt	*lætt*
more	mai-ri/flai-ri	*meiri/fleiri*
less	min-ni	*minni*
too much/many	o mic-hi/o nehgv	*ov mikið/ov nógv*
many	nehgv	*nógv*
enough	noh mi-chi/noh nehgv	*nóg mikið/nónógv*
also	ai-sin-i	*eisini*
a little bit	aitt sin-dur	*eitt sindur*

HEALTH

Where is ...?	kvaer ehr ...?	*Hvar er ...?*
the chemist	uh-po-teh-cheh	*apotekið*
a doctor	ain luhk-neh	*ein lækni*
a dentist	ain tuhn-luhk-neh	*ein tannlækni*
the hospital	shook-ruh-hoos-eh	*sjúkrahúsið*

I'm sick.
eh ehr-i shook/-ur — *Eg eri sjúk/-ur.* (f/m)

My friend is sick.
veen-ur mooin ehr shook-ur — *Vinur mín er sjúkur.*

Could I see a female doctor?
kuhn eh slehp-puh uh tos-uh vee ain kvin-neh-li-yuhn luhk-nuh? — *Kann eg sleppa at tosa við ein kvinnuligan lækna?*

What's the matter?
kvaet bae-yir? — *Hvat bagir ?*

Where does it hurt?
kvaer heh-vur too ilt? — *Hvar hevur tú ilt?*

It hurts here.
eh haev-i ilt hehr — *Eg havi ilt her.*

Ailments

I have (a/an) ...	eh haev-i ...	*Eg havi ...*
allergy	o-vee-kvae-meh	*ovviðkvæmi*
anaemia	bloh-muhng-ul	*blóðmangul*
blister	bler-ru	*bløðru*
burn	bruhnd-swahr	*brandsár*
cold	krooim	*krím*
constipation	haer-uhn book	*harðan búk*
cough	hos-tuh	*hosta*
diarrhoea	lehst looiv	*leyst lív*
fever	fehb-ur	*fepur*
headache	her-vu-pooin-eh	*høvuðpínu*
hepatitis	liv-ruh-brun-uh	*livrabruna*
indigestion	ilt ooi boo-chin-un	*ilt í búkinum*
infection	brun-uh	*bruna*
influenza	in-flu-ehn-suh	*influensa*
lice	loois	*lýs*
low/high	logt/herkt	*lágt/høgt*
blood pressure	bloh-trooist	*blóðtrýst*
sore throat	ilt ooi hol-sin-un	*ilt í hálsinum*
a sprained foot	kok-tuhn foht	*keiktan fót*
stomachache	boo-kil-sku	*búkilsku*
temperature	fehb-ur	*fepur*
venereal disease	cheen-shoo-ku	*kynssjúku*
worms	orm	*orm*

Parts of the Body

ankle	er-kul	*økul*
arm	uhrm-ur	*armur*
back	baek	*bak*
chest	bring-uh/brerst	*bringa/bróst*
ear	oy-ruh	*oyra*
eye	uhy-yuh	*eyga*
finger	fing-ur	*fingur*
foot	foht-ur	*fótur*
hand	hond	*hond*
head	herdd	*høvd*

heart	yuhrt-uh	*hjarta*
leg	bain	*bein*
mouth	mun-nur	*munnur*
ribs	riv-yuh-bain	*rivjabein*
skin	hoo	*húð*
stomach	book-ur	*búkur*
teeth	tehn	*tenn*
throat	hols-ur	*hálsur*

Some Useful Words & Phrases

I'm ...	eh ehr-i ...	*Eg eri ...*
diabetic	su-kur-shook/-ur	*sukursjúk/-ur* (f/m)
epileptic	eh-pi-lehp-ti-kuhr-eh	*epileptikari*
asthmatic	uhs-muh-shook/-ur	*astmasjúk/-ur* (f/m)

I'm allergic to antibiotics/penicillin.
eh tol-i i-cheh uhn-ti-bi-o-tik-uh/ pehn-i-sill-een — *Eg toli ikki antibiotika/ penisillin.*

I'm pregnant.
eh ehr-i up wah veh-yin — *Eg eri upp á vegin.*

I haven't had my period for ... months.
eh haevi- i-cheh huhft mwah-nuh-shook-un-uh ooi ... mwahn-uhr — *Eg havi ikki havt mánasjúkuna í ... mánaðar.*

I have been vaccinated.
eh ehr-i vuhk-si-nehr-uh/-vur — *Eg eri vaksinerað/-ur.* (f/m)

accident	oh-luk-kuh	*ólukka*
addiction	trongd	*trongd*
aspirin	pooin-eh-tuhb-leht-tir	*pínutablettir*
a bandage	for-bind-ing	*forbinding*
blood test	bloh-roynd	*blóðroynd*
contraceptive	fi-ri-bir-djing	*fyribyrging*
medicine	hai-li-vwah-vur	*heilivágur*
nausea	vuhml	*vaml*
oxygen	soo-rehv-ni	*súrevni*
vitamins	vi-tuh-meen-ir	*vitaminir*

At the Chemist

I need medication for ...
kuhn eh fwah hail-i-vwah fi-ri ...? — *Kann eg fáa heilivág fyri ...?*

I have a prescription.
eh haev-i reh-sehpt — *Eg havi resept.*

At the Dentist

I have a toothache.
eh haev-i tuhn-nuh-pooin-eh — *Eg havi tannapínu.*

I've lost a filling.
eh haev-i mist ain-uh plom-beh — *Eg havi mist eina plombu.*

I've broken a tooth.
eh haev-i brot-i ain-uh ton — *Eg havi brotið eina tonn.*

My gums hurt.
tae pooin-ir ooi tuhn-huhl-din-un — *Tað pínir í tannhaldinum.*

Please give me an anaesthetic.
kuhn eh fwah doy-ving? — *Kann eg fáa doyving?*

TIME & DATES

What date is it today?
kverr dae-vur ehr ooi dae? — *Hvør dagur er í dag?*

What time is it?
kvaet ehr klok-kuhn? — *Hvat er klokkan?*

It's ... am/pm.
hon ehr ... — *Hon er ...*

in the morning	um mor-gun-in	*um morgunin*
in the afternoon	said-nuh-puhrst-in	*seinnapartin*
in the evening	um kverl-deh	*um kvøldið*

Days of the Week

Monday	mwah-nuh-dae-vur	*Mánadagur*
Tuesday	tooís-dae-vur	*Týsdagur*
Wednesday	mee-ku-dae-vur	*Mikudagur*
Thursday	hers-dae-vur	*Hósdagur*
Friday	frooi-djuh-dae-vur	*Fríggjadagur*
Saturday	luhy-yuhr-dae-vur	*Leygardagur*
Sunday	sun-nu-dae-vur	*Sunnudagur*

Months

January	djuhn-vwahr	*Januar*
February	feh-bruv-uhr	*Februar*
March	muhrs	*Mars*
April	uhp-rooil	*Apríl*
May	mai	*Mai*
June	dju-ni	*Juni*
July	dju-li	*Juli*
August	uhu-gust	*August*
September	sehp-tehm-bir	*September*
October	ok-to-bir	*Oktober*
November	no-vehm-bir	*November*
December	dehs-ehm-bir	*Desember*

Seasons

summer	sumuhr	*summar*
autumn	hehst	*heyst*
winter	veh-tur	*vetur*
spring	vwahr	*vár*

Present

today	ooi dae	*í dag*
this morning	ooi mor-gun	*í morgun*
tonight	ooi kverld/ooi nott	*í kvøld/í nátt*
this week/ this year	heh-suh vee-ku-nuh/ ooi wahr	*hesa vikuna/ í ár*
now	noo	*nú*

Past

yesterday	ooi djwahr	*í gjár*
day before yesterday	ooi fir-ruh-dae-yin	*í fyrradagin*
yesterday morning	ooi djwahr-uh-mor-gun-in	*í gjáramorgunin*
last night	djwahr-kverl-di	*í gjárkvøldið*
last week/last year	ooi soois-tu vee-ku/ soois-tuh wahr	*í síðstu viku/ síðsta ár*

Future

tomorrow	ooi mor-djin	*í morgin*
day after tomorrow	o-vur-mor-djin	*ovurmorgin*
tomorrow morning	ooi mor-djin-wahr-i	*í morgindri*
tomorrow afternoon	said-nuh-puhrs-tin	*seinnapartin*
	ooi mor-djin	*í morgin*
tomorrow evening	ooi uhn-nuh-kverld	*í annaðkvøld*
next week	nuhs-tu vee-ku	*næstu viku*
next year	nuhs-uh wahr	*næsta ár*

During the Day

afternoon	said-nuh-puhrs-tur	*seinnapartur*
dawn	ooi loois-in-djin-i	*í lýsingini*
day	dae-vur	*dagur*
early	tooil-yuh	*tíðliga*
midnight	mid-nott	*midnátt*
morning	mor-gun	*morgun*
night	nottt	*nátt*
noon	wah mid-deh-yi	*á miðdegi*

NUMBERS & AMOUNTS

0	null	*null*
1	aitt	*eitt*
2	tvuhy	*tvey*
3	trooi	*trý*
4	fooir-uh	*fira*
5	fim	*fimm*
6	sehks	*seks*
7	shuhy	*sjey*
8	ot-tuh	*átta*
9	nooi-djeh	*níggju*
10	tooi-djeh	*tíggju*
11	ehd-lehv-eh	*ellivu*
12	terlv	*tólv*
13	treht-tuhn	*trettan*
14	fdjürs-tuhn	*fjúrtan*
15	fim-tuhn	*fimtan*
16	sehks-tuhn	*sekstan*
17	suhy-chuhn	*seytjan*
18	wah-chuhn	*átjan*
19	nooi-chuhn	*nítjan*
20	choo-vu	*tjúgu*
21	ain-o-choo-vu	*einogtjúgu*
30	treh-di-veh	*tretivu*
40	fyerr-it-eh	*fjøruti*
50	fim-ti	*fimti*
60	sehks-ti	*seksti*
70	shoo-ti	*sjúti*
80	waht-tuh-ti	*áttati*
90	nooi-ti	*níti*
100	hun-druh	*hundrað*
1000	too-sin	*túsund*
one million	ain mil-liohn	*ein millión*

1st	fis-teh	*fyrsti*
2nd	uhn-nuhr	*annar*
3rd	tree-yi	*triðji*
1/4	ain fyoh-ring-ur	*ein fjórðingur*
1/3	ain tree-ying-ur	*ein triðjingur*
1/2	aitt holt	*eitt hálvt*
3/4	trooi-djir fyoh-ring-uhr	*tríggir fjórðingar*

Some Useful Words

a little (amount)	aitt sin-dur	*eitt sindur*
double	du-bult	*dupult*
enough	noh mi-chi/noh nehgv	*nóg mikið/nógv*
few	fwahr/fwah-yir/fwah	*fáar/fáir/fá* (f/m/n)
less	min-ni	*minni*
many	nehg-vuhr/nehg-vir/nehgv	*nógvar/nógvir/nógv* (f/m/n)
more	mai-ri/flai-ri	*meiri/fleiri*
once	ain-uh-fehr	*einaferð*
a pair	aitt paer/tvuhy	*eitt par/tvey*
percent	pro-sehnt	*procent*
some	naek-ruhr/naek-rir/nerk-ur	*nakrar/nakrir/nøku* (f/m/n)
too much	o nehgv	*ov nógv*
twice	tvaer fehr-ir	*tvær ferðir*

FAROESE

ABBREVIATIONS

SLS	*trandfaraskip Landsins*	Faroese national ferry company
ES	*Evropasamveldið*	European Community
ST	*Sameindu tjóðir*	United Nations
AA	*Atlantic Airways*	Faroese national airlines
km		kilometres
FO		Faroe Islands (letters used on cars/com puter adresses, etc.)

EMERGENCIES

I'm lost.	eh ehr-i vilst/-ur	*Eg eri vilst/-ur.* (f/m)
I've been raped.	eh ehr-i nuhy-ti-chin	*Eg eri neyðtikin.*
Go away!	faer burs-tur!	*Far burtur!*
Help!	djolp!	*Hjálp!*
Thief!	choh-vur!	*Tjóvur!*

SIGNS

LØGREGLA	POLICE

It's an emergency! heht-tuh ehr ain nuhy-ster-vuh!	*Hetta er ein neyðstøða!*
There's been an accident! ain oh-luk-kuh ehr hehnd!	*Ein ólukka er hend!*
Call a doctor/an ambulance! rin-ji eht-tir luhk-uht/ shook-ruh-bee-li!	*Ringið eftir lækna/ sjúkrabili!*
Call the police! rin-dji eht-tir lerg-rehg-lu-neh!	*Ringið eftir løgregluni!*
Where is the police station? kvaer ehr lerg-rehg-lus-ter-yin?	*Hvar er løgreglustøðin?*
I'll call the police! eh rin-dji eht-tir lerg-rehg-lu-neh!	*Eg ringi eftir løgregluni!*
I'm/My friend is ill. eh ehr-í/veen-ur mooin ehr shook-ur	*Eg eri/vinur mín er sjúkur.*
Where are the toilets? kvaer ehr-u veh-seh-ni?	*Hvar eru vesini?*
Could you (pol) help me please? kun-nu ti-yun djeh-ruh so vael uh djol-puh maer?	*Kunnu tygum gera so væl at hjálpa mær?*
Could I please use the telephone? kuhn eh lae-nuh teh-leh-fon-in-uh?	*Kann eg læna telefonina?*
I didn't do it. eh hae-vi i-chi djerrt duh	*Eg havi ikki gjørt tað.*

I'm sorry. I apologise.
um-shil-duh. eh bi-yeh um fi-ri-djehv-ing — *Umskylda. Eg biði um fyrigeving.*

I didn't realise I was doing anything wrong.
eh vis-ti i-chi aet eh djerr-di nae-guh sgaift — *Eg visti ikki, at eg gjørdi nakað skeivt.*

I wish to contact my embassy/consulate.
eh veel to-suh vee mooi-nuh uhm-buhs-suh-du/mooitt kon-su-lwaht — *Eg vil tosa við mína ambassadu/mítt konsulát.*

I speak English.
eh to-si ain-djilst — *Eg tosi eingilskt.*

I have medical insurance.
eh hae-vi shook-ruh-tri-djing — *Eg havi sjúkratrygging.*

My possessions are insured.
Mooi-nuhr og-nir ehr-u tri-djuh-yuhr — *Mínar ognir eru tryggjaðar.*

My ...	mooin/mooitt ...	*Mín/Mítt ...*
was stolen.	ehr sto-lin/sto-li	*er stolin/stolið.*
I've lost my ...	eh hae-vi mist ...	*Eg havi mist ...*
bags	mooi-nuhr tuhs-kur	*mínar taskur*
handbag	mooi-nuh hond-tuhs-ku	*mína hondtasku*
money	mooi-nuhr pehng-uhr	*mínar pengar*
passport	mooitt puhs	*mítt pass*
travellers cheques	mooi-nuhr feh-ruh-chehk-kuhr	*mínar ferðakekkar*

FINNISH

QUICK REFERENCE

Hello.	*hay/ tehrr*-veh	*Hei/Terve.*
Goodbye.	*na*-keh-meen	*Näkemiin.*
Yes.	*kül*-lah/yoo	*Kyllä/Joo.*
No.	ay	*Ei.*
Excuse me.	*uhn*-teehk-si	*Anteeksi.*
Sorry.	*o*-lehn *puh*-hoyl-luh-ni; *so*-rri	*Olen pahoillani; Sori.*
Thank you.	*kee*-toss	*Kiitos.*
You're welcome.	*o*-leh *hü*-va	*Ole hyvä.*
I understand.	*üm*-marr-rran	*Ymmärrän.*
I don't understand.	*ehn üm*-marr-rra	*En ymmärrä.*
Where is ...?	*mis*-sa *on* ...?	*Missä on ...?*
Go straight ahead.	*kul*-yeh *su-o*-rrahn	*Kulje suoraan.*

Turn left/right. *kaan*-nü *vuh*-sehm-pahn/ *oy*-keh-ahn.	*Käänny vasempaan/ oikeaan.*
Do you speak English? *pu*-hut-ko *ehng*-luhn-ti-uh?	*Puhutko englantia?*
Do you have any rooms available? *on*-ko *tayl*-la *vuh*-pah-tuh *hu-o*-neht-tuh?	*Onko teillä vapaata huonetta?*
Where is a public toilet? *mis*-sa *on ü*-lays-ta *vehs*-sah/ *ü*-lay-nehn *vehs*-suh?	*Missä on yleistä vessaa/ yleinen vessa?*

I'd like ...	*sahn*-ko ...	*Saanko ...*
a one-way ticket	*meh*-no-*li*-pun	*menolipun*
a return ticket	*meh*-no-*pa*-loo-*li*-pun	*meno-pa luulipun*

1	*ük*-si	*yksi*	6	*koo*-si	*kuusi*
2	*kuhk*-si	*kaksi*	7	*sayt*-seh-man	*seitsemän*
3	*kol*-meh	*kolme*	8	*kuhkh*-dehk-suhn	*kahdeksan*
4	*nehl*-ya	*neljä*	9	*ükh*-dehk-san	*yhdeksän*
5	*vee*-si	*viisi*	10	*küm*-meh-nehn	*kymmenen*

FINNISH

Finnish, or **suomi** as it's called in Finland, is almost unique. It's not closely related to any language other than Estonian and Karelian and a handful of other rare languages. Linguistically, Finnish belongs to the Finnic (or more widely, Finno-Ugric) group of languages. Hungarian is the most widely spoken of the Finno-Ugric languages, but similarities with Finnish are extremely few.

Finnish is spoken by some five million people. It isn't related to any Indo-European languages. There are, however, many loan words from Baltic, Slavonic and Germanic languages, and many words deriving from French and, especially, English.

The main difficulties with Finnish are the suffixes (endings) added to noun and verb roots, which often alter in this process, and the habit of constructing long words by putting several small words together.

Outside the large towns, few people speak fluent English, so it's advisable to learn some phrases in Finnish to make your visit more rewarding. Finns appreciate any effort made by a non-native speaker and are eager to help further. Finnish is by no means an easy language to master, but it's easy to read out loud and the phonetics are not difficult – and mistakes made by foreigners are usually disregarded. There is also a notable Swedish-speaking minority in Finland, and all Finns learn Swedish in school, so you may need your Swedish vocabulary in Finland from time to time.

PRONUNCIATION

Pronunciation is given in the pronunciation guide at the front of this book, with the following exceptions:

Vowels

Finnish has eight vowels and the alphabet also includes Swedish å (see page 308).

FINNISH	GUIDE	SOUNDS
u	**u**	as in 'pull'

WHAT COMES AFTER Z?

The last three letters of the alphabet are **å**, **ä** and **ö**. So, while **Aatami** would be one of the first entries in a telephone book, **Äänekoski** would be one of the last.

Vowel Harmony

Finnish divides vowels into two groups: those formed 'in the front of the mouth' (**e**, **i**, **y**, **ä**, **ö**) and those formed 'in the back of the mouth' (**a**, **o**, **u**). This distinction is very important when forming words with suffixes, because the vowels in the suffixes must be of the same type as the vowels in the root word. For example, **koulussa**, 'in school', is formed by adding **-ssa**, not **-ssä**, to the root.

Double Vowels

Double vowels are tricky to pronounce, so follow the pronunciation guide carefully. You will find that some double vowels are pronounced as one sound within one syllable, others as diphthongs, and some as separate syllables.

FINNISH	GUIDE	SOUNDS
ää	**aa**	as the 'a' in American 'fast', but even longer

Consonants

There are only 13 consonants in Finnish, although the alphabet includes English consonants. The letter x can be written as ks, and z can be written, and is pronounced, as *ts*. Finns consider v and w more or less as the same letter, and in phone books you will find both under 'V'. In literature of a certain type, w makes a word look 'older.' Vanha is 'old', but wanha is 'definitely old'.

FINNISH	GUIDE	SOUNDS
p	p	soft, as in 'spirit'
b	b	explosive, as the 'b' in 'bug'
t	t	soft, as in 'steak'
k	k	soft, as in 'skate'
g	g	explosive, as the 'g' in 'gutter'
s	s	as in 'sun', but weaker
h	h	as in 'horse'
	kh	almost as strong as the 'ch' in Scottish 'loch'

PRONOUNS		
SG		
I	*mi*-na	*minä*
you	*si*-na	*sinä*
he/she/it	*han/han/seh*	*hän/hän/se*
PL		
we	*meh*	*me*
you (pl & pol)	*teh*	*te*
they	*heh/neh*	*he/ne* (inf)

Double Consonants

Double consonants like kk in viikko, 'week', or mm in summa, 'sum', are held longer and they always split the word into two syllables. Note that ng and nk both make two syllables, and are pronounced as -*ng*-ng- and -*ng*-k-. For example, vangit, 'prisons', is *vuhng*-ngit. Note also that np is pronounced as mp, as in olenpa, *o*-lehm-puh, 'I am'.

SIGNS

AUKI/SULJETTU	OPEN/CLOSED
KIELLETTY	PROHIBITED
KUUMA/KYLMÄ	HOT/COLD
LÄHTÖSELVITYS	CHECK-IN COUNTER
MATKATAVARAT	BAGGAGE COUNTER
OPASTUS/NEUVONTA	INFORMATION
PUHELIN	TELEPHONE
PÄÄSY KIELLETTY	NO ENTRY
SISÄÄN	ENTRANCE
TULLI	CUSTOMS
TUPAKOINTI KIELLETTY	NO SMOKING
ULOS	EXIT
VAPAA PÄÄSY	FREE ADMISSION
VARATTU	RESERVED
VARAULOSKÄYNTI	EMERGENCY EXIT
WC	TOILETS

GREETINGS & CIVILITIES

Top Useful Phrases

Hello.	*hay/tehrr*-veh/*moy*	*Hei/Terve/Moi.* (pol/inf)
Goodbye.	*na*-keh-meen/*moy*	*Näkemiin/Moi.* (pol/inf)
Yes.	*kül*-lah/yoo	*Kyllä/Joo.* (pol/inf)
No.	ay	*Ei.*
Excuse me.	*uhn*-teehk-si	*Anteeksi.*
Thank you.	*kee*-toss/*keet*-ti	*Kiitos/Kiitti.* (inf)
Many thanks.	*puhl*-yon *kee*-tok-si-uh	*Paljon kiitoksia.*

May I? Do you mind?
sai-sin-ko? — *Saisinko?*

Sorry.
o-lehn *puh*-hoyl-luh-ni; *so*-rri — *Olen pahoillani; Sori.* (inf)

That's fine. You're welcome.
o-leh *hü*-va; *ay*-pa *kehs*-ta — *Ole hyvä; Eipä kestä.* (inf)

There's no frequently used word for 'please' in Finnish. Often **kiitos** (thank you) is used. Another useful expression is 'could you', **voisitteko**, plus a verb. If you assume equality, or generally deal with informal situations, you are free to use less formal expressions. Speaking to a young clerk at a ticket booth or in a bank, you can say **voitko**, or even **voitsä**, 'are you able to', whereas an elderly lady would like to hear **voisitteko**, 'could you'.

Greetings

Good morning.
(*hü*-vaa) *hu*-o-mehn-tuh *(Hyvää) huomenta.*
Good afternoon.
hü-vaa *pa*-i-vaa/*pa*-i-vaa *Hyvää päivää./Päivää.* (inf)

Good evening/night.	*hü*-vaa *il*-tah/*ü-er*-ta	*Hyvää iltaa/yötä.*
How are you?	*mi-ta koo*-loo?	*Mitä kuuluu?*
Well, thanks.	*kee*-toss *hü*-vaa	*Kiitos hyvää.*

Forms of Address

Madam/Mrs	*rrohv*-vuh	*Rouva*
Sir/Mr	*hehrr*-rruh	*Herra*
Miss	*nay*-ti	*Neiti*
companion/friend	*üs*-ta-va/*kuh*-veh-rri	*ystävä/kaveri* (inf)

SMALL TALK

When you ask for a favour, use the most polite word: **Te** ('you' in the plural).

Minä means 'I', **sinä** is 'you'. Not everyone uses these words, however. In southern Finland, especially in Helsinki, most people say **mä** and **sä**. In Turku, Tampere and Oulu it's **mää**, for 'I', and **sää** for 'you' (**nää** in Oulu). In southern Savo they say **mie** and **sie**. In Helsinki it would be better to use **mä** instead of **minä**, to express that you don't place yourself above the other person. In northern Savo and places in Karelia, people still use **minä** – elsewhere you may sound rather egoistic if you use it. An asterisk (*) indicates where you could consider using some other form as you tour Finland.

Meeting People

What's your name?

mi-ka *tay*-dan *ni*-mehn-neh *on*?;	*Mikä teidän nimenne on?;*
mi-ka *sun ni*-mi *on*?	*Mikä sun nimi on?* (inf)

My name is ...

mi-nun *ni*-mehn-ni *on* ...;	*Minun nimeni on ...;*
mun ni-mi *on* ...	*Mun nimi on ...* (inf)

I'd like to introduce you to ...

huh-lu-ai-sin	*Haluaisin*
eh-si-tehl-la *si*-nut ...	*esitellä sinut ...-lle.*

I'm pleased to meet you.

hows-kuh *tuh*-vuh-tuh	*Hauska tavata.*

Nationalities

Where are you from?

mis-ta *si*-na *o*-let *ko*-toy-sin?	*Mistä sinä* olet kotoisin?*

I'm from ...	*o*-lehn ...	*Olen ...*
Australia	*owst*-rruh-li-uhs-tuh	*Australiasta*
Canada	*kuh*-nuh-duhs-tuh	*Kanadasta*
England	*ehng*-luhn-nis-tuh	*Englannista*
Finland	*su*-o-mehs-tuh	*Suomesta*
Ireland	*irr*-luhn-nis-tuh	*Irlannista*
New Zealand	*oo*-dehs-tuh	*Uudesta-*
	seeh-luhn-nis-tuh	*Seelannista*
Scotland	*scot*-luhn-nis-tuh	*Skotlannista*
the USA	*ükh*-düs-vuhl-loys-tuh/	*Yhdysvalloista/*
	uh-meh-rri-kuhs-tuh	*Amerikasta*
Wales	*wayl*-sis-ta	*Walesistä*

DID YOU KNOW ... In Finnish, the word for Finland is Suomi and the word for Finnish (the language) is suomi

Age

How old are you?

ku-in-kuh *vuhn*-huh *si*-na *o*-leht? *Kuinka vanha sinä* olet?*

I'm ... years old.

o-lehn ... *vu-o*-ti-uhs *Olen ...-vuotias.*

Occupations

What work do you do?

mi-ta *si*-na *teeht tüh-erk*-seh-si? *Mitä sinä* teet työksesi?*

I'm (a/an) ...	*o*-lehn ...	*Olen ...*
artist	*tai*-tay-li-yuh	*taiteilija*
businessperson	*lee*-keh-mi-ehs	*liikemies*
engineer	*in*-si-ner-rri	*insinööri*
farmer	*mahn-vil*-yeh-li-ya	*maanviljelijä*
journalist	*yohrr*-nuh-lis-ti/ *lekh*-ti-*mi-ehs*	*journalisti/ lehtimies*
lawyer	*yu*-rris-ti/ *luh*-ki-*mi-ehs*	*juristi/ lakimies*
mechanic	*meh*-kaa-nik-ko	*mekaanikko*
doctor	*laa*-ka-rri	*lääkäri*
nurse	*sai*-rrahn-*hoy*-tuh-yuh	*sairaanhoitaja*
office worker	*toy*-mis-to-*tü-ern-teh*-ki-ya	*toimistotyöntekijä*
scientist	*tut*-ki-yuh/ *ti-eh*-deh-*mi*-ehs	*tutkija/ tiedemies*
student	*o*-pis-keh-li-yuh	*opiskelija*
teacher	*o*-peht-tuh-yuh	*opettaja*
waiter	*tuhrr*-yoy-li-yuh	*tarjoilija*
writer	*kihrr*-yai-li-yuh	*kirjailija*

Religion

What is your religion?
mi-ka ***on si-nun us***-kon-to-si? *Mikä on sinun uskontosi?*

I'm not religious.
ehn o-leh ***us***-kon-nol-li-nehn/ ***us***-ko-vai-nehn *En ole uskonnollinen/ uskovainen.*

I'm (a) ...	***o***-lehn ...	*Olen ...*
Buddhist	***bud***-huh-lai-nehn	*buddhalainen*
Catholic	***kuh***-to-li-nehn	*katolinen*
Christian	***krris***-tit-tü	*kristitty*
Hindu	***hin***-du-lai-nehn	*hindulainen*
Jewish	***yoo***-tuh-lai-nehn	*juutalainen*
Lutheran	***lu***-teh-rri-lai-nehn	*luterilainen*
Muslim	***mus***-li-mi	*muslimi*

Family

Are you married? ***o***-leht-ko ***nai***-mi-sis-suh? *Oletko naimisissa?*

I'm ...	***o***-lehn ...	*Olen ...*
single	***nai***-muh-ton	*naimaton*
married	***nai***-mi-sis-suh	*naimisissa*
in a relationship	uhvo-lee-tos-suh	*avoliitossa*

How many children do you have?
ku-in-kuh ***mon***-tuh ***luhs***-tuh ***sul***-luh ***on***? *Kuinka monta lasta sinulla on?*

I don't have any children.
mul-luh ***ay o***-leh ***luhp***-si-uh *Minulla ei ole lapsia.*

I have a daughter/a son.
mul-luh ***on tü***-tarr/***poy***-kuh *Minulla on tytär/poika.*

How many brothers/sisters do you have?
ku-in-kuh ***mon***-tuh ***vehl***-yeh-a/ ***sis***-uhrr-tuh ***si***-nul-luh ***on***? *Kuinka monta veljeä/ sisarta sinulla on?*

Do you have a boyfriend/girlfriend?
on-ko ***sul***-luh ***poy***-kuh-***üs***-ta-vaa/ ***tüt***-ter-***üs***-ta-vaa? *Onko sinulla poikaystävää/ tyttöystävää?*

brother	*veh*-li	*veli*
children	*luhp*-set	*lapset*
daughter	*tü*-tarr	*tytär*
family	*pehrr*-heh	*perhe*
father	*i*-sa	*isä*
grandfather	*i*-so-*i*-sa/*vah*-rri/*uk*-ki	*isoisä/vaari/ukki*
grandmother	*i*-so-*a*-*i*-ti/*mum*-mi	*isoäiti/mummi*
husband	*uh*-vi-o *mi*-ehs	*aviomies*
mother	*a*-*i*-ti	*äiti*
partner	*e*-lam-an-*kump*-puh-ni	*elämänkumppani*
sister	*sis*-ko	*sisko*
son	*poy*-kuh	*poika*
wife	*vai*-mo	*vaimo*

Kids' Talk

How old are you? *ku*-in-kuh *vuhm*-huh *si*-na *o*-let?	*Kuinka vanha sinä olet?*
When's your birthday? *kos*-kuh *sun sünt*-ta-rrit *on?*	*Koska sun synttärit on?*
What do you do after school? *mi*-ta *si*-na *te*-eht *koh*-lun *jal*-keehn?	*Mitä sinä teet koulun jälkeen?*
Do you have a pet at home? *on*-ko *si*-nul-luh *lehm*-mik-ki-*eh*-la-in-ta *ko*-to-nuh?	*Onko sinulla lemmikkieläintä kotona?*

I have a ...	*mi*-nul-luh *on* ...	*Minulla on* ...
bird	*lin*-tu	*lintu*
budgerigar	*un*-du-laht-ti	*undulaatti*
canary	*kuh*-nuhrr-i-uhn-*lin*-tu	*kanarianlintu*
cat	*kis*-suh	*kissa*
dog	*koy*-rruh	*koira*
goldfish	*kul*-tuh-*kuh*-luh	*kultakala*

Feelings

I like ...	*pi*-dan ...-sta/stuh	*Pidän ...-sta/stä.*
I don't like ...	*ehn pi*-da ...-sta/stuh	*En pidä ...-sta/stä.*
I'm well.	*voyn hü*-vin	*Voin hyvin.*
I'm ...	*mi*-nul-luh *on* ...	*Minulla on ...*
cold	*kül*-ma	*kylmä*
hot	*koo*-muh	*kuuma*
in a hurry	*kee*-rreh	*kiire*
I'm ...	*o*-lehn ...	*Olen ...*
angry	*vi*-hai-nehn	*vihainen*
grateful	*kee*-tol-li-nehn	*kiitollinen*
happy	*i*-loy-nehn	*iloinen*
right	*oy*-keh-uhs-suh	*oikeassa*
sad	*su*-rrul-li-nehn	*surullinen*
sleepy	*u*-ni-nehn	*uninen*
tired	*va*-sü-nüt	*väsynyt*
worried	*hu-o*-lis-suh-ni	*huolissani*

I'm sorry. (condolence)

o-tuhn *o*-sah *o*-lehn	*Otan osaa, olen*
puh-hoyl-luh-ni	*pahoillani.*

BREAKING THE LANGUAGE BARRIER

Do you speak English?

pu-hut-ko *ehng*-luhn-ti-uh?	*Puhutko englantia?*

Does anyone speak English?

pu-hoo-ko ku-kahn *ehng*-luhn-ti-uh?	*Puhuuko kukaan englantia?*
I speak a little ...	*pu*-hun va-han ...	*Puhun vähän ...*
I don't speak ...	*ehn pu*-hu ...	*En puhu ...*
I understand.	*üm*-marr-rran	*Ymmärrän.*
I don't understand.	*ehn üm*-marr-rra	*En ymmärrä.*

Could you speak more slowly please?	
voy-sit-ko *pu*-hu-uh *hi*-tahm-min?	*Voisitko puhua hitaammin?*
Could you repeat that?	
voyt-ko *toys*-tah?	*Voitko toistaa?*
How do you say ...?	
mi-tehn *suh*-no-tahn ...?	*Miten sanotaan ...?*
What does ... mean?	
mi-ta ... *tuhrr*-koyt-tah?	*Mitä ... tarkoittaa?*

I speak ...	*pu*-hun ...	*Puhun ...*
English	*ehng*-luhn-ti-uh	*englantia*
French	*rruhns*-kah	*ranskaa*
German	*suhk*-sah	*saksaa*
Swedish	*rru*-ot-si-uh	*ruotsia*

Some Useful Phrases

Just a minute.	*heht*-ki-nehn	*Hetkinen.*
Wait!	*o*-do-tuh!	*Odota!*

Good luck!	
on-neh-uh! (*lükh*-kü-a *tüh*-ker!)	*Onnea! (Lykkyä tykö!)*
It's (not) important.	
seh on (*ay o*-leh) *tarr*-keh-aa	*Se on (ei ole) tärkeää.*
It's (not) possible.	
seh on (*ay o*-leh) *muhkh*-dol-lis-tuh	*Se on (ei ole) mahdollista.*

BODY LANGUAGE

You are in the country of the 'silent Finn': it's not felt necessary to make small talk all the time, and lack of eye contact doesn't indicate shiftiness or rudeness. If there are empty seats on a bus or in the cinema (and there always are), it's not usual to sit down right next to a stranger – leave a 'buffer zone.'

Shake hands when you meet someone for the first time.

PAPERWORK

address	*o*-soy-teh	*osoite*
age	*i*-ka	*ikä*
birth certificate	*sün*-tü-ma-*to*-dis-tus	*syntymätodistus*
border	*rruh*-yuh	*raja*
car registration	*rreh*-kis-teh-rri *nu*-meh-rro	*rekister inumero*
customs	*tul*-li	*tulli*
date of birth	*sün*-tü-ma *ai*-kuh/ *hen*-ki-ler-*tun*-nus	*syntymäaika/ henkilötunnus*
driver's licence	*uh*-yo-korrt-ti	*ajokortti*
identification	*hehn*-ki-ler-*puh*-peh-rrit	*henkilöpaperit*
make of car	*ow*-ton *mehrrk*-ki	*auton merkki*
marital status	*si*-vee-li-*saa*-tü	*siviilisääty*
name	*ni*-mi	*nimi*
nationality	*kuhn*-suh-lai-soos	*kansalaisuus*
passport	*puhs*-si	*passi*
passport number	*puhs*-sin *nu*-meh-rro	*passin numero*
place of birth	*sün*-tü-ma-*paik*-kuh	*syntymäpaikka*
profession	*uhm*-muht-ti	*ammatti*
reason for travel	*muht*-kuhn *tuhrr*-koy-tus	*matkan tarkoitus*
religion	*us*-kon-to	*uskonto*
sex	*su*-ku-*pu*-*o*-li	*sukupuoli*
visa	*vee*-su-mi	*viisumi*

SIGNS

AIKATAULU	TIMETABLE
ALIKULKUKÄYTÄVÄ	SUBWAY (pedestrian)
ASEMA	STATION
BUSSI/RATSIKKA PYSÄKKI	BUS/TRAM STOP
LIPPUTOIMISTO	TICKET OFFICE
LÄHTEVÄT	DEPARTURES
METRO	SUBWAY (train)
RAUTATIEASEMA	TRAIN STATION
SAAPUVAT	ARRIVALS

GETTING AROUND

As you look for places, visit them and leave them, you'll use different words in each case, and a little grammar is needed to gain an understanding of how words are constructed. Finnish grammar is extremely complicated. With all the possible suffixes and meanings, you can construct over 450 different words from any noun root.

-ssa or **-ssä**, 'in something': **koulu-ssa**, 'in school'
-sta or **-stä**, 'from something': **koulu-sta**, 'from school'
-double vowel plus **n**, 'to something': **koulu-un**, 'to school'
-lla or **-llä**, 'on', 'at' or 'in something' or 'somebody': **koulu-lla**, 'at school'
-lta or **-ltä**, 'from something' or 'somebody': **koulu-lta**, 'from school'
-lle, 'to something' or 'somebody': **koulu-lle**, 'to school'

Consider the following examples of expressing 'in ...', and 'to ...' (a town):

Helsinki:	**Helsingi-ssä**	**Helsinki-in**
Turku:	**Turku-ssa**	**Turku-un**
Varkaus:	**Varkaude-ssa**	**Varkaute-en**
Tampere:	**Tamperee-lla**	**Tamperee-lle**
Rovaniemi: (and others ending **-niemi**)	**Rovanieme-llä**	**Rovanieme-lle**
Seinäjoki: (and others ending **-joki**)	**Seinäjoe-lla**	**Seinäjoe-lle**
Kemijärvi: (and others ending **-järvi**)	**Kemijärve-llä**	**Kemijärve-lle**

To express being inside a vehicle, hotel etc, the **-ssa** suffix is used for 'in', and a double vowel plus **-n** for 'to': **juna-ssa/juna-an**, **hotelli-ssa/hotelli-in**. When you use a vehicle, you use the **-lla** suffix, as **matkustaa juna-lla**, 'to travel by train'.

What time does ...	*mi*-hin *ai*-kahn ...	*Mihin aikaan ...*
leave/arrive?	*lakh*-teeh/*sah*-poo?	*lähtee/saapuu?*
the (aero)plane	*lehn*-to-*ko*-neh	*lentokone*
the boat	*lai*-vuh	*laiva*
the bus (city)	*bus*-si	*bussi*
the bus (intercity)	*bus*-si/*lin*-yuh-*ow*-to	*bussi/linja-auto*
the train	*yu*-nuh	*juna*
the tram	*rrai*-ti-o-*vow*-nu/ *rruh*-tik-kuh	*raitiovaunu/ ratikka* (inf)

Directions

Where is ...?	*mis*-sa *on* ...?	*Missä on ...?*
How do I get to ...?		
mi-ten *mi*-na *paa*-sen ...?		*Miten minä* pääsen ...?*
Is it far from/near here?		
on-ko *seh kow*-kuh-nuh/ *la*-hehl-la?		*Onko se kaukana/ lähellä?*
Can I walk there?		
voy-ko *sin*-neh *ka*-vehl-la?		*Voiko sinne kävellä?*
Can you show me (on the map)?		
voyt-ko *na-üt*-taa *mul*-leh (*kuhrr*-tuhs-tuh)?		*Voitko näyttää minulle (kartasta)?*
Are there other means of getting there?		
paa-seeh-ker sin-neh *yol*-luh-kin *mool*-luh *tuh*-vuhl-luh?		*Pääseekö sinne jollakin muulla tavalla?*
I want to go to ...		
huh-lu-uhn *men*-na ...		*Haluan mennä ...*
Go straight ahead.		
kul-yeh *su-o*-rrahn		*Kulje suoraan.*
It's two blocks down.		
seh on kuhkh-den *korrt*-teh-lin *paas*-sa		*Se on kahden korttelin päässä.*

Turn left/right ...	*kaan*-nü *vuh*-sehm-pahn/ *oy*-keh-ahn ...	*Käänny vasempaan/ oikeaan ...*
at the next corner	*seh-u*-rrah-vuhs-tuh	*seuraavasta*
	kuh-dun-*kul*-muhs-tuh	*kadunkulmasta*
at the traffic lights	*lee*-kehn-neh-*vuh*-loys-suh	*liikenne valoissa*
behind	...-n *tuh*-kuh-nuh	*...-n takana*
far	*kow*-kuh-nuh	*kaukana*
near	*la*-hehl-la	*lähellä*
in front of	*eh*-dehs-sa	*edessä*
opposite	*vuhs*-tuh *paa*-ta ... -ta/-tuh	*vastapäätä ... -ta/-tä*

Booking Tickets

Where can I buy a ticket?	
mis-ta *voy os*-tah *li*-pun?	*Mistä voi ostaa lipun?*
I want to go to ...	
ha-lu-uhn *men*-na ...	*Haluan mennä ...-lle/ ...*vowel + *n*
Do I need to book?	
ta-ü-tüü-ker *vuh*-rruh-tuh?	*Täytyykö varata?*
I'd like to book a seat to ...	
ha-lu-ai-sin *vuh*-rruh-tuh	*Haluaisin varata*
is-tu-muh-*pai*-kuhn ...	*istumapaikan ...lle/...*vowel + *n*

I'd like ...	*sahn*-ko ...	*Saanko ...*
a one-way ticket	*meh*-no-*li*-pun	*menolipun*
a return ticket	*meh*-no-*pa*-loo-*li*-pun	*menopaluulipun*
two tickets	*kuhk*-si *lip*-pu-uh	*kaksi lippua*
a student's fare	*o*-pis-keh-li-ya-*li*-pun	*opiskelijalipun*
a child's fare	*lu̇hs*-tehn-*li*-pun	*lastenlipun*
a pensioner's fare	*eh*-la-keh-la-is-tehn *li*-pun	*eläkeläisten lipun*
1st class	*en*-sim-ma-i-nehn *lu-ok*-kuh	*ensimmäinen luokka*
2nd class	*toy*-nehn *lu-ok*-kuh	*toinen luokka*

Is it completely full?
on-ko *se ai*-vuhn *ta-ün*-na? — *Onko se aivan täynnä?*
Can I get a stand-by ticket?
voyn-ko *sah*-duh — *Voinko saada*
li-pun *il*-muhn — *lipun ilman*
paik-kuh-*vuh*-rrows-tuh? — *paikkavarausta?*

Air

Is there a flight to ...?
on-ko ... *len*-to-uh? — *Onko ...-lle/* (vowel + *n) lentoa?*
How long does the flight take?
kow-uhn-ko *len*-to *kehs*-taa? — *Kauanko lento kestää?*
What is the flight number?
mi-ka *on len*-non — *Mikä on lennon*
nu-meh-rro? — *numero?*
You must check in at ...
tay-dan (*sun*) *taü*-tüü — *Teidän (sun) täytyy*
kheh-kuh-tuh ... -la — *tsekata ...-lla*

airport tax	*lehn*-to-*kehnt*-ta *veh*-rro	*lentokenttävero*
boarding pass	*tuhrr*-kuhs-tus-*korrt*-ti	*tarkastuskortti*
customs	*tul*-li/*tul*-li-*tuhrr*-kuhs-tus	*tulli/tullitarkastus*

Bus

Does this bus go to ...?
meh-neeh-ker *ta*-ma — *Meneekö tämä*
bus-si ...? — *bussi ...* vowel + *n/...lle?*
Could you let me know when we get to ...?
voyt-ko *suh*-no-uh, *mil*-loyn — *Voitko sanoa, milloin*
tul-ehm-meh ...-n *lu-o*-nuh? — *tulemme ...-n luona?*
I want to get off!
mi-na *huh*-lu-uhn — *Minä* haluan*
jaa-da *poys*! — *jäädä pois!*

What time is the ... bus?	*mi*-hin *ai*-kahn *on* ... *bus*-si?	*Mihin aikaan on ... bussi?*
next	*seh-u*-rrah-vuh	*seuraava*
first	*ehn*-sim-ma-i-nehn	*ensimmäinen*
last	*vee*-may-nehn	*viimeinen*

Train

Is this the right platform for ...?
on-ko *ta*-ma *oy*-keh-uh *rrai*-deh ...? — *Onko tämä oikea raide* ... vowel + *n*/...*lle*?

Passengers must change trains.
muht-kus-tuh-yi-ehn *on vaikh*-deht-tuh-vuh *yu*-nah — *Matkustajien on vaihdettava junaa*

The train leaves from platform ...
yu-nuh *lakh*-teeh *rrai*-teehl-tuh ... — *Juna lähtee raiteelta* ...

dining car	*rruh*-vin-to-luh-vow-nu	*ravintolavaunu*
express	*pi*-kuh-*yu*-nuh	*pikajuna*
local	*pai*-kuhl-lis-*yu*-nuh	*paikallisjuna*
sleeping car	*muh*-koo-*vow*-nu	*makuuvaunu*

Metro

Which direction takes me to ...?
kum-pahn *soon*-tahn *paa*-seeh ...? — *Kumpaan suuntaan pääsee* ...*lle*/...vowel + *n*?

What is the next station?
mi-ka *on seh-u*-rrah-vuh *uh*-seh-muh? — *Mikä on seuraava asema?*

SIGNS

KAUKOLIIKENNE	LONG-DISTANCE TRAFFIC
KOLIKOT	CHANGE (for coins)
LAITURIALUE	PLATFORM AREA (for ticket check)
LÄHILIIKENNELIPPUJA	LOCAL TRAIN TICKETS
LÖYTÖTAVARAT	LOST AND FOUND
RAIDE	PLATFORM NO
VR MATKAPALVELU	TRAVEL SERVICE

Taxi

How much does it cost to go to ...?
puhl-yon-ko *muhk*-sah *muht*-kuh ...?
Paljonko maksaa matka ...vowel + *n/...lle?*

Here is fine, thank you!
tas-sa *on hü*-va *kee*-toss! — *Tässä on hyvä, kiitos!*

Continue!
yuht-kuh *vi*-eh-la! — *Jatka vielä!*

Stop here!
pü-sa-ü-ta *tas*-sa! — *Pysäytä tässä!*

The next street to the left/right.
seh-u-rrah-vah *kuh*-tu-uh *vuh*-sehm-muhl-leh/ *oy*-keh-uhl-leh — *Seuraavaa katua vasemmalle/oikealle.*

Please slow down.
hi-das-tuh *va*-han — *Hidasta vähän.*

Please wait here.
voyt-ko *o*-dot-tah *tas*-sa *va*-han — *Voitko odottaa tässä vähän.*

TAXI!

When directing a taxi driver, people usually just say their destination without any civilities.

Some Useful Phrases

The train is delayed/cancelled.
yu-nuh *on mü-er*-has-sa/ *peh*-rroo-teht-tu — *Juna on myöhässä/ peruutettu.*

How long will it be delayed?
kow-uhn-ko *seh onmu-er*-has-sa? — *Kauanko se on myöhässä?*

There is a delay of ... hours.
seh on ... *tun*-ti-uh *mu-er*-has-sa — *Se on ... tuntia myöhässä.*

How long does the trip take?
kow-uhn-ko *muht*-kuh *kehs*-taa? — *Kauanko matka kestää?*

Is it a direct route?
on-ko *se su-o*-rruh *rrayt*-ti? — *Onko se suora reitti?*

Is that seat taken?
on-ko *toy paik*-kuh *vuh*-rruht-tu? — *Onko tuo paikka varattu?*

I want to get off at ...
mi-na *jaan poys* ...-ssa/lla — *Minä* jään pois ...-ssa/-lla.*
Where can I hire a bicycle?
mis-ta *mi*-na *voyn vu-ok*-rruh-tuh *pol*-ku-*pü-er*-rran? — *Mistä minä* voin vuokrata polkupyörän?*
Is there room for the bicycle?
makh-too-ko *tan*-neh *pol*-ku-*pü-er*-rra? — *Mahtuuko tänne polkupyörä?*

Car

Where can I rent a car?
mis-ta *mi*-na *voy*-sin *vu-ok*-rruh-tuh *ow*-ton? — *Mistä minä* voisin vuokrata auton?*
daily/weekly
pehrr pa-i-va/*pehrr veek*-ko — *per päivä/per viikko*
Does that include insurance/unlimited mileage?
koo-loo-ko *see*-hen *vuh*-koo-tus/*rruh*-yoyt-tuh-muh-ton *ki*-lo-meht-rri *maa*-rra? — *Kuuluuko siihen vakuutus/rajoittamaton kilometrimäärä?*
Where's the next petrol station?
mis-sa *on la*-hin *ben*-suh *uh*-seh-muh? — *Missä on lähin bensa -asema?*
How long can I park here?
kow-uhn-ko *tas*-sa *sah parrk*-keeh-rruh-tuh? — *Kauanko tässä saa parkkeerata?*
Does this road lead to ...?
meh-neeh-ker *ta*-ma *ti-eh* ...? — *Meneekö tämä tie* ...vowel + *n/...lle?*

I need a mechanic.
mi-na *tarr*-vit-sehn *korr*-yah-yah — *Minä* tarvitsen korjaajaa.*
The battery is flat.
uhk-ku *on tükh*-ya — *Akku on tyhjä.*
The radiator is leaking.
yaakh-dü-tin *vu-o*-tah — *Jäähdytin vuotaa.*
I have a flat tyre.
rrehng-nguhs *on tükh*-ja — *Rengas on tyhjä.*

It's overheating.
seh koo-meh-neeh *lee*-kah — *Se kuumenee liikaa.*
It's not working.
seh ay toy-mi — *Se ei toimi.*

air (for tyres)	*il*-muh	*ilma*
battery	*uhk*-ku	*akku*
brakes	*yuhrr*-rrut	*jarrut*
clutch	*küt*-kin	*kytkin*
driver's licence	*uh*-yo-*korrt*-tih	*ajokortti*
engine	*morrt*-to-rri/*ko*-neh	*moottori/kone*
lights	*vuh*-lot	*valot*
oil	*erl*-yü	*öljy*
puncture	*rrehng*-nguhs-*rrik*-ko	*rengasrikko*
radiator	*yaakh*-dü-tin	*jäähdytin*
road map	*ti-eh*-kuhrrt-tuh	*tiekartta*
tyres	*rrehn*-kaht	*renkaat*
windscreen	*too*-li-*luh*-si	*tuulilasi*

SIGNS

BENSA-ASEMA	FILLING STATION
HUOLTOASEMA	GARAGE
ITSEPALVELU	SELF SERVICE
JÄINEN TIE	ICE ON ROAD
KELIRIKKO	BAD ROAD
KIELLETTY AJOSUUNTA	NO ENTRY
KIERTOTIE	DETOUR
KORJAAMO	MECHANIC
LYIJYTÖN 95E	UNLEADED
MOOTTORITIE	FREEWAY
PYSÄKÖINTI KIELLETTY	NO PARKING
STOP	STOP
TIETYÖ	ROADWORKS
YKSISUUNTAINEN AJOTIE	ONE WAY
97 OKTAANIA	NORMAL LEADED
99 OKTAANIA	SUPER LEADED

ACCOMMODATION

Where is ...?	*mis*-sa *o*-li-si ...?	*Missä olisi ...?*
a cheap hotel	*huhl*-puh *ho*-tehl-li	*halpa hotelli*
a good hotel	*hü*-va *ho*-tehl-li	*hyvä hotelli*
a nearby hotel	*la*-hin *ho*-tehl-li	*lähin hotelli*

What is the address?	
mi-ka *on o*-soy-teh?	*Mikä on osoite?*
Could you write the address, please?	
voy-sit-teh-ko *kirr*-yoyt-tah *o*-soyt-teen	*Voisitteko kirjoittaa osoitteen.*

At the Hotel

Do you have any rooms available?		
on-ko *tayl*-la *vuh*-pah-tuh *hu-o*-neht-tuh?		*Onko teillä vapaata huonetta?*
I'd like ...	*ha*-lu-ai-sin ...	*Haluaisin ...*
a single room	*ükh*-dehn *hehng*-ngehn *hu-o*-neehn	*yhden hengen huoneen*
a double room	*kuhkh*-dehn *hehng*-ngehn *hu-o*-neehn	*kahden hengen huoneen*
to share a dorm	*muh*-koo-*suh*-lin *san*-kü-*pai*-kuhn	*makuusalin sänkypaikan*
a bed	*sang*-ngün	*sängyn*
I want a room with a ...	*mi*-na *huh*-lu-uhn *hu-o*-neehn ...	*Minä* haluan huoneen ...*
bathroom	*kül*-pü-*hu*-o-neehl-luh	*kylpyhuoneella*
shower	*su*-ih-kul-luh	*suihkulla*
television	*yos*-suh *on teh*-leh-vi-si-o	*jossa on televisio*
window	*yos*-suh *on ik*-ku-nuh	*jossa on ikkuna*
I'm going to stay for ...	*mi*-na *ai*-on *vee*-pü-a ...	*Minä* aion viipyä ...*
one day	*ükh*-dehn *pai*-van	*yhden päivän*
two days	*kuhk*-si *pai*-vaa	*kaksi päivää*
one week	*vee*-kon	*viikon*

Do you have identification?
on-ko *tayl*-la/*sul*-luh *hehn*-ki-ler-*puh*-peh-rray-tuh? — *Onko teillä/sulla henkilöpapereita?* (pol/inf)

Your membership card, please.
sahn-ko *ya*-sehn-*korrt*-tin — *Saanko jäsenkortin.*

Sorry, we're full.
vuh-li-teht-tuh-vuhs-ti *mayl*-la *on ta-üt*-ta — *Valitettavasti meillä on täyttä.*

How many nights?
ku-in-kuh *mon*-tuh *u-er*-ta? — *Kuinka monta yötä?*

How much is it per night/per person?
puhl-yon-ko *seh on ü-erl*-ta/ *hehng*-ngehl-ta? — *Paljonko se on yöltä/ hengeltä?*

Can I see it?
voyn-ko *mi*-na *nakh*-da *sehn*? — *Voinko minä* nähdä sen?*

Are there any others?
on-ko *mi*-taan *mu-i*-tuh? — *Onko mitään muita?*

Are there any cheaper rooms?
on-ko *huhl*-vehm-pah *hu-o*-neht-tuh? — *Onko halvempaa huonetta?*

Can I see the bathroom?
voyn-ko *mi*-na *nakh*-da *kül*-pü-*hu-o*-neehn? — *Voinko minä* nähdä kylpyhuoneen?*

Is there a reduction for students/children?
sah-ko *o*-pis-keh-li-yuh/*luhp*-si *uh*-lehn-nus-tuh? — *Saako opiskelija/lapsi alennusta?*

Does it include breakfast?
koo-loo-ko *ah*-mi-ai-nehn *hin*-tahn? — *Kuuluuko aamiainen hintaan?*

It's fine, I'll take it.
se on hü-va *mi*-na *o*-tuhn *sen* — *Se on hyvä, minä* otan sen.*

I'm not sure how long I'm staying.
mi-na *ehn ti-eh*-da *ku-in*-kuh *kow*-uhn *mi*-na *vii*-vün *taal*-la — *Minä* en tiedä kuinka kauan minä* viivyn täällä.*

Is there a lift?
on-ko *taal*-la *his*-si-a? — *Onko täällä hissiä?*

Where is the bathroom?
mis-sa *on kül*-pü *hu-o*-neh (*vehs*-suh)? — *Missä on kylpyhuone (vessa)?*

Is there hot water all day?
on-ko *koo*-mah *veht*-ta *ko*-ko *pai*-van? — *Onko kuumaa vettä koko päivän?*

Do you have a safe where I can leave my valuables?
on-ko *tayl*-la *sa*-ilü-tüs-*lo*-kehrr-oy-tuh *arr*-vo-*tuh*-vuhrr-uhl-le? — *Onko teillä säilytyslokeroa arvotavaralle?*

Is there somewhere to wash clothes?
voy-ko *taal*-la *yos*-sain *pehs*-ta *vaht*-tay-tuh? — *Voiko täällä jossain pestä vaatteita?*

Can I use the kitchen?
voyn-ko *ka-üt*-taa *kayt*-ti-er-ta? — *Voinko käyttää keittiötä?*

Can I use the telephone?
voyn-ko *ka-üt*-taa *pu*-heh-lin-tuh? — *Voinko käyttää puhelinta?*

Is your sauna warm?
on-ko *sow*-nuh *lam*-min? — *Onko sauna lämmin?*

Do you have a smoke sauna?
on-ko *tayl*-la *suh*-vu-*sow*-nah? — *Onko teillä savusaunaa?*

SIGNS

HOTELLI	**HOTEL**
MATKUSTAJAKOTI	**GUESTHOUSE**
MOTELLI	**MOTEL**
RETKEILYMAJA	**YOUTH HOSTEL**

Requests & Complaints

Please wake me up at ...
voyt-teh-ko *heh*-rrat-taa — *Voitteko herättää*
mi-nut *kehl*-lo ... — *minut kello ...*

The room needs to be cleaned.
hu-o-neh *ta-ii*-tü-i-si *see*-vo-tuh — *Huone täytyisi siivota.*

Please change the sheets.
voyt-teh-ko *vaikh*-tah — *Voitteko vaihtaa*
luh-kuh-nuht — *lakanat.*

I can't open/turn on ...	*ehn sah ... ow*-ki	*En saa ... auki.*
I can't close/turn off ...	*ehn sah ... keen*-ni	*En saa ... kiinni.*
the window	*ik*-ku-nah	*ikkunaa*
the door	*o*-veh-uh	*ovea*
the heating	*puht*-teh-rri-uh	*patteria*
the TV	*tee*-veeh-ta	*TV:ta*

I left my key in the room.
uh-vai-meh-ni *ya-i* — *Avaimeni jäi*
hu-o-neeh-seehn — *huoneeseen.*

The toilet won't flush.
vehs-suh *ay veh*-da — *Vessa ei vedä.*

I don't like this room.
mi-na *ehn oy*-kayn *pi*-da — *Minä* en oikein*
tas-ta *hu-o*-neehs-tuh — *pidä tästä huoneesta.*

It's too small.	*se on lee*-uhn *pi-eh*-ni	*Se on liian pieni.*
It's noisy.	*si-ehl*-la *on meh*-lu-uh	*Siellä on melua.*
It's too dark.	*se on lee*-uhn *pi*-meh-a	*Se on liian pimeä.*
It's expensive.	*se on kuhl*-lis	*Se on kallis.*

Some Useful Words & Phrases

I'm/We're leaving now/tomorrow.

mi-na *luh*-dehn/*meh*	*Minä* lähden/Me*
lakh-deh-taan *nüt/hu-o*-mehn-nuh	*läh-detään nyt/huomenna.*

I'd like to pay the bill.

mi-na *muhk*-sai-sin *luhs*-kun	*Minä* maksaisin laskun.*

name	*ni*-mi	*nimi*
given names	*eh*-tu *ni*-meht	*etunimet*
surname	*su*-ku-*ni*-mi	*sukunimi*
address	*o*-soy-teh	*osoite*
room number	*hu-o*-neen	*huoneen*
	nu-meh-rro	*numero*
air-conditioned	*il*-muhs-toy-tu	*ilmastoitu*
balcony	*puhrr*-veh-keh	*parveke*
bathroom	*kül*-pü-*hu-o*-neh	*kylpyhuone*
bed	*san*-kü	*sänky*
bill	*luhs*-ku	*lasku*
blanket	*payt*-to	*peitto*
candle	*künt*-ti-la	*kynttilä*
chair	*tu-o*-li	*tuoli*
clean	*puh*-duhs	*puhdas*
cupboard	*kahp*-pi	*kaappi*
dirty	*li*-kai-nehn	*likainen*
double bed	*puh*-rri-*san*-kü	*parisänky*
electricity	*sakh*-ker	*sähkö*
excluded	*ay koo*-lu *hin*-tahn	*ei kuulu hintaan*
included	*koo*-loo *hin*-tahn	*kuuluu hintaan*
key	*uh*-vain	*avain*
lift (elevator)	*his*-si	*hissi*
light bulb	*heh*-ku-*luhmp*-pu/ *luhmp*-pu	*hehkulamppu/ lamppu*
a lock	*luk*-ko	*lukko*
mattress	*puht*-yuh	*patja*
mirror	*pay*-li	*peili*
padlock	*mu*-nuh-*luk*-ko	*munalukko*

pillow	*tüü*-nü	*tyyny*
quiet	*hil*-jai-nehn	*hiljainen*
room (in hotel)	*hu-o*-neh/*ho*-tehl-li- *hu-o*-neh	*huone/hotelli* *huone*
sauna	*sow*-nuh	*sauna*
sheet	*luh*-kuh-nuh	*lakana*
shower	*su-ih*-ku	*suihku*
soap	*saip*-pu-uh	*saippua*
suitcase	*muht*-kuh-*lowk*-ku	*matkalaukku*
swimming pool	*u-i*-muh-*uhl*-luhs	*uima-allas*
table	*per-ü*-ta	*pöytä*
toilet	*veeh*-seeh/*vehs*-suh	*WC/vessa*
toilet paper	*vehs*-suh-*puh*-peh-rri	*vessapaperi*
towel	*püü*-heh	*pyyhe*
(some) water	*veht*-ta	*vettä*
cold water	*kül*-muh vesi	*kylmä vesi*
hot water	*koo*-mah vet-ta	*kuumaa vettä*
window	*ik*-ku-nuh	*ikkuna*

STRAIGHT TO THE POINT

When buying a pack of cigarettes or a beer, you just state the merchandise. Pitkä! means 'Could you give me a large glass of beer, please!'.

AROUND TOWN

Where is ...?	*mis*-sa *on* ...?	*Missä on ...?*
the art gallery	*tai*-deh-*guhl*-leh-rri-ah/	*taidegalleriaa/*
	tai-deh-*guhl*-leh-rri-uh	*taidegalleria*
a bank	*puhnk*-ki-uh/*puhnk*-ki	*pankkia/pankki*
the church	*kirrk*-ko-uh/*kirrk*-ko	*kirkkoa/kirkko*
the city centre	*kehs*-kus-tah/	*keskustaa/*
	kehs-kus-tuh	*keskusta*
the ...embassy	...-n *soorr*	*...-n suur*
	la-heh-tüs-ter-a/	*lähetystöä/*
	...-n *soorr la*-heh-tüs-ter	*suurlähetystö*
my hotel	*ho*-tehl-li-ni	*hotellini*
a mail box	*pos*-ti-*lah*-tik-ko-uh/	*postilaatikkoa/*
	pos-ti-*lah*-tik-ko	*postilaatikko*
the market	*to*-rri-uh/*to*-rri	*oria/tori*
the museum	*mu*-seh-o-tuh/*mu*-seh-o	*museota/museo*
the police	*po*-lee-si-uh/*po*-lee-si	*poliisia/poliisi*
the post office	*pos*-ti-uh/*pos*-ti	*postia/posti*
a public toilet	*ü*-lays-ta *vehs*-sah/	*yleistä vessaa/*
	ü-lay-nehn *vehs*-suh	*yleinen vessa*
a telephone	*pu*-heh-lin-tuh/	*puhelinta/*
	pu-heh-lin	*puhelin*
the tourist	*muht*-kay-lu	*matkailu*
information	*toy*-mis-to-uh/	*toimistoa/*
office	*toy*-mis-to	*toimisto*

What time does it open/close?
mil-loyn *seh uh*-vuh-tahn/ *sul*-jeh-tahn?

Milloin se avataan/ suljetaan?

What ... is this?	*mi*-ka ... *ta*-ma *on*?	*Mikä ... tämä on?*
street	*kuh*-tu	*katu*
suburb	*kow*-pung-ngin-*o*-suh/	*kaupunginosa/*
	eh-si-*kow*-pung-ki	*esikaupunki*

For directions, see the Getting Around section, page 144.

At the Post Office

I'd like to send ...	*huh*-lu-ai-sin	*Haluaisin*
	la-heht-taa ...	*lähettää ...*
a fax	*fuhk*-sin	*faksin*
a letter	*kirr*-yeehn	*kirjeen*
a postcard	*pos*-ti-*korr*-tin	*postikortin*
a parcel	*puh*-keh-tin	*paketin*
a telegram	*sakh*-keehn	*sähkeen*

I'd like some stamps.
huh-lu-ai-sin — *Haluaisin*
pos-ti-*mehrrk*-keh-ja — *postimerkkejä.*

How much does it cost to send this to ...?
puhl-yon-ko *muhk*-sah — *Paljonko maksaa*
la-heht-taa ta-ma ...? — *lähettää tämä ...*vowel + *n?*

an aerogram	*uh-eh*-rro-grruhm-mi	*aerogrammi*
air mail	*lehn*-to-*pos*-ti-nuh	*lentopostina*
envelope	*kirr*-jeh	*kirje*
registered mail	*kirr*-juht-tu *kirr*-jeh	*kirjattu kirje*
surface mail	*mah-pos*-ti-nuh	*maapostina*

CHEAP ACCESS!

You can find cybercafés in most large towns, but the best and cheapest way to access the Internet is at a public library.

Telephone & Internet

I want to ring ...
huh-lu-ai-sin *soyt*-tah ... — *Haluaisin soittaa ...*

The number is ...
pu-heh-lin-*nu*-meh-rro *on* ... — *Puhelinnumero on ...*

How much does a three-minute call cost?
puhl-yon-ko *muhk*-sah *kol*-mehn *mi*-noo-tin *pu*-heh-lu? — *Paljonko maksaa kolmen minuutin puhelu?*

How much does each extra minute cost?
puhl-yon-ko *muhk*-sah *jo*-kai-nehn *li*-sa-*mi*-noot-ti? — *Paljonko maksaa jokainen lisäminuutti?*

I'd like to speak to (Mr Nieminen).
huh-lu-ai-sin *pu*-hu-uh *(hehrr*-rruh *ni-eh*-mi-sehn) *kuhns*-suh — *Haluaisin puhua (herra Niemisen) kanssa.*

I want to make a reverse-charges phone call.
huh-lu-uhn *soyt*-tah *vuhs*-tuh-*pu*-heh-lun — *Haluan soittaa vastapuhelun.*

It's engaged.
seh on vuh-rruht-tu — *Se on varattu.*

I've been cut off.
pu-heh-lu *kuht*-keh-si — *Puhelu katkesi.*

cellular phone
kan-nük-ka — *kännykkä*

Where can I access the Internet?
mis-sa *paa*-sehn *in*-tehrr-neht-tiin? — *Missä pääsen Internettiin?*

I'd like to send an e-mail.
huh-lu-ai-sin *la*-heht-taa *suh*-ker-*pos*-ti-uh — *Haluaisin lähettää sähköpostia.*

At the Bank

I want to change some money/ travellers cheques.
huh-lu-ai-sin *vaikh*-tah *rruh*-hah/ *muht*-kuh *shehk*-keh-ja
Haluaisin vaihtaa rahaa/ matkashekkejä.

What is the exchange rate?
mi-ka *on kurrs*-si?
Mikä on kurssi?

How many marks per dollar?
puhl-yon-ko *dol*-luh-rril-luh *sah muhrrk*-ko-yuh?
Paljonko dollarilla saa markkoja?

Can I have money transferred here from my bank?
voyn-ko *mi*-na *sah*-duh *rruh*-hah *seö*-rreht-tü-a *o*-muhs-tuh *puhn*-kis-tuh-ni?
Voinko minä saada rahaa siirrettyä omasta pankistani?*

How long will it take to arrive?
kow-uhn-ko *sehn tu*-lo *kehs*-taa?
Kauanko sen tulo kestää?

Has my money arrived yet?
on-ko *mi*-nun *rruh*-huh-ni *sah*-pu-nut *vi-eh*-la?
Onko minun rahani saapunut vielä?

(some) banknotes	*seh*-teh-leh-i-ta	*seteleitä*
cashier	*kuhs*-suh	*kassa*
some coins	*ko*-li-koy-tuh	*kolikoita*
credit card	*lu-ot*-to-*korrt*-ti	*luottokortti*
exchange	*rruh*-huhn-*vaikh*-to	*rahanvaihto*
loose change	*pik*-ku-*rruh*-hah/ *vaikh*-to-*rruh*-hah	*pikkurahaa/ vaihtorahaa*
money transfer	*ti*-li-*seer*-to	*tilisiirto*
signature	*uhl*-leh-*kirr*-yoy-tus	*allekirjoitus*

INTERESTS & ENTERTAINMENT

Sightseeing

Do you have a guidebook/ local map?	
on-ko *si*-nul-luh *muht*-kuh-*o*-puhs-tuh/*kuhrrt*-tah?	*Onko sinulla matkao pasta/karttaa?*
What are the main attractions?	
mit-ka *o*-vuht *tarr*-kaym-mat *nakh*-ta-vüü- deht?	*Mitkä ovat tärkeimmät nähtävyydet?*
What is that?	
mi-ka *tu-o on*?	*Mikä tuo on?*
How old is it?	
ku-in-kuh *vuhn*-huh *seh* on?	*Kuinka vanha se on?*
Can I take photographs?	
voyn-ko *mi*-na *ot*-tah *vuh*-lo-*ku*-vi-uh?	*Voinko minä* ottaa valokuvia?*
What time does it open/close?	
mil-loyn *seh ow*-keh-ah/ *sul*-yeh-tahn?	*Milloin se aukeaa/ suljetaan?*

ancient	*vuhn*-huh	*vanha*
archaeological	*uhrr*-keh-o-lo-gi-nehn	*arkeologinen*
beach	*u-i*-muh *rruhn*-tuh	*uimaranta*
building	*rruh*-kehn-nus	*rakennus*
castle	*lin*-nuh	*linna*
cathedral	*tu-o*-mi-o-*kirrk*-ko/ *kuh*-tehd-rrah-li	*tuomiokirkko/ katedraali*
church	*kirrk*-ko	*kirkko*
concert hall	*kon*-sehrrt-ti-*huhl*-li	*konserttihalli*
library	*kirr*-juhs-to	*kirjasto*
main square	*kehs*-kus *to*-rri	*keskustori*
market	*to*-rri/*kowp*-puh-*to*-rri/ *muhrrk*-ki-nuht	*tori/kauppatori/ markkinat*
monastery	*lu-os*-tuh-rri	*luostari*
monument	*mu-is*-to-*mehrrk*-ki/ *mo*-nu-mehnt-ti	*muistomerkki/ monumentti*

mosque	*mos*-kay-yuh	*moskeija*
old city	*vuhn*-huh-*kow*-pun-ki	*vanhakaupunki*
palace	*puh*-luht-si	*palatsi*
opera house	*orrp*-peh-rruh-*tuh*-lo	*oopperatalo*
ruins	*rrow*-ni-ot	*rauniot*
stadium	*stuh*-di-on	*stadion*
some statues	*puht*-sai-tuh	*patsaita*
synagogue	*sü*-nuh-gorr-guh	*synagooga*
temple	*tehmp*-peh-li	*temppeli*
university	*ü-li-o*-pis-to/ *korr*-keh-uh *koh*-lu	*yliopisto/ korkeakoulu*

Going Out

What's there to do in the evening?
mi-ta *taal*-la *voy teh*-da *il*-tai-sin? *Mitä täällä voi tehdä iltaisin?*
Are there any discos?
on-ko *taal*-la *üch*-taan *dis*-ko-uh? *Onko täällä yhtään diskoa?*
Are there places where you can hear local folk music?
voy-ko *taal*-la *mis*-saan *kool*-luh *pai*-kal-lis-tuh *mu*-seek-ki-uh? *Voiko täällä missään kuulla paikallista musiikkia?*
How much does it cost to get in?
puhl-yon-ko *on paa*-sü *muhk*-su? *Paljonko on pääsymaksu?*

cinema	*eh*-lo-ku-vuh-*teh-uht*-teh-rri	*elokuvateatteri*
concert	*kon*-sehrrt-ti	*konsertti*
discotheque	*dis*-ko	*disko*
theatre	*teh*-uht-teh-rri	*teatteri*

FRIENDS FOREVER

Traditionally Finns had to make a deal, sinunkaupat, to call each other sinä instead of Te. The deal involved an exchange of names and a formal handshake, after which you were friends forever.

Sports & Interests

What do you do in your spare time?

mi-ta *si*-na *teeht*	*mitä sinä teet*
va-pah-*ai*-kuh-nuh-si?	*vapaa-aikanasi?*

What sport do you play?

mi-ta *urr*-hay-lu-*luh*-yi-uh	*mitä urheilulajia*
huhrr-rruhs-tat?	*harrastat?*

art	*tai*-deh	*taide*
basketball	*ko*-rri-puhl-lo	*koripallo*
boxing	*nürrk*-kay-lü	*nyrkkeily*
cooking	*rru*-uuhn-*lait*-to	*ruuanlaitto*
fishing	*kuh*-luhs-tus	*kalastus*
football	*yuhl*-kuh-puhl-lo	*jalkapallo*
going out	*ul*-ko-nuh-*ka*-ün-ti	*ulkonakäynti*
going to the cinema	*eh*-lo-ku-vis-suh-*ka*-ün-ti	*elokuvissakäynti*
music	*mu*-seek-ki	*musiikki*
photography	*vuh*-lo-kuv-ows	*valokuvaus*
reading	*luk*-ehm-in-ehn	*lukeminen*
shopping	*shop*-pai-luu	*shoppailu*
soccer	*yuhl*-kuh-puhl-lo	*jalkapallo*
sport	*orr*-hay-loo	*urheilu*
the theatre	*the*-uht-teh-rri	*teatteri*
travelling	*muht*-kust-uh-min-ehn	*matkustaminen*
writing	*kirr*-yoy-tuh-min-ehn	*kirjoittaminen*

Festivals

The best film festival is held in Sodankylä (above the Arctic Circle) in June. The longest-established summer events are both held in July: **Pori Jazz** and the huge festival of world and traditional music at Kaustinen in Ostrobothnia. The biggest rock festivals are held near Turku (**Ruisrock**, July) and Seinäjoki (**Provinssirock**, June). One of Europe's leading and most remarkable Chamber Music events is held in Kuhmo on the Eastern border (July). To hear some of the best choirs for which the Nordic countries are famous, go to the **Choirs Festival** in Vaasa in May.

IN THE COUNTRY

Weather

What's the weather like?	*mi*-ka *on saa ti*-luh?/ *mil*-lai-nehn *saa on*?	*Mikä on säätila?/ Millainen sää on?*
It's ... today.	*ta*-naan *on* ...	*Tänään on ...*
Will it be ... tomorrow?	*on*-ko *hu-o*-mehn-nuh?	*Onko huomenna... ?*
cloudy	*pil*-vis-ta	*pilvistä*
cold	*kül*-maa	*kylmää*
foggy	*su*-mu-is-tuh	*sumuista*
forest fire alert	*meht*-sa-*puh*-lo-*vuh*-rroy-tus	*metsäpalo varoitus*
frosty	*puhk*-kuhs-tuh	*pakkasta*
hot	*koo*-muh	*kuuma*
raining	*suh*-deht-tuh	*sadetta*
snowing	*lun*-tuh/ *lu*-mih-*suh*-deht-tuh	*lunta/ lumisadetta*
summer night frost	*huhl*-lah	*hallaa*
sunny	*ow*-rrin-koys-tuh	*aurinkoista*
thunderstorm	*uk*-kos-tuh	*ukkosta*
sleet	*rran*-taa	*räntää*
windy	*too*-lihs-tuh	*tuulista*

Camping

Am I allowed to camp here?
sah-ko *taal*-la *lay*-rri-ü-tü-a? — *Saako täällä leiriytyä?*

Is there a campsite nearby?
on-ko *taal*-la *yos*-sain *la*-hehl-la *lay*-rrint-tuh-*uh*-luh-eh? — *Onko täällä jossain lähellä leirintäaluetta?*

backpack	*rrehp*-pu	*reppu*
can opener	*purr*-kin-*uh*-vah-yuh	*purkinavaaja*
compass	*kom*-puhs-si	*kompassi*
some firewood	*polt*-to-*poo*-tuh	*polttopuuta*
foam mattress	*muh*-koo-*uh*-lou-tuh	*makuualusta*
gas cartridge	*kah*-su-*sa*-*i*-li-ö	*kaasusäiliö*
mattress	*puht*-yuh	*patja*
penknife	*link*-ku-*vayt*-si	*linkkuveitsi*
rope	*ker*-*ü*-si	*köysi*
tent	*tehlt*-tuh	*teltta*
torch (flashlight)	*tuhs*-ku-*luhmp*-pu	*taskulamppu*
sleeping bag	*muh*-koo-*pus*-si	*makuupussi*
stove	*rreht*-ki-*kay*-tin	*retkikeitin*
water bottle	*veh*-si-*pul*-lo	*vesipullo*

SIGNS

LEIRINTÄALUE	CAMPING GROUND

FOOD

Some Useful Words & Phrases

breakfast	*ah*-mi-ai-nehn	*aamiainen*
lunch	*loh*-nuhs	*lounas*
early/late dinner	*pa-i*-val-li-nehn/ *il*-luhl-li-nehn	*päivällinen/ illallinen*

Table for ..., please.
sah-dahn-ko *meh per-ü*-ta ...? — *Saadaanko me pöytä ... lle?*
Can I see the menu please?
voyn-ko *mi*-na *nakh*-da *meh*-nun? — *Voinko minä* nähdä menun?*
I'd like the set lunch, please.
sahn-ko *pa-i*-van *loh*-nahn — *Saanko päivän lounaan.*
What does it include?
mi-ta *see*-hehn *koo*-loo? — *Mitä siihen kuuluu?*
Service is included in the bill.
tuhrr-yoy-lu *koo*-loo *hin*-tahn — *Tarjoilu kuuluu hintaan.*

ashtray	*tuh*-kuh-*kup*-pi	*tuhkakuppi*
the bill	*luhs*-ku	*lasku*
a cup	*kup*-pi	*kuppi*
dessert	*yal*-ki-*rru-o*-kuh	*jälkiruoka*
a drink	*yu-o*-muh	*juoma*
a fork	*hah*-rruk-kuh	*haarukka*
fresh	*tu-o*-rreh	*tuore*
a glass	*luh*-si	*lasi*
a knife	*vayt*-si	*veitsi*
a plate	*low*-tuh-nehn	*lautanen*
spicy	*tu*-li-nehn	*tulinen*
spoiled	*pi*-lahn-tu-nut	*pilaantunut*
a spoon	*lu*-sik-kuh	*lusikka*
sweet	*muh*-keh-uh	*makea*
teaspoon	*teeh-lu*-sik-kuh	*teelusikka*
toothpick	*huhm*-muhs-*tik*-ku	*hammastikku*

Vegetarian Meals

I'm a vegetarian.
o-lehn *kuhs*-vis-*sü-er*-ya — *Olen kasvissyöjä.*

I don't eat meat.
ehn sü-er *li*-hah — *En syö lihaa.*

I don't eat chicken, fish, or ham.
ehn sü-er *kuh*-nah *kuh*-lah *ehn*-ka *kink*-ku-uh — *En syö kanaa, kalaa enkä kinkkua.*

Staple Foods

bread	*lay*-paa	*leipää*
macaroni	*muh*-kuh-rro-ni	*makaroni*
oats	*kow*-rruh	*kaura*
rice	*rree*-si	*riisi*
rye	*rru*-is	*ruis*

Breakfast Menu

butter	*voi*	*voi*
boiled egg	*kay*-teht-tu *mu*-nuh	*keitet munah*
cereal	*hiu*-tuh-lay-ta	*hiualeitä*
cheese	*yuus*-to	*juusto*
coffee	*kuh*-vi	*kahvi*
fresh juice	*tuo*-rreh-*meh*-hu	*tuoremehu*
fried egg	*pais*-teht-tu *mun*-uh	*paisettu munah*
marmalade	*ap*-pehl-see-ni-*hil*-lo	*appelsiinihillo*
milk	*mai*-to	*maito*
oatmeal/porridge	*poo*-rro	*puuro*
orange juice	*ap*-pehl-see-ni-*meh*-hu	*appelsiinimehu*
sugar	*so*-kehrr-i	*sokeri*
tea	*teeh*	*tee*
toast	*pah*-to-*lay*-pa	*paahtoleipä*
yoghurt	*yog*-urrt-ti	*jogurtti*

Meat

beef	*now*-tuh/*harr*-ka	*nauta/härkä*
chicken	*kuh*-nuh/*brroy*-leh-rri	*kana/broileri*
ham	*kink*-ku	*kinkku*
liver	*muhk*-suh	*maksa*
minced meat	*yow*-heh-*li*-huh	*jauheliha*
pork	*porr*-sahs/*pos*-su	*porsas/possu*
reindeer	*po-rron*	*poron*
sausage	*muhk*-kuh-rruh	*makkara*
steak	*pih*-vi	*pihvi*

Seafood

Baltic herring	*si*-luhk-kuh	*silakka*
fish	*kuh*-lah	*kala*
herring	*sil*-li	*silli*
salmon	*loh*-hi	*lohi*
seafood (not fish)	*a*-ü-rri-ai-nehn	*äyriäinen*
shrimp	*kuht*-kuh-rruh-pu	*katkarapu*

Vegetables

cabbage	*kah*-li	*kaali*
carrot	*porrk*-kuh-nuh	*porkkana*
cucumber	*kurrk*-ku	*kurkku*
garlic	*val*-ko-*si*-pu-li	*valkosipuli*
mushroom	*si*-ehn-i	*sieni*
onion	*si*-pu-li	*sipuli*
pea	*hehrr*-ne	*herne*
potato	*peh*-rru-nuh	*peruna*
swede	*luhnt*-tu	*lanttu*
tomato	*to*-maht-ti	*tomaatti*
vegetable	*vi*-huhn-nehs	*vihannes*

Fruit

apple	*om*-ehn-a	*omena*
banana	bah-*nah*-ni	*banaani*
blueberry	*mus*-tik-kuh	*mustikka*
grapes	*vee*-ni-*rü*-pa-leh	*viinirypäle*
lemon	*si*-troo-nah	*sitruuna*
lingonberry	*puo*-kuk-kuh	*puolukka*
orange	*ap*-pehl-see-ni	*appelsiini*
pear	*paa*-rü-na	*päärynä*
pineapple	*uhn*-uhn-uhs	*ananas*
strawberry	*muhn*-sik-kuh	*mansikka*

MENU DECODER

Prepared Food

kiisseli laatikko *kees*-seh-li *lah*-tik-ko
berry or fruit soup minced vegetables and/or meat, baked in an oven

rieska *rrieh*-ska
thin barley bread, like chappati

herkku	*hehrrk*-ku	tidbit
kastike	*kuhs*-ti-keh	sauce
keitto/soppa	*kayt*-toh/*sop*-puh	soup
munakas	*mu*-nuh-kuhs	omelette
paistos	*pais*-tos	scalloped food or pie
pannu	*puhn*-nu	pan-fried food
piiras	*pee*-rruhs	pie
salaatti	*suh*-laht-ti	salad
sämpylä	*sam*-pü-la	roll
voileipä	*voy-lay*-pa	open sandwich

'Grilli' Food

The grilli can also be called katukeittiö snägäri or nakkikioski. Enormously popular, they prepare fast food by order until the early hours when everything else is closed. You can also find local specialities, such as mikkeliläinen in Mikkeli.

atomi *uh*-to-mi
meat pie with ham or fried egg

kebakko *keh*-buhk-ko
finger-shaped meat ball

lihapiirakka *li*-huh-*pee*-rruhk-kuh
pie with meat & rice filling

makkaraperunat *muhk*-kuh-rruh-*peh*-rrun-uht
sausage with French fries

munakukkaro *mu*-nuh-*kuk*-kuh-rro
hamburger with fried egg

nakkipiiras *nuhk*-ki-*pee*-rruhs
small sausage inside a pie

porilainen *po*-rri-lai-nehn
thick slice of sausage in a burger roll

reissumies *rrays*-su-*miehs*
two slices of rye bread with filling
vety *veh*-tü
meat pie with ham and eggs

camping	*kuhm*-ping	sausage
kalapuikot	*kuh*-luh-pu-i-kot	fish fingers
kuumakoira	*koo*-muh-*koi*-rruh	hot dog
nakki/nakit	*nuhk*-ki/*nuh*-kit	small sausage
publiski	*pub*-lis-ki	kind of hot dog
ranskalaiset	*rruhn*-skuh-lai-seht	French fries

Other Meals

janssonin kiusaus *yuhns*-son-in *kiu*-sows
potato and herring prepared in oven
kaalikääryleet *kah*-li-*kaa*-rrü-leeht
minced meat covered with cabbage leaves
kesäkeitto *ke*-sa-*kayt*-to
vegetable soup (lit. 'summer soup')
lihamureke *li*-huh-*mu*-rreh-keh
seasoned minced meat prepared in the oven
metsästäjänpihvi *mehts*-ast-ay-an-*pih*-vi
minced meat with mushroom sauce (lit. 'Hunter's steak')
pyttipannu *püt*-ti-*puhn*-nu
ham and potatoes fried in butter

lihapullat	*li*-huh-*pul*-luht	meatballs
lipeäkala	*li*-peh-a-*kuh*-luh	lutefish

Local Specialities

karjalanpiirakka *kuhrr*-yuh-luhn-*pee*-rruhk-kuh
rye pie with rice, barley or potato filling (Eastern)
lanttusupikas *luhnt*-tu-*su*-pik-uhs
kind of rye pita bread with swede filling (Savo)
lörtsy *lert*-sü
flat doughnut with apple or meat filling (Eastern)
kukkonen *kuk*-ko-nehn
rice porridge on bread (Karelian)

leipäjuusto *lay*-puh-*joo*-sto
flat dessert cheese eaten with jam in the west and north of the country (Pohjanmaa & Kainuu)

loimulohi *loi*-mu-lo-hi
salmon prepared on open fire (Eastern)

mustamakkara *mus*-tuh-*muhk*-kuh-rruh
rice-filled black sausage (Tampere)

muurinpohjalettu *muu*-rrin-*poh*-yuh-*leht*-tu
thin large fried pancake (Eastern)

neulamuikut *neh*-ul-uh-*mu*-ik-ut
small whitefish (Karelian)

poronkäristys *po*-rron-*ka*-rris-tüs
reindeer casserole (Lapland)

rönttönen *rrernt*-tern-ehn
round pie with rye, potato and lingon filling (Kuhmo)

sultsina *sult*-si-na
kind of chappati bread stuffed with porridge (Karelian)

vatruska *vuht*-rrus-kuh
thick pancake made of mashed potato and wheat flour (Karelian)

kukko *kuk*-ko
large rye bread loaf with filling (Eastern)

ahvenkukko	*uh*-vehn-*kuk*-ko	pork and perch
kalakukko	*kuh*-luh-*kuk*-ko	pork and fish
lanttukukko	*luhnt*-tu-*kuk*-ko	pork and swede
muikkukukko	*muik*-ku-*kuk*-ko	pork and whitefish
perunakukko	*peh*-rru-nuh-*kuk*-ko	pork and potato

Alcoholic Drinks

kossu *kos*-su
another name for strong Koskenkorva spirit

kotikal ja *ko*-ti-*kuhl*-yuh
lit. 'home-brewed malt drink'

lonkero *lon*-keh-rro
another name for a long gin and lemon

pitkä *pit*-ka
large glass of strong beer (lit. 'long')

huurteinen *huurr*-tay-nehn
cold beer, (lit. 'frosty')

Non-Alcoholic Drinks

berry drink	*meh*-hu	*mehu*
coffee	*kuh*-vi	*kahvi*
(drinking) water	(*juo*-muh-)*veh*-si	*(juoma)vesi*
fresh juice	*tuo*-rreh-*meh*-hu	*tuoremehu*
hot chocolate	*kah*-kao	*kaakao*
iced water	*yaa-veh*-si	*jäävesi*
milk	*mai*-to	*maito*
soft drink	*lim*-on-uh-di/ *li*-mu/*limp*-puh-rri/ *lim*-suh	*limonadi/ limu/ limppari/limsa*
soured milk	*pee*-ma	*piimä*
tea	*teeh*	*tee*

Alcoholic Drinks

beer	*o*-lut/*kuhl*-yuh	*olut/kalja* (lit. 'malt drink')
cocktail	*drrink*-ki	*drinkki*
light beer	*iik*-kers *o*-lut	*I-olut/ykkös olut*
medium strong beer	*kehs-ki-kuhl*-ya/ kol-mon-ehn/ *kol*-mos *o*-lut	*keskikalja/ kolmonen/ III-olut*
red wine	*pu*-nuh-*vee*-ni	*punaviini*
strong alcohol, vodka	*vee*-nah	*viina*
strong beer	*neh*-los-*o*-lut	*IV A-olut/ nelosolut*
white wine	*vuhl*-ko-*vee*-ni	*valkoviini*

TIME FOR A COFFEE BREAK

A **kahvila** is a normal cafe, whereas a **kahvio** serves coffee in, say, a petrol station or a supermarket, but basically these two are similar places, also called **kuppila**

AT THE MARKET

Basics

bread	*lay*-paa	*leipää*
butter	*voi*	*voi*
cereal	*hiu*-tuh-lay-ta	*hiualeitä*
cheese	*yuus*-to	*juusto*
chocolate	*suk*-lah	*suklaa*
eggs	*kuh*-nuh-*mu*-ni-uh	*kanamunia*
flour	*yow*-ho-uh	*jauhoa*
margarine	*muhrr*-guhrr-een-i-uh	*margariinia*
marmalade	*ap*-pehl-see-ni-	*appelsiinihilloa*
milk	*mai*-to	*maito*
macaroni	*mah*-kah-ro-ni	*makaroni*
olive oil	*ol*-ee-vi-*erl*-yü-uh	*oliiviöljyä*
rice	*ree*-si	*riisi*
sugar	*so*-kehrr-i	*sokeri*
(drinking) water	(*juo*-muh-)*veh*-si	(*juoma*)*vesi*
yoghurt	*yog*-urrt-ti	*jogurtti*

Meat & Poultry

beef	*now*-tuh/*harr*-ka	*nauta/härkä*
chicken	*kuh*-nuh/*brroy*-leh-rri	*kana/broileri*
ham	*kink*-ku	*kinkku*
pork	*porr*-sahs/*pos*-su	*porsas/possu*
reindeer	*po*-*rron*	*poron*
sausage	*muhk*-kuh-rruh	*makkara*

AT THE MARKET

Vegetables

cabbage	*kah*-li	*kaali*
carrot	*porrk*-kuh-nuh	*porkkana*
cucumber	*kurrk*-ku	*kurkku*
garlic	*val*-ko-*si*-pu-li	*valkosipuli*
mushroom	*si*-ehn-i	*sieni*
onion	*si*-pu-li	*sipuli*
pea	*hehrr*-ne	*herne*
potato	*peh*-rru-nuh	*peruna*
swede	*luhnt*-tu	*lanttu*
tomato	*to*-maht-ti	*tomaatti*
vegetable	*vi*-huhn-nehs	*vihannes*

Seafood

Baltic herring	*si*-luhk-kuh	*silakka*
fish	*kuh*-lah	*kala*
herring	*sil*-li	*silli*
salmon	*loh*-hi	*lohi*
seafood (not fish)	*a*-ü-rri-ai-nehn	*äyriäinen*
shrimp	*kuht*-kuh-rruh-pu	*katkarapu*

Fruit

apple	*om*-ehn-a	*omena*
banana	bah-*nah*-ni	*banaani*
grapes	*vee*-ni-*rü*-pa-leh	*viinirypäle*
lemon	*si*-troo-nah	*sitruuna*
orange	*ap*-pehl-see-ni	*appelsiini*
pear	*paa*-rü-na	*päärynä*
strawberry	*muhn*-sik-kuh	*mansikka*

SHOPPING

bookshop	*kirr*-yuh *kowp*-puh	*kirjakauppa*
camera shop	*vuh*-lo-*ku*-vows-*lee*-keh	*valokuvausliike*
clothing store	*vah*-the-*kowp*-puh	*vaatekauppa*
delicatessen	*hehrrk*-ku-*kowp*-puh	*herkkukauppa*
general store, shop	*kowp*-puh	*kauppa*
laundry	*peh*-su-luh	*pesula*
market	*kowp*-puh *to*-rri/ *muhrrk*-ki-nuht/ *buh*-sah-rri	*kauppatori/ mark-kinat/ basaari*
newsagency/ stationers	*lekh*-ti *ki-os*-ki/ *puh*-peh-rri-*kowp*-puh	*lehtikioski/ paperikauppa*
pharmacy	*uhp*-teehk-ki	*apteekki*
shoe shop	*kehn*-ka-*kowp*-puh	*kenkäkauppa*
souvenir shop	*muht*-kuh *mu-is*-to *miüü*-ma-la	*matkamuisto-myymälä*
supermarket	*su*-pehrr *muhrr*-keht	*supermarket*
vegetable shop	*vi*-huhn-nehs-*kowp*-puh	*vihanneskauppa*

I'd like to buy ...
huh-lu-ai-sin *os*-tah ... — *Haluaisin ostaa ...*

Do you have others?
on-ko *tayl*-la *mu-i*-tuh? — *Onko teillä muita?*

I don't like it.
ehn oy-kayn *pi*-da *see*-ta — *En oikein pidä siitä.*

Can I look at it?
voyn-ko mi-na *kuht*-so-uh *si*-ta? — *Voinko minä* katsoa sitä?*

I'm just looking.
mi-na *vain kuht*-seh-lehn — *Minä* vain katselen.*
How much is it?
puhl-yon-ko *seh muhk*-sah? — *Paljonko se maksaa?*
Can you write down the price?
voyt-teh-ko *kirr*-yoyt-tah *hin*-nuhn? — *Voitteko kirjoittaa hinnan?*

Do you accept credit cards?
voy-ko *muhk*-sah *lu-ot*-to-*korrt*-til-luh? — *Voiko maksaa luottokortilla?*
Could you lower the price?
voyt-ko *luhs*-keh-uh *hin*-tah? — *Voitko laskea hintaa?*
I don't have much money.
mul-luh *ay o*-leh *puhl*-yon *rruh*-hah — *Mulla ei ole paljon rahaa.*

Can I help you?
voyn-ko *owt*-tah? — *Voinko auttaa?*
Will that be all?
yuh tu-leeh-ko *moo*-tuh? — *Ja tuleeko muuta?*
Sorry, this is the only one.
ta-ma *on may*-dan *ai*-no-uh — *Tämä on meidän ainoa.*
How much/many do you want?
puhl-yon-ko *si*-na *huh*-lu-uht?/ *ku-in*-kuh *mon*-tuh *pis*-teh-taan? — *Paljonko sinä* haluat?/ Kuinka monta pistetään?*

SAMI HANDICRAFTS

Sami handicrafts, made according to Sami traditions, make great souvenirs. They're made in the traditional way, using traditional materials such as bone, wood, metals and hides. Check for a token with the word Duodji, as this indicates that the item is genuine.

Essential Groceries

I'd like ...	*huh*-lu-ai-sin ...	*Haluaisin ...*
batteries	*puhrr*-is-to-ya	*paristoja*
bread	*lay*-paa	*leipää*
butter	*voi*-tuh	*voita*
cheese	*yuus*-to-uh	*juustoa*
chocolate	*suk*-lah	*suklaa*
eggs	*kuh*-nuh-*mu*-ni-uh	*kanamunia*
flour	*yow*-ho-uh	*jauhoa*
gas cylinder	*kah*-su-*sai*-li-er	*kaasusäiliö*
ham	*kink*-ku-uh	*kinkkua*
honey	*hun*-uh-yah	*hunajaa*
margarine	*muhrr*-guhrr-een-i-uh	*margariinia*
marmalade	*ap*-pehl-see-ni-*hil*-lo-uh	*appelsiinihilloa*
matches	*tu*-li-*tik*-ku-yuh	*tulitikkuja*
milk	*mai*-to-uh	*maitoa*
olive oil	*ol*-ee-vi-*erl*-yü-uh	*oliiviöljyä*
pepper	*pip*-pu-rri-uh	*pippuria*
salt	*su*-ol-ah	*suolaa*
shampoo	*sam*-porr-tuh	*shampoota*
soap	*saip*-pu-uh	*saippua*
sugar	*so*-kehrr-iuh	*sokeria*
toilet paper	*vehs*-suh-*puhp*-ehrr-iuh	*vessapaperia*
toothpaste	*huhm*-muhs-*tuh*-nah	*hammastahnaa*
washing powder	*peh*-su-*yow*-heht-tuh	*pesujauhetta*

Souvenirs

some earrings	*korr*-vuh-*ko*-rru-yuh	*korvakoruja*
some handicrafts	*ka*-si-*ter*-*i*-ta	*käsitöitä*
necklace	*kow*-luh-*ko*-rru	*kaulakoru*
pottery	*keh*-rruh-meek-kuh	*keramiikka*
ring	*sorr*-mus	*sormus*
rug	*muht*-to/*rrah*-nu	*matto/raanu*

Clothing

clothing	*vaht*-teeht	*vaatteet*
coat	*tuhk*-ki	*takki*
dress	*pu*-ku	*puku*
jacket	*tuhk*-ki	*takki*
jumper (sweater)	*pu*-seh-rro/ *vil*-luh-*pai*-tuh	*pusero/ villapaita*
shirt	*pai*-tuh	*paita*
shoes	*kehng*-ngat	*kengät*
skirt	*huh*-meh	*hame*
trousers	*hoh*-sut	*housut*

It doesn't/They don't fit.
ta-ma/*na*-ma *ay muhkh*-du *Tämä/Nämä ei mahdu.*

It's too ...	*seh on lee*-uhn ...	*Se on liian ...*
big/small	*i*-so/*pi-eh*-ni	*iso/pieni*
short/long	*lü*-hüt/*peet*-ka	*lyhyt/pitkä*
tight/loose	*ki*-rreh-a/*ler-ü*-sa	*kireä/löysä*

Materials

cotton	*poo*-vil-lah	*puuvillaa*
handmade	*ka*-sin-*teh*-tüh/ *ka*-si-*tü-er*-ta	*käsintehty/ käsityötä*
leather	*nuhkh*-kah	*nahkaa*
brass	*mehs*-sin-ki-a	*messinkiä*
gold	*kul*-tah	*kultaa*
silver	*ho*-peh-ah	*hopeaa*
flax	*pehl*-luh-vah	*pellavaa*
pure alpaca	*uhl*-puhk-kah	*alpakkaa*
silk	*silk*-ki-a	*silkkiä*
wool	*vil*-lah	*villaa*

Colours

black	*mus*-tuh	*musta*
blue	*si*-ni-nehn	*sininen*
brown	*rrus*-keuh	*ruskea*
green	*vih*-rreh-a	*vihreä*
orange	*o*-rruhns-si	*oranssi*
pink	*vah*-leh-uhn-*pu*-nai-nehn (*pink*-ki)	*vaaleanpunainen (pinkki)*
purple	*vi*-o-leht-ti	*violetti*
red	*pu*-nai-nehn	*punainen*
white	*vuhl*-koy-nehn	*valkoinen*
yellow	*kel*-tai-nehn	*keltainen*

Toiletries

comb	*kuhm*-pa	*kampa*
some condoms	*kon*-do-meh-yuh	*kondomeja*
deodorant	*deh-o*-do-rruhnt-ti	*deodorantti*
hairbrush	*hi-us-huhrr*-yuh	*hiusharja*
moisturising cream	*kos*-te-us-*voy*-deh	*kosteusvoide*
razor	*puhrr*-tuh *teh*-rra	*partaterä*
sanitary napkins	*tehrr*-veh-üs-*si*-deh/ *pik*-ku-*hoh*-sun-*su-o*-yuh	*terveysside/ pikkuhousunsuoja*
shampoo	*suhmp*-porr	*shampoo*
shaving cream	*puhrr*-tuh-*vahh*-to	*partavaahto*
some tampons	*tuhm*-po-neh-yuh	*tamponeja*
tissues	*neh*-na-*lee*-nuh	*nenäliina*
toilet paper	*vehs*-suh-*puh*-peh-rri	*vessapaperi*
toothbrush	*huhm*-muhs-*huhrr*-yuh	*hammasharja*
toothpaste	*huhm*-muhs-*tuh*-nuh	*hammastahna*

Stationery & Publications

map	*kuhrrt*-tuh	*kartta*
newspaper (in English)	(*ehng*-luhn-nin *ki-eh*-li-nehn)	*(englannin kielinen)*
	suh-no-muh-*lekh*-ti	*sanomalehti*
novels in English	*ehng*-luhn-nin *ki-eh*-li-si-a	*englannin kielisiä*
	rro-mah-neh-yuh	*romaaneja*
paper	*puh*-peh-rri	*paperi*
pen (ballpoint)	*kü*-na	*kynä*
	(*koo*-luh-*karr*-ki-*kü*-na)	*(kuulakärkikynä)*
scissors	*suhk*-seht	*sakset*

Photography

How much is it to process this film?
puhl-yon-ko *muhk*-sah — *Paljonko maksaa*
keh-hit-taa *ta*-ma *fil*-mi? — *kehittää tämä filmi?*

When will it be ready?
kos-kuh *seh on vuhl*-mis? — *Koska se on valmis?*

I'd like a film for this camera.
mi-na *huh*-lu-ai-sin *fil*-min — *Minä* haluaisin filmin*
ta-han *kuh*-meh-rrahn — *tähän kameraan.*

B&W (film)	*mus*-tuh-*vuhl*-koy-nehn	*mustavalkoinen*
camera	*kuh*-meh-rruh	*kamera*
colour (film)	*va*-rri-*fil*-mi	*värifilmi*
film	*fil*-mi	*filmi*
flash	*suh*-luh-muh	*salama*
lens	*ob*-yehk-tee-vi/*lins*-si	*objektiivi/linssi*
light meter	*vuh*-lo-tus-*mit*-tuh-rri	*valotusmittari*

HOLY MOLEY!

Pyhä, 'holy', is used of Sundays, religious festivals and holidays like May Day and Midsummer when nearly everything is shut and special timetables apply. The day before these events, often used for heating up the sauna and celebrating, is aatto 'eve'.

Smoking

A packet of cigarettes, please.
sahn-ko *tu*-puhk-kuh *uhs*-kin *kee*-toss — *Saanko tupakka askin, kiitos.*

Are these cigarettes strong/mild?
o-vuht-ko *na*-ma *tu*-puh-kuht *vakh*-vo-yuh/*mi-eh*-to-yuh? — *Ovatko nämä tupakat vahvoja/mietoja?*

Do you have a light?
on-ko *sul*-luh *tul*-tuh? — *Onko sinulla tulta?*

cigarette papers	*suh*-vu-keh-*puh*-peh-rri-uh	*savuke paperia*
some cigarettes	*tu*-puhk-kah	*tupakkaa*
filtered	*filt*-teh-rri	*filteri*
lighter	*sü*-tü-tin/*süt*-ka	*sytytin/sytkä* (inf)
matches	*tu*-li-*ti*-kut/*ti*-kut	*tulitikut/tikut* (inf)
menthol	*menth*-torr-li	*menthol*
pipe	*peep*-pu	*piippu*
tobacco	*tu*-puhk-kuh	*tupakka*

Sizes & Comparisons

small	*pi-eh*-ni	*pieni*
big	*soo*-rri/*i*-so	*suuri/iso*
heavy	*pai*-nuh-vuh	*painava*
light	*keh*-vüt	*kevyt*
more	*eh*-nehm-man	*enemmän*
less	*va*-hehm-man	*vähemmän*
too much/many	*lee*-kah/*lee*-uhn *mon*-tuh	*liikaa/liian monta*
many	*mon*-tuh	*monta*
enough	*tuhrr*-peehk-si	*tarpeeksi*
also	*mü*-ers	*myös*
a little bit	*va*-han	*vähän*

ALL DAY

Finns use Päivää! (lit. 'Day!') as a general greeting during most of the day.

HEALTH

Where is the ...?	*mis*-sa *on* ...?	*Missä on ...?*
doctor	*la*-a-ka-rri	*lääkäri*
hospital	*sai*-rrah-luh	*sairaala*
chemist	*uhp*-teehk-ki	*apteekki*
dentist	*huhm*-muhs-*laa*-ka-rri	*hammaslääkäri*

I'm/My friend is sick.
o-lehn/*iis*-ta-va-ni *on sai*-rruhs — *Olen/Ystäväni on sairas.*

Could I see a female doctor?
on-ko muhkh-dol-lis-tuh *saa*-duh *nais laa*-ka-rri? — *Onko mahdollista saada naislääkäri?*

What's the matter?	*mi*-ka *on ha*-ta-na?	*Mikä on hätänä?*
Where does it hurt?	*mis*-ta *suht*-too?	*Mistä sattuu?*
My ... hurts.	*mi*-nun ... *on ki*-peh-a	*Minun ... on kipeä.*

Parts of the Body

ankle	*nilk*-kuh	*nilkka*
arm	*ka*-si	*käsi*
back	*sehl*-ka	*selkä*
chest	*rrin*-tuh/*rrin*-tuh-*keh*-ha	*rinta/rintakehä*
ear	*korr*-vuh	*korva*
eye	*sil*-ma	*silmä*
finger	*sorr-mi*	*sormi*
foot	*yuhl*-kuh	*jalka*
hand	*ka*-si	*käsi*
head	*paa*	*pää*
heart	*sü*-dan	*sydän*
leg	*saa*-rri	*sääri*
mouth	*soo*	*suu*
nose	*neh*-na	*nenä*
ribs	*kül*-ki-*loot*	*kylkiluut*
skin	*i*-ho	*iho*
stomach	*muh*-huh/*vuht*-suh	*maha/vatsa*
teeth	*huhm*-paht	*hampaat*
throat	*kurrk*-ku	*kurkku*

Ailments

I have (a/an) ...	*mul*-luh *on* ...	*Minulla on ...*
allergy	*uhl*-lehrr-gi-uh	*allergia*
anaemia	*uh*-neh-mi-uh	*anemia*
blister	*rruhk*-ko	*rakko*
burn	*puh*-lo-*vuhm*-muh	*palovamma*
cold	*fluns*-suh	*flunssa*
constipation	*um*-meh-tus-tuh	*ummetusta*
cough	*üs*-ka	*yskä*
diarrhoea	*rri*-pu-li	*ripuli*
fever	*koo*-meht-tuh	*kuumetta*
headache	*paan sarr*-kü	*päänsärky*
hepatitis	*muhk*-suh-*tu*-leh-dus/ *heh*-puh-teet-ti	*maksatulehdus/ hepatiitti*
indigestion	*rroo*-uhn-*su*-luh-tos *ha*-*i*-rri-er	*ruuansulatus-häiriö*
infection	*tu*-leh-dus	*tulehdus*
influenza	*in*-flu-ehns-suh	*influenssa*
lice	*ta*-*i*-ta	*täitä*
low/high blood pressure	*muh*-tuh-luh/ *korr*-keh-uh *veh*-rrehn-*pai*-neh	*matala/ korkea verenpaine*
sore throat	*kurrk*-ku *ki*-peh-a	*kurkku kipeä*
sprain	*nilk*-kuh *nürr*-yakh-ta-nüt	*nilkka nyrjähtänyt*
stomachache	*muh*-huh *ki*-pu	*mahakipu*
sunburn	*i*-ho *puh*-luh-nut	*iho palanut*
venereal disease	*su*-ku *pu*-*o*-li-*tow*-ti	*sukupuolitauti*

Some Useful Words & Phrases

I'm pregnant.	
o-lehn *rruhs*-kah-nuh	*Olen raskaana.*
I'm on the pill.	
sü-ern *eh*-pil-lehrr-ayt-a	*Syön e-pillereitä*
I haven't had my period for ... months.	
mul-luh *ay o*-leh *ol*-lut *koo*-kow-ti-si-uh ... *koo*-kow-teehn	*Minulla ei ole ollut kuukautisia* ...vowel + *n kuukauteen.*

I have been vaccinated. *min*-ut *on rro*-ko-teht-tu	*Minut on rokotettu.*
I have my own syringe. *mul*-luh *on o*-muh *rru-is*-ku/*neh-u*-luh	*Minulla on oma ruisku/neula.*
I feel better/worse. *voyn*-ti-ni *on puh*-rrehm-pi/ *hu-o*-nom-pi	*Vointini on parempi/ huonompi.*

I'm ...	*o*-lehn ...	*Olen ...*
asthmatic	*uhst*-mah-tik-ko	*astmaatikko*
diabetic	*di-uh*-beeh-tik-ko	*diabeetikko*
epileptic	*eh*-pi-lehp-tik-ko	*epileptikko*
I'm allergic to ...	*mi*-na *o*-lehn *uhl*-lehrr-gi-nehn ...	*Minä* olen allerginen ...*
antibiotics	*uhn*-ti-bi-orr-tayl-leh	*antibiooteille*
penicillin	*peh*-ni-sil-lee-nil-leh	*penisilliinille*
accident	*on*-neht-to-moos	*onnettomuus*
addiction	*rreep*-pu-voos	*riippuvuus*
antiseptic	*uhn*-ti-sehp-ti-nehn	*antiseptinen*
aspirin	*uhs*-pi-rree-ni	*aspiriini*
bandage	*si*-deh	*side*
blood test	*veh*-rri-*ko*-eh	*verikoe*
contraceptive	*ekh*-ka-i-sü-*va*-li-neh	*ehkäisyväline*
injection	*rru-is*-keh	*ruiske*
injury	*vuhm*-muh	*vamma*
medicine	*laa*-keh	*lääke*
nausea	*puh*-hoyn-*voyn*-ti	*pahoinvointi*
oxygen	*huhp*-pi	*happi*
some vitamins	*vi*-tuh-mee-neh-yuh	*vitamiineja*

At the Chemist

I need medication for ...
tuhrr-vit-sen *laa*-ki-tüs-ta ...-uh/ a *vuhrr*-tehn — *Tarvitsen lääkitystä ...-a/ ä varten.*

I have a prescription.
mi-nul-luh *on rreh*-sehp-ti — *Minulla on resepti.*

At the Dentist

I have a toothache.
mi-nun *huhm*-muhs-tuh-ni *sarr*-keeh — *Minun hammastani särkee.*

I've lost a filling.
mi-nul-tuh *on irr*-rron-nut *paik*-kuh — *Minulta on irronnut paikka.*

I've broken a tooth.
mi-nul-tuh *on loh*-yehn-nut *huhm*-muhs — *Minulta on lohjennut hammas.*

My gums hurt.
i-keh-neh-ni *o*-vuht *ki*-peh-uht — *Ikeneni ovat kipeät.*

I don't want it extracted.
ehn huh-lu-uh *eht*-ta *huhm*-muhs *poys*-teh-tahn — *En halua, että hammas poistetaan.*

Please give me an anaesthetic.
voyt-teh-ko *poo*-dut-tah — *Voitteko puuduttaa.*

SOCK IT TO ME COLD & STEAMY

In the traditional Finnish smoke sauna, savusauna water is thrown over the log-heated stove to produce steam. You may see people lightly hit themselves with small, leafy birch branches, to improve circulation. Then, it's outside to jump into a lake or the sea, even in winter, when they may first cut a hole in the ice.

TIME & DATES

What date is it today?
mi-ka *pa-i*-va *ta*-naan *on*? — *Mikä päivä tänään on?*
What time is it?
puhl-yon-ko *kehl*-lo *on*? — *Paljonko kello on?*

It's in the ...	*kehl*-lo *on* ...	*Kello on* ...
morning	*ah*-mul-luh	*aamulla*
afternoon	*il*-tuh-*pa-i*-val-la	*iltapäivällä*
evening	*il*-luhl-luh	*illalla*

Days of the Week

Monday	*mah*-nuhn-tai	*maanantai*
Tuesday	*tees*-tai	*tiistai*
Wednesday	*kehs*-ki-*veek*-ko	*keskiviikko*
Thursday	*torrs*-tai	*torstai*
Friday	*pehrr*-yuhn-tai	*perjantai*
Saturday	*low*-uhn-tai	*lauantai*
Sunday	*sun*-nun-tai	*sunnuntai*

Months

January	*tuhm*-mi-koo	*tammikuu*
February	*hehl*-mi-koo	*helmikuu*
March	*mah*-lis-koo	*maaliskuu*
April	*huh*-ti-koo	*huhtikuu*
May	*toh*-ko-koo	*toukokuu*
June	*keh*-sa-koo	*kesäkuu*
July	*hay*-na-koo	*heinäkuu*
August	*eh*-lo-koo	*elokuu*
September	*süüs*-koo	*syyskuu*
October	*lo*-kuh-koo	*lokakuu*
November	*muhrr*-rruhs-koo	*marraskuu*
December	*yoh*-lu-koo	*joulukuu*

Seasons

summer	*keh*-sa	*kesä*
autumn	*sük*-sü	*syksy*
winter	*tuhl*-vi	*talvi*
spring	*keh*-vat	*kevät*

Present

today	*ta*-naan	*tänään*
this morning	*ta*-na *ah*-mu-nuh	*tänä aamuna*
tonight	*ta*-na *il*-tuh-nuh	*tänä iltana*
this week	*tal*-la *vee*-kol-luh	*tällä viikolla*
this year	*ta*-na *vu-on*-nuh	*tänä vuonna*
now	*nüt*	*nyt*

Past

yesterday	*ay*-lehn	*eilen*
day before yesterday	*toys*-suh-*pa-i*-va-na	*toissapäivänä*
yesterday morning	*ay*-lehn *ah*-mul-luh	*eilen aamulla*
last night	*vee*-meh *ü-er*-na	*viime yönä*
last week	*vee*-meh *vee*-kol-luh	*viime viikolla*
last year	*vee*-meh *vu-on*-nuh	*viime vuonna*

Future

tomorrow	*hu-o*-mehn-nuh	*huomenna*
day after tomorrow	*ü*-li *hu-o*-mehn-nuh	*ylihuomenna*
tomorrow morning	*hu-o*-mehn *ah*-mu-nuh	*huomen aamuna*
tomorrow afternoon	*hu-o*-mehn-nuh *il*-tuh-*pa-i*-val-la	*huomenna iltapäivällä*
tomorrow evening	*hu-o*-mehn *il*-tuh-nuh	*huomeniltana*
next week	*ehn*-si *vee*-kol-luh	*ensi viikolla*
next year	*ehn*-si *vu-on*-nuh	*ensi vuonna*

During the Day

afternoon	*il*-tuh-*pa*-*i*-val-la	*iltapäivällä*
dawn	*ah*-mun *koyt*-to	*aamunkoitto*
very early morning	*ah*-mul-luh *ai*-kai-sin	*aamulla aikaisin*
day	*pa*-*i*-va	*päivä*
early	*ai*-kai-sin	*aikaisin*
midnight	*kehs*-ki-*ü*-*er*	*keskiyö*
morning	*ah*-mu	*aamu*
night	*ü*-*er*	*yö*
noon	*kehs*-ki-*pa*-*i*-va	*keskipäivä*
sunset	*ow*-rring-ngon-*luhs*-ku	*auringonlasku*
sunrise	*ow*-rring-ngon-*noh*-su	*auringonnousu*

NUMBERS & AMOUNTS

0	*nol*-luh	*nolla*
1	*ük*-si	*yksi/yks* (inf)
2	*kuhk*-si	*kaksi/kaks* (inf)
3	*kol*-meh	*kolme*
4	*nehl*-ya	*neljä*
5	*vee*-si	*viisi/viis* (inf)
6	*koo*-si	*kuusi/kuus* (inf)
7	*sayt*-seh-man	*seitsemän/seittemän* (inf)
8	*kuhkh*-dehk-suhn	*kahdeksan/kasi/kaheksan* (inf)
9	*ükh*-dehk-san	*yhdeksän/ysi/yheksän* (inf)
10	*küm*-meh-nehn	*kymmenen*
11	*ük*-si-*toys*-tuh	*yksitoista*
12	*kuhk*-si-*toys*-tuh	*kaksitoista*
13	*kol*-meh-*toys*-tuh	*kolmetoista*
14	*nehl*-ya-*toys*-tuh	*neljätoista*
15	*vee*-si-*toys*-tuh	*viisitoista*
20	*kuhk*-si-*küm*-mehn-ta	*kaksikymmentä*
30	*kol*-meh-*küm*-mehn-ta	*kolmekymmentä*
40	*nehl*-ya-*küm*-mehn-ta	*neljäkymmentä*
50	*vee*-si-*küm*-mehn-ta	*viisikymmentä*
60	*koo*-si-*küm*-mehn-ta	*kuusikymmentä*
70	*sayt*-seh-man-*küm*-mehn-ta	*seitsemänkymmentä*

80	*kuhkh*-dehk-suhn-*küm*-mehn-ta	*kahdeksankymmentä*
90	*ükh*-dehk-san-*küm*-mehn-ta	*yhdeksänkymmentä*
100	*suh*-tuh	*sata*
1000	*tu*-huht	*tuhat*
one million	*mihl*-yorr-nuh	*miljoona*
1st	*ehn*-sin-ma-i-nehn/*eh*-kuh	*ensimmäinen/eka* (inf)
2nd	*toy*-nehn/*to*-kuh	*toinen/toka* (inf)
3rd	*kol*-muhs	*kolmas*
1/4	*nehl*-yas *o*-suh/*nehl*-yan-nehs	*neljäsosa/neljännes*
1/3	*kol*-muhs *o*-suh/*kol*-muhn-nehs	*kolmasosa/kolmannes*
1/2	*pu-o*-leht	*puolet*
3/4	*kol*-meh *nehl*-yas *o*-sah	*kolme neljäsosaa*

Some Useful Words

Enough!	*rreet*-taa!	*Riittää!*
a little	*va*-han	*vähän*
double	*tup*-luht	*tuplat*
a dozen	*tu*-si-nuh	*tusina*
few	*huhrr*-vuh	*harva*
less	*va*-hehm-man	*vähemmän*
many	*mon*-tuh/*mo*-ni-uh	*monta/monia*
more	*eh*-nehm-man	*enemmän*
once	*kehrr*-rruhn	*kerran*
a pair	*puh*-rri	*pari*
percent	*prro*-sehnt-ti	*prosentti*
some	*yo*-tuh-kin/*va*-han/*yon*-kin *vehrr*-rruhn	*jotakin/vähän/jonkin verran*
too much	*lee*-kah/*lee*-uhn *puhl*-yon	*liikaa/liian paljon*
twice	*kuhkh*-dehs-ti/*kuhk*-si *kehrr*-tah	*kahdesti/kaksi kertaa*

ABBREVIATIONS

ALE – alennusmyynti	sale
ark – arkisin	on weekdays (Monday to Saturday)
as. – asema	station
eiL – ei lauantaisin	not on Saturdays
EP – erikoispikajuna	special express train
EU – Euroopan Unioni	European Union
FIN/fi.	Official abbreviations of Finland
Hki	Helsinki
IC	Intercity
k. – katu	Street
ke – keskiviikko	Wednesday
-kj. – -kuja	Alley
kpl – kappaletta	amount of something, or pieces
la – lauantai	Saturday
ma – maanantai	Monday
mk – markka	Finnish marks (currency)
n:o/nro – numero	number
pe – perjantai	Friday
PL – Postilokero	PO Box
puh./p. – puhelinnumero	telephone number
-t. – -tie	Road
SRM – Suomen Retkeilymajajärjestö	Finnish YHA
SS	(in timetables only) when there are two consecutive holidays, buses run on the second holiday only
su – sunnuntai	Sunday
ti – tiistai	Tuesday
Tku	Turku
to – torstai	Thursday
Tre	Tampere
v. – vuonna	year
VR – Valtion Rautatiet	National Railways

EMERGENCIES

Help!
uh-pu-uh!
Apua!

It's an emergency!
ta-ma *on ha*-ta-tuh-pows!
Tämä on hätätapaus!

There's been an accident!
nüt on tuh-puh-tu-nut *on*-neht-to-moos! — *Nyt on tapahtunut onnettomuus!*

Call a doctor!
kut-su-kah *laa*-ka-rri! — *Kutsukaa lääkäri!*

Call an ambulance!
soyt-tuh-kah *uhm*-bu-luhns-si! — *Soittakaa ambulanssi!*

I've been raped.
mi-nut *on rrais*-kuht-tu — *Minut on raiskattu.*

I've been robbed.
mi-nut *on rrii-ers*-teht-tü — *Minut on ryöstetty.*

Call the police!
soyt-tuh-kah *po*-lee-si! — *Soittakaa poliisi!*

Where is the police station?
mis-sa *on po*-lee-si *uh*-seh-muh? — *Missä on poliisiasema?*

Go away!
meh-neh *poys!/ha-i*-vü! — *Mene pois!/Häivy!* (inf)

I'll call the police!
mi-na *kut*-sun *po*-lee-sin! — *Minä* kutsun poliisin!*

Thief!
vuh-rruhs! — *Varas!*

I'm/My friend is ill.
mi-na *o*-lehn/ *mun üs*-ta-va *on sai*-rruhs — *Minä* olen/ Minun ystäväni on sairas.*

I'm lost.
mi-na *o*-lehn *ehk*-sü-nüt — *Minä* olen eksynyt.*

SIGNS

POLIISI
POLICE

POLIISIASEMA
POLICE STATION

Where are the toilets?
mis-sa *on vehs*-suh? — *Missä on vessa?*

Could you help me please?
voyt-teh-ko (*voyt*-ko) *owt*-tah — *Voitteko (voitko) auttaa.*

Could I please use the telephone?
sahn-ko *ka-üt*-taa *pu*-heh-lin-tuh? — *Saanko käyttää puhelinta?*

I'm sorry. I apologise.
oh-lehn *puh*-hoyl-luh-ni. *püü*-dan *uhn*-teehk-si — *Olen pahoillani. Pyydän anteeksi.*

I didn't realise I was doing anything wrong.
ehn tuh-yun-nut *teh*-keh-va-ni *mi*-taan *vaa*-rrin — *En tajunnut tekeväni mitään väärin.*

I didn't do it.
ehn teh-nüt *si*-ta — *En tehnyt sitä.*

I wish to contact my embassy/consulate.
huh-lu-uhn *ot*-tah *ükh*-teh-üt-ta *soorr-la*-heh-tüs-ter-ni/ *kon*-su-laht-teen — *Haluan ottaa yhteyttä suurlä-hetystööni/ konsulaattiin.*

I speak English.
pu-hun *ehng*-luhn-ti-uh — *Puhun englantia.*

I have medical insurance.
mi-nul-luh *on vuh*-koo-tus — *Minulla on vakuutus.*

My possessions are insured.

tuh-vuh-rruh-ni *on*	*Tavarani on*
vuh-koo-teht-tu	*vakuutettu.*

My ... was stolen.

mi-nul-tuh *on*	*Minulta on*
vuh-rruhs-teht-tu	*varastettu ...*

I've lost my...	*mi*-na *o*-lehn *hu*-kuhn-nut ...	*Minä* olen hukannut ...*
bag	*lowk*-ku-ni	*laukkuni*
handbag	*ka*-si *-owk*-ku-ni	*käsilaukkuni*
money	*rruh*-huh-ni	*rahani*
travellers cheques	*muht*-kuh-*shehk*-ki-ni	*matkashekkini*
passport	*puhs*-si-ni	*passini*

ICELANDIC

QUICK REFERENCE

Hello.	hahl-loh	*Halló.*
Goodbye.	blehs	*Bless.*
Yes./No.	yow/nay	*Já./Nei.*
Excuse me. (forgive me)	ahf-sahk-ith	*Afsakið.*
Sorry.	myehrr thi-kirr thahth layht	*Mér þykir það leitt.*
Please.	gyer-thö svo vehl	*Gjörðu svo vel.*
Thank you.	tahk firr-irr	*Takk fyrir.*
You're welcome.	ehk-ehrrt ahth thahk-ah	*Ekkert að þakka.*
I'd like ...	gyai-ti yehkh fayn-khith ...	*Gæti ég fengið ...*
a one-way ticket	mith-ah/ahth-rrah layth-in-ah	*miða/aðra leiðina*
a return ticket	mith-ah/bowth-ahrr layth-irr	*miða/báðar leiðir*

I (don't) understand.
yehkh skil (ehk-i) — *Ég skil (ekki).*

Do you speak English?
tah-lahrr thoo ehn-skö? — *Talar þú ensku?*

Where is ...?
kvahrr ehrr ...? — *Hvar er ...?*

Go straight ahead.
fahrr-thö baynt owfrram — *Farðu beint áfram.*

Turn left/right.
baykh-thö til vinst-rri/haikh-rri. — *Beygðu til vinstri/hægri.*

Do you have any rooms available?
ehrr-ö hehrr-behrr-khi leörs? — *Eru herbergi laus?*

I'm looking for a public toilet.
yehkh ehrr ahth lay-tah ahth ahl-mehn-inkhs-sahl-ehrr-dni — *Ég er að leita að almenningssalerni.*

1	aydn	*einn*	6	sehks	*sex*
2	tvayrr	*tveir*	7	syer	*sjö*
3	thrreer	*þrír*	8	owt-dah	*átta*
4	fyoh-rrirr	*fjórir*	9	nee-ö	*níu*
5	fimm	*fimm*	10	tee-ö	*tíu*

ICELANDIC

Icelandic is a North Germanic language. Iceland was settled primarily by Norwegians in the 9th and 10th centuries. By the 14th century Icelandic (Old Norse) and Norwegian had grown apart considerably. This was due to changes in Norwegian, while Icelandic changed remarkably little through the centuries. In fact, it has an unbroken literary tradition, dating from about 1100. The treasures of the Sagas and the poetic **Edda**, written about 700 years ago, can be enjoyed by a modern-day speaker of Icelandic.

Icelanders are proud of their literary heritage. They are particularly conservative when it comes to the written word. Borrowed vocabulary is ill tolerated and the policy of keeping the language pure is very strong. After all, Icelandic is spoken by a mere 280,000 people, and outside pressures on the language, in these times of easy travel and worldwide communications, are enormous.

The practice of creating neologisms (new words) instead of adopting foreign words is well established in Iceland. Neologisms, such as **útvarp**, 'radio', **sjónvarp**, 'television', **tölva**, 'computer', and **þota**, 'jet', are just a few that have become part of the Icelandic vocabulary in the last 50 years.

Icelanders are a rather informal people. A person is very rarely addressed by title and/or surname. Icelanders use the ancient patronymic system, where **son**, 'son' or **dóttir**, 'daughter' is attached to the genitive form of the father's or, less commonly, the mother's, first name. The telephone book entries are listed according to first names.

As one might expect, most Icelanders speak English, and often as many as three or four other languages, although among themselves they only converse in Icelandic. Your efforts to speak Icelandic will most certainly be met with great enthusiasm.

STRESS

Stress is generally on the first syllable.

PRONUNCIATION

Double consonants are pronounced as such. The Icelandic alphabet consists of 33 letters: a, á, b, d, ð, e, é, f, g, h, i, í, j, k, l, m, n, o, ó, p, r, s, t, u, ú, v, x, y, ý, z, þ, æ, ö.

Pronunciation is given in the general pronunciation guide at the front of this book, with the following exceptions:

Diphthongs

ICELANDIC	GUIDE	SOUNDS
au	eör	there is no equivalent sound in English

Semiconsonants

é	yeh	as in the 'ye' in 'yes'

Consonants

f	f	as in English. When between vowels or at the end of a word it's pronounced as 'v'. When followed by *l* or *n* it's pronounced as 'b'.
g	g	as the 'g' in 'get'
	kh	between vowels or before *r* or *ð*, *g* has a guttural sound, as the 'ch' in Scottish 'loch'
h	h	as in English, except when followed by *v*, when it's pronounced as 'k'
þ	th	as the 'th' in 'thin'
ð	th	as the 'th' in 'lather'

PRONOUNS		
SG		
I	yehkh	ég
you	thoo	þú
she/he/it		
PL	hoon/hahn/thahth	hún/hann/það
we	vith	við
you (pol)	thoo	þú
you (pl)	thith	þið
they	thayrr/thairr/theör	þeir/þær/þau

MIND YOUR þ's & ð's

Remember, the Icelandic letter þ, represented as th in the pronunciation guide, is pronounced as the 'th' in 'thin', while ð, represented as th, is pronounced as the 'th' in 'lather'.

GREETINGS & CIVILITIES

Top Useful Phrases

Hello.	hahl-loh	*Halló.*
Goodbye.	blehs	*Bless.*
Yes./No.	yow/nay	*Já./Nei.*
Excuse me. (forgive me)	ahf-sahk-ith	*Afsakið.*
Sorry.	myehrr thi-kirr thahth layht	*Mér þykir það leitt.*
Please.	gyer-thö svo vehl	*Gjörðu svo vel.*
Thank you.	tahk firr-irr	*Takk fyrir.*
That's fine.	ahlt ee lai-i	*Allt í lagi.*
You're welcome.	ehk-ehrrt ahth thahk-ah	*Ekkert að þakka.*

Forms of Address

Madam/Mrs	frroo	*frú*
Sir/Mr	hehrr-rrah	*herra*
Miss	frrer-kehn	*fröken*
companion/friend	vin-ko-nah/vin-örr	*vinkona/vinur* (f/m)

Greetings

Good morning.	gohth-ahn dai-in	*Góðan daginn.*
Good afternoon.	gohth-ahn dai-in	*Góðan daginn.*
Good evening/night.	khot kverld/khoh-th-ah noht	*Gott kvöld./Góða nótt.*
How are you?	kvehrr-dnikh heh-vörr thoo thahth?	*Hvernig hefur þú það?*
Well, thanks.	khot tahk	*Gott, takk.*

SMALL TALK

Meeting People

What's your name?	kvahth hay-tirr-thoo?	*Hvað heitir þú?*
My name is ...	yehkh hay-ti ...	*Ég heiti ...*
I'm pleased to meet you.	kon-dö sail/saidl	*Komdu sæl/sæll.* (f/m)

DID YOU KNOW ...

Family names are illegal in Iceland, unless they were adopted before the Personal Names Act which was passed by Iceland's parliament, Alþing, in 1925.

Nationalities

Where are you from? kvahth-ahn ehrrt thoo? *Hvaðan ert þú?*

I'm from ...	yehkh ehrr frrow ...	*Ég er frá ...*
Australia	owst-rrah-lee-ö	*Ástralíu*
Canada	kaha-nah-dah	*Kanada*
England	aynkh-lahn-di	*Englandi*
Ireland	eer-lahn-di	*Írlandi*
New Zealand	nee-ah syow-lahn-di	*Nýja Sjálandi*
Scotland	skot-lahn-di	*Skotlandi*
the USA	bahnd-ah-rree-kyö-nöm	*Bandaríkjunum*

Age

How old are you?
kvahth ehrr-dö ger-möl/gahm-ahdl? *Hvað ertu gömul/gamall?* (f/m)

I'm ... years old.
yehkh ehrr ... ow-rrah *Ég er ... ára.*

Occupations

What do you do?	kvahth gehrr-irr thoo?	*Hvað gerir þú?*
I'm (a/an) ...	yehkh ehrr ...	*Ég er ...*
in business	ee vith-skift-öm	*í viðskiptum*
journalist	frryeht-ah-mahth-örr	*fréttamaður*
manual worker	vehrrk-ah-mahth-örr	*verkamaður*
nurse	hyook-rrön-ahrr-frraith-ing-örr	*hjúkrunar-fræðingur*
office worker	skrrif-stof-ö-mahth-örr	*skrifstofumaður*
scientist	vee-sin-dah-mahth-örr	*vísindamaður*
student	nowms-mahth-örr	*námsmaður*
teacher	kehn-ah-rri	*kennari*
waiter	thyohdn/ thyohn-ös-dö-stool-kah	*þjónn/ þjónustustúlka*
writer	rrit-hehrf-önd-örr	*rithöfundur*

Religion

What is your religion?		
kvehrr-ahrr trroo-ahrr ehrrt thoo?		*Hverrar trúar ert þú?*
I'm not religious.		
yehkh ehrr ehk-i trroo-öth/ trroo-ahth-örr		*Ég er ekki trúuð/ trúaður.* (f/m)
I'm ...	yehkh ehrr ...	*Ég er ...*
Buddhist	boo-dah-trroo-ahrr	*búddatrúar*
Catholic	kah-tholsk/ kah-thol-skörr	*kapólsk/ kapólskur* (f/m)
Christian	krrist-in-ahrr trroo-ahrr	*kristinnar trúar*
Hindu	hin-doo trroo-ahrr	*hindú trúar*
Jewish	gith-ing-örr	*gyðingur*
Muslim	moo-hah-mehths-trroo-ahrr	*múhameðs-trúar*

Family

Are you married?
ehrrt-ö gift/gift-örr? *Ert þú gift/giftur?* (f/m)

I'm single.
yehkh ehrr ayn-hlayp/ ayn-hlayp-örr *Ég er einhleyp/ einhleypur.* (f/m)

I'm married.
yehkh ehrr gift/gift-örr *Ég er gift/giftur.* (f/m)

How many children do you have?
kvahth owt thoo merg berdn? *Hvað átt þú mörg börn?*

I don't have any children.
yehkh ow ayn-gin berdn *Ég á engin börn.*

Do you have a boyfriend/girlfriend?
owt thoo kairr-ahs-dah/ kairr-ös-dö? *Átt þú kærasta/ kærustu?*

brother	**brroh-thirr**	*bróðir*
children	**berdn**	*börn*
daughter	**doht-irr**	*dóttir*
family	**fyerl-skil-dah**	*fjölskylda*
father	**fahth-irr**	*faðir*
grandfather	**ah-vi**	*afi*
grandmother	**ahm-mah**	*amma*
husband	**ay-in-mahth-örr**	*eiginmaður*
mother	**mohth-irr**	*móðir*
sister	**sist-irr**	*systir*
son	**son-örr**	*sonur*
wife	**ay-in-ko-nah**	*eiginkona*

Kids' Talk

How old are you?
kvahth ehrr-tö ger-möl/ gahm-ahdl? *Hvað ertu gömul/ gamall?* (f/m)

When's your birthday?
kveh-nayrr owh-tö ahm-mai-li? *Hvenær áttu afmæli?*

What do you do after school?
kvath geh-rrirr-thoo ehf-tirr skoh-la? *Hvað gerirðu eftir skóla?*

Do you have a pet at home?
owt-tö gyai-lö-deer hehi-ma? *Áttu gæludýr heima?*

I have a ...	yehkh ow ...	*Ég á ...*
bird	fögl	*fugl*
budgerigar	pow-va-geörk	*páfagauk*
canary	kah-nah-rree-fögl	*kanarífugl*
cat	kerht	*kött*
dog	hönd	*hund*
frog	frrosk	*frosk*

Feelings

I (don't) like ...
yehkh ehrr (ehk-i) hrri-vin ahv ... *Ég er (ekki) hrifinn af...*
I'm cold/hot.
myehrr ehrr kahlt/hayt *Mér er kalt/heitt.*

I'm ...	yehkh ehrr ...	*Ég er ...*
angry	rrayth/rrayth-örr	*reið/reiður* (f/m)
grateful	thahk-lowt/	*þakklát/*
	thahk-law-törr	*þakklátur* (f/m)
happy	ow-naikhth/	*ánægð/*
	aw-naikhth-örr	*ánægður* (f/m)
hungry	sveörnkh/svown-görr	*vöng/svangur* (f/m)
sad	hrrig/hrrig-görr	*hrygg/hryggur* (f/m)
tired	thrrayt/thrrayt-örr	*þreytt/þreyttur* (f/m)
well	frreesk/frrees-görr	*frisk/friskur* (f/m)

I'm worried.
yehkh hehf ow-hig-yörr *Ég hef áhyggjur.*
I'm sorry. (condolence)
myehrr thik-irr thahth layht *Mér þykir það leitt.*

Some Useful Phrases

Sure.	viss-ö-lehkh-ah	*Vissulega.*
Just a minute.	bee-dö ahth-ayns	*Bíddu aðeins.*
Good luck!	gown-gi thyehrr vehl!	*Gangi þér vel!*

BREAKING THE LANGUAGE BARRIER

Do you speak English?
tah-lahrr thoo ehn-skö? *Talar þú ensku?*

Does anyone speak English?
tah-lahrr ayn-kvehrr ehn-skö? *Talar einhver ensku?*

I speak a little Icelandic.
yehkh tah-lah svoh lit-lah ees-lehn-skö *Ég tala svolitla íslensku.*

I don't speak ...
yehkh tah-lah ehki ... *Ég tala ekki ...*

I (don't) understand.
yehkh skil (ehk-i) *Ég skil (ekki).*

Could you speak more slowly please?
gyai-tirr thoo tah-lahth svo-lee-tith haikh-ahrr? *Gætir þú talað svolítið hægar?*

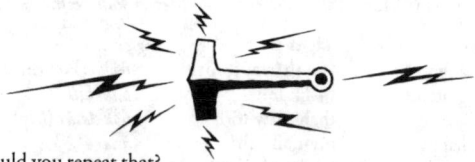

Could you repeat that?
gyai-tirr thoo ehn-dörr-tehk-ith theht-ah? *Gætir þú endurtekið þetta?*

How do you say ...?
kvehrr-dnikh say-irr mahth-örr ...? *Hvernig segir maður ...?*

What does ... mean?
kvahth theeth-irr? *Hvað þýðir ...?*

I speak ...	**yehkh tah-lah ...**	*Ég tala ...*
English	**ehn-skö**	*ensku*
French	**frrern-skö**	*frönsku*
German	**thees-kö**	*þýsku*
Italian	**ee-terl-skö**	*ítölsku*
Spanish	**spern-skö**	*spönsku*

BODY LANGUAGE

Icelandic society is small and it's possible to recognise Icelanders abroad because of the way they watch people directly, even in a big city, as if they expect to meet someone they know. Icelanders also tend – or at least used to, they're becoming more sophisticated now – to stare at foreigners.

Possibly the reason Icelanders crowd each other is that they have a different sense of bodily space from other westerners. An interesting idea, which may also account for the large number of automobile collisions, is that they have a different sense of 'car space' – a sense that there is much more space around themselves and their cars than in fact there is.

In the old Icelandic rural culture, people used to kiss a lot when they met. Nowadays most people only shake hands or put a little kiss on one cheek only. Icelanders are rather reserved and it takes time to get to know them, but they're known for their hospitality and they're used to fixing things (for themselves or anyone who needs it), so even if they don't seem very friendly you may experience their helpfulness all the same.

SIGNS

AÐGANGUR BANNAÐUR	NO ENTRY
BANNAÐ	PROHIBITED
FARANGUR	BAGGAGE COUNTER
FRÁTEKIÐ	RESERVED
INNGANGUR/INN	ENTRANCE
INNRITUN	CHECK-IN COUNTER
KONUR/KARLAR	LADIES/GENTLEMEN
NEYÐARÚTGANGUR	EMERGENCY EXIT
OPIÐ/LOKAÐ	OPEN/CLOSED
ÓKEYPIS	FREE ADMISSION
REYKINGAR BANNAÐAR	NO SMOKING
SÍMI	TELEPHONE
SNYRTING	TOILETS
TOLLUR	CUSTOMS
UPPLÝSINGAR	INFORMATION
ÚTGANGUR/ÚT	EXIT

PAPERWORK

address	hay-mil-is-fowng	*heimilisfang*
age	ahld-örr	*aldur*
birth certificate	faith-ing-ahrr-vot-orrth	*fæðingarvottorð*
car owner's title	ayg-nahrr-voth-orrth	*eignarvottorð*
car registration	biv-rrayth-ah-skoth-ön	*bifreiðaskoðun*
customs	todl-skoth-ö	*tollskoðun*
date of birth	faith-ing-ahrr-dahkh-örr	*fæðingardagur*
driver's licence	er-kö-skeer-tay-ni	*ökuskírteini*
identification	skil-rree-ki	*skilríki*
immigration	vehkh-ah-brryehvs-skoth-ön	*vegabréfsskoðun*
name	nahbn	*nafn*
nationality	thyohth-ehrr-dni	*þjóðerni*
passport	vehkh-ah-brryehv	*vegabréf*
(number)	(s-noo-ehrr)	*(snúmer)*
place of birth	faith-ing-ahrr-stahth-örr	*fæðingarstaður*
profession	aht-vin-ah	*atvinna*
reason for travel	ow-staith-ah	*ástæða*
	fehrrth-ah-lahkhs-ins	*ferðalagsins*
religion	trroo	*trú*
sex	kin	*kyn*
tourist card	fehrrth-ah-mahn-ah-spyahld	*ferðamannaspjald*
visa	vehkh-ah-brryehvs-ow-rrit-ön	*vegabréfsáritun*

GETTING AROUND

What time does the ... leave/arrive?	kveh-nayrr fehrr/keh-mörr ...?	*Hvenær fer/kemur ...?*
aeroplane	flökh-vyehl-in	*flugvélin*
boat	bow-törr-in	*báturinn*
(city)bus	vahgn-in	*vagninn*
tram	sporr-vahgn-in	*sporvagninn*

Directions

Where is ...?	
kvahrr ehrr ...?	*Hvar er ...?*
How do I get to ...?	
kvehrr-dnikh kyehmst yehkh til ...?	*Hvernig kemst ég til ...?*
Is it far from here?	
ehrr thahth lowngt hyehth-ahn?	*Er það langt héðan?*
Can I walk there?	
ehrr thahth ee gern-gö fai-rri?	*Er það í göngufæri?*
Can you show me (on the map)?	
geh-törr thoo seent myehrr (ow korrt-in-ö)?	*Getur þú sýnt mér (á kortinu)?*
I want to go to ...	
migh lown-gahrr ahth fah-rrah til ...	*Mig langar að fara til ...*
Go straight ahead.	
fahrr-thö baynt owfrram	*Farðu beint áfram.*
It's two blocks down.	
thahth ehrr tvaym-örr gert-öm nehth-ahrr	*það er tveimur götum neðar.*

Turn left/right at the ...	**baykh-thö til vinst-rri/haikh-rri vith ...**	*Beygðu til vinstri/hægri við ...*
next corner	**nais-dah horrdn**	*næsta horn*
traffic lights	**öm-fehrrth-ahrr-ljohs-in**	*umferðarljósin*
behind	**firr-irr ahft-ahn**	*fyrir aftan*
in front of	**firr-irr frrahm-ahn**	*fyrir framan*
far	**lownkht ee börr-dö**	*langt í burtu*
near	**now-laikht**	*nálægt*
opposite	**ow moh-ti**	*á móti*

Booking Tickets

Where can I buy a ticket?
kvahrr geht yehkh kayft mith-ah? *Hvar get ég keypt miða?*

I want to go to ...
yehkh vil fah-rrah til ... *Ég vil fara til ...*

Do I need to book?
thahrrf yehkh ahth pahn-tah? *Þarf ég að panta?*

I'd like to book a seat to ...
gyai-ti yehkh pahn-tahth fahrr til ... *Gæti ég pantað far til ...*

I'd like ...	gyai-ti yehkh fayn-khith ...	*Gæti ég fengið ...*
a one-way ticket	mith-ah/ ahth-rrah layth-in-ah	*miða/ aðra leiðina*
a return ticket	mith-ah/ bowth-ahrr layth-irr	*miða/ báðar leiðir*
two tickets	tvo mith-ah	*tvo miða*
a student's fare	nowms-mahn-ah-mith-ah	*námsmanna-miða*
1st class	firrst-ah fahrr-rreem-i	*fyrsta farrými*
2nd class	ahn-ahth fahrr-rreem-i	*annað farrými*

Is it completely full?
ehrr ahl-vehkh fölt? *Er alveg fullt?*

Can I get a stand-by ticket?
gyeht yehkh fayn-gith forr-fahd-lah-mith-ah? *Get ég fengið forfallamiða?*

Can I have a refund?
gyeht yehkh fayn-gith ehnd-örr-grrayths-lö? *Get ég fengið endurgreiðslu?*

DID YOU KNOW ... There are no trains in Iceland, but there are plenty of buses!

SIGNS

BROTTFÖR	DEPARTURES
KOMA	ARRIVALS
MIÐASALA	TICKET OFFICE
STRÆTISVAGNABIÐSTÖÐ	BUS STOP
STÖÐ	STATION
TÍMAÁÆTLUN	TIMETABLE

Air

Is there a flight to ...?
ehrr flo-yith til ...? *Er flogið til ...?*
How long does the flight take?
kvahth ehrr theh-tah lowngt flüg? *Hvað er þetta langt flug?*

airport tax	flü-vadla-skah-türr	*fluhvallaskattur*
boarding pass	brroht-fah-rrahrr-spyald	*brottfaraspjald*

Bus

Where is the bus stop?
kvahrr ehrr bith-sterth-in? *Hvar er biðstöðin?*
Which bus goes to ...?
kvahth-ah vahkhn fehrr til ...? *Hvaða vagn fer til ...?*
Could you let me know
when we get to ...?
gyai-tirr thoo low-tith mikh *Gætir þú látið mig*
vi-tah thehkh-ahrr *vita þegar*
vith kom-öm til ...? *við komum til ...?*
I want to get off!
yehkh vil fah-rrah oot! *Ég vil fara út!*

What time is the ... bus?	kveh-nairr kehm-örr ... vahgn-in?	*Hvenær kemur ... vagninn?*
first	firrst	*fyrst*
next	naist	*næst*
last	seeth-ahst	*síðast*

Taxi

Please take me to ...
gyai-tir thoo ehkith myehrr til ...? *Gætir þú ekið mér til ...?*
How much does it cost to go to ...?
kvahth kost-ahrr ahth fah-rrah til ...? *Hvað kostar að fara til ...?*
Here is fine, thank you.
hyehrr-dnah ehrr ow-gyait tahk *Hérna er ágætt, takk.*
The next street to the left/right.
nais-tah gah-tah til vinst-rri/haikh-rri *Næsta gata til vinstri/hægri.*

Continue. **hahl-dö ow-frrahm** *Haltu áfram.*
Stop here! **stahn-sah hyehrr-dnah!** *Stansa hérna!*

Car

Where's the next petrol station?
kvahrr ehrr nais-dah behn-seen-sterth? *Hvar er næsta bensínstöð?*
The battery is flat.
gaym-irr-in ehrr rahv-mahgns-leös *Geymirinn er rafmagnslaus.*
The radiator is leaking.
vahs-kahs-in leh-körr *Vatnskassinn lekur.*
I have a flat tyre.
thahth ehrr sprroon-ghith hyow myer *Það er sprungið hjá mér.*
It's overheating.
hahn heh-vör of-hit-nath *Hann hefur ofhitnað.*
It's not working.
hahn virrk-ahrr ehk-i *Hann virkar ekki.*

air (for tyres)	loft (ee dehk)	*loft (í dekk)*
battery	rrahf-gay-mirr	*rafgeymir*
brakes	brrehm-sörr	*bremsur*
clutch	koop-leeng	*kúpling*
driver's licence	ehr-kö-skeer-tay-ni	*ökuskírteini*
engine	vyehl	*vél*
lights	lyohs	*ljós*
radiator	vahss-kahss-i	*vatnskassi*
road map	vehkh-ah-korrt	*vegakort*
tyres	dehk	*dekk*
windscreen	frrahm-rrooth-ah	*framrúða*

SIGNS

ALLUR AKSTUR BANNAÐUR	**NO ENTRY**
BIÐSKYLDA	**GIVE WAY**
BLÝLAUST	**UNLEADED**
EÐLILEGT	**NORMAL**
EINSTEFNA	**ONE WAY**
ENGIN BÍLASTÆÐI	**NO PARKING**
SJÁLFSAFGREIÐSLA	**SELF SERVICE**
STANS	**STOP**
SUPER	**SUPER**
VERKSTÆÐI	**GARAGE**
VÉLVIRKI	**MECHANIC**
VIÐGERÐIR	**REPAIRS**

ACCOMMODATION

Where is a ...	kvahrr ehrr ...	*Hvar er ...*
hotel?	ho-tehl?	*hótel?*
cheap	oh-deert	*ódýrt*
nearby	now-laikht	*nálægt*
clean	hrraynt	*hreint*

What is the address?
kvahth ehrr hay-mil-is-fown-gith? *Hvað er heimilisfangið?*
Could you write the address, please?
gyai-tirr thoo skrrif-ahth nith-örr hay-mil-is fown-gith? *Gætir þú skrifað niður heimilisfangið?*

At the Hotel

Do you have any rooms available?
ehrr-ö hehrr-behrr-khi leörs? *Eru herbergi laus?*

I'd like ...	gyai-ti yehkh fayn-khith ...	*Gæti ég fengið ...*
a single room	ayn-stahk-lings-hehrr-behrr-khi	*einstaklingsherbergi*
a double room	tvehg-yah-mahn-ah-hehrr-behrr-gi	*tveggjamannaherbergi*
a room with a bathroom	hehrr-behrr-khi mehth bahth-i	*herbergi með baði*
to share a dorm	ahth day-lah hehrr-behrr-khi mehth erth-rröm	*að deila herbergi með öðrum*
a bed	rroom	*rúm*

I'm going to stay for ...	yehkh vehrrth ee ...	*Ég verð í ...*
one day	aydn dahkh	*einn dag*
two days	tvo dahkh-ah	*tvo daga*
one week	ay-nah vi-kö	*eina viku*

Sorry, we're full.
myehrr thi-kirr thahth layt thahth ehrr födl boh-kahth *Mér þykir það leitt, það er fullbókað.*

How long will you be staying?
kvahth ait-lahrr thoo ahth veh-rra layn-gi? *Hvað ætlar þú að vera lengi?*

How many nights?
kvahth mahrr-gahrr nai-törr? *Hvað margar nætur?*

How much is it per night/per person?
kvahth kost-ahrr noht-in firr-irr mahn-in? *Hvað kostar nóttin fyrir manninn?*

Requests & Complaints

Can I see it?
mow yehkh syow thahth? *Má ég sjá það?*

Are there any other/cheaper rooms?
eh-rrö nok-örr ern-örr/ oh-deer-ah-rri hehrr-behrr-gi? *Eru nokkur önnur/ ódýrari herbergi?*

Is there a reduction for students/children?
ehrr ahf-slowt-örr firr-irr nowms-mehn/berdn? *Er afsláttur fyrir námsmenn/börn?*

Does it include breakfast?
ehrr morrkh-ön-maht-örr in-i-fahl-in? *Er morgunmatur innifalinn?*

It's fine, I'll take it.
thahth ehrr ow-gyait yehkh fai thahth *Það er ágætt, ég fæ það.*

I'm not sure how long I'm staying.
yehkh ehrr ehk-i viss öm kvahth yehkh vehrrth layn-gi *Ég er ekki viss um hvað ég verð lengi.*

Where is the bathroom?
kvahrr ehrr bahth-hehrr-behrr-gith? *Hvar er baðherbergið?*

May I leave these in your safe?
mow yehkh gay-mah theh-dah ee er-ikh-is-hohl-vi? *Má ég geyma þetta í öryggishólfi?*

Is there somewhere to wash clothes?
ehrr ayn-kvehrrs-stahth-ahrr haikht ahth thvo thvoht? *Er einhversstaðar hægt að þvo þvott?*

Can I use the kitchen?
mow yehkh no-tah ehld-hoo-sith? *Má ég nota eldhúsið?*

Can I use the telephone?
mow yehkh no-tah see-mahn? *Má ég nota símann?*

Some Useful Words & Phrases

We're leaving now/tomorrow.
vith ehrr-öm ahth fah-rrah noo-nah/ow morr-goon — *Við erum að fara núna/á morgun.*

I'd like to pay the bill.
yehkh vil borr-khah rraykn-inkh-in — *Ég vil borga reikninginn.*

bathroom	bahth-hehrr-behrr-gi	*baðherbergi*
bed	rroom	*rúm*
blanket	teh-bi	*teppi*
clean	hrraydn	*hreinn*
dirty	ow-hrraydn	*óhreinn*
double bed	tvee-brrayt rroom	*tvíbreitt rúm*
electricity	rrahv-mahgn	*rafmagn*
excluded	firr-irr öt-ahn	*fyrir utan*
fan	vif-dah	*vifta*
included	in-i-fahl-ith	*innifalið*
key	li-kidl	*lykill*
lift (elevator)	lif-dah	*lyfta*
light bulb	lyow-sah-peh-rrah	*ljósapera*
a lock	lows	*lás*
mirror	spay-idl	*spegill*
pillow	kod-di	*koddi*
quiet	hlyoht	*hljótt*
sheet	lahk	*lak*
shower	störr-dah	*sturta*
soap	sow-pah	*sápa*
toilet	kloh-seht/sahl-ehrr-dni	*klósett/salerni*
toilet paper	klow-seht-pah-peer	*klósettpappír*
towel	hahnd-klai-thi	*handklæði*
(cold/hot) water	(kahlt/hayt) vahtn	*(kalt/heitt) vatn*
window	khlö-khi	*gluggi*

AROUND TOWN

I'm looking	**yehkh ehrr ahth**	*Ég er að*
for a/the ...	**lay-tah ahth ...**	*leita að ...*
bank	**bown-kah**	*banka*
city centre	**mith-bai-nöm**	*miðbænum*
... embassy	**... sehn-di-rrow-thi-nö**	*... sendiráðinu*
hotel	**hoh-tehl-i-nö mee-nö**	*hótelinu mínu*
market	**mahrrk-ahth-nöm**	*markaðnum*
police	**lerkh-rrehgl-ö-ni**	*lögreglunni*
post office	**pohst-hoos-i-nö**	*pósthúsinu*
public toilet	**ahl-mehn-inkhs-sahl-ehrr-dni**	*almennings-salerni*
telephone centre	**seem-sterthin-i**	*símstöðinni*
tourist information office	**öp-lees-een-gah-thjohn-öst-ö firr-irr fehrrth-ah-fohlk**	*upplýsinga-þjónustu fyrir ferðafólk*

What time does it open/close? **kveh-nairr ehrr op-nahth/ lo-kahth?**	*Hvenær er opnað/ lokað?*
What street/suburb is this? **kvahth-ah gah-tah/ kvehrr-vi ehrr theh-dah?**	*Hvaða gata/ hverfi er þetta?*

For directions, see the Getting Around section, page 207.

SIGNS

FARFUGLAHEIMILI	**YOUTH HOSTEL**
GISTIHEIMILI	**GUESTHOUSE**
GISTIHÚS	**MOTEL**
HÓTEL	**HOTEL**

At the Post Office

I'd like	yehkh ait-lah	*Ég ætla*
to send a ...	ahth sehn-dah ...	*að senda ...*
letter	brreef	*bréf*
postcard	korrt	*kort*
parcel	pahk-ah	*pakka*
telegram	skay-ti	*skeyti*

I'd like some stamps.
yehkh aid-lah ahth fow nok örr frree-mehrr-gi — *Ég ætla að fá nokkur frímerki.*

How much does it cost to send this to ...?
kvahth kos-dahrr ahth sehn-dah <u>th</u>eh-dah til ...? — *Hvað kostar að senda þetta til ...?*

an aerogram	flökh-brreef	*flugbréf*
airmail	flookh-pohst-örr	*flugpóstur*
envelope	öm-slahkh	*umslag*
mailbox	pohst-kahss-i	*póstkassi*
registered mail	ow-birrth-ahrr-pohst-örr	*ábyrgðarpóstur*
surface mail/sea mail	syoh-pohst-örr	*sjópóstur*

Telephone & Internet

I want to ring ...
yehkh <u>th</u>ahrrv ahth hrreen-gya ... — *Ég þarf að hringja ...*

The number is ...
noo-mehrr-ith ehrr ... — *Númerið er ...*

How much does a three-minute call cost?
kvahth kos-dahrr <u>th</u>rri-khjah-meen-oot-nah sahm-tahl? — *Hvað kostar þriggja mínútna samtal?*

How much does each extra minute cost?
kvahth kos-dahrr kvehrr meen-oo-tah? — *Hvað kostar hver mínúta?*

I'd like to speak to (Jón Pálsson).
gyai-ti yehkh fayn-gith ahth tahlah vith (yohn powls-sohn)? *Gæti ég fengið að tala við (Jón Pálsson)?*

I want to make a reverse-charges phone call.
yehkh ait-lah ahth hrreen-khyah okh vith-tahk-ahn-di borr-gahrr *Ég ætla að hringja og viðtakandi borgar.*

It's engaged. thahth ehrr ow tah-li *Það er á tali.*
I've been cut off. thahth slit-nahth-i *Það slitnaði.*

Where can I get Internet access?
kvahr gyeht yehkh fayn-gyith ahth noh-tah in-tehrr-neh-tith? *Hvar get ég fengið að nota internetið?*

I'd like to send an email.
Mig lown-guhrr til ahth sen-duh terl-vü-pohst *Mig langar til að senda tölvupóst.*

At the Bank

I want to exchange some money/travellers cheques.
yehkh thahrrf ahth skif-dah pehn-inkh-öm/fehrrth-ah-tyehköm *Ég þarf að skipta peningum/ferðatékkum.*

What is the exchange rate?
kvehrrt ehrr gehngith? *Hvert er gengið?*

How many kronas per dollar?
kvahth ehrr-ö mahrr-gahrr krrohn-örr ee dol-ah-rrah-nöm? *Hvað eru margar krónur í dollaranum?*

bank notes	sehth-lahrr	*seðlar*
cashier	gyahld-kehrr-i	*gjaldkeri*
coins	smow-mint	*smámynt*
credit card	grrayth-slö-korrt	*greiðslukort*
exchange	skif-dah	*skipta*
loose change	rrayth-ö-fyeh	*reiðufé*
signature	ön-dirr-skrrift	*undirskrift*

INTERESTS & ENTERTAINMENT

Sightseeing

Do you have a guidebook/local map?
owt-ö fehrrth-ah-hahnd-bohk/ korrt ahv stahth-nöm? *Áttu ferðahandbók/ kort af staðnum?*

What are the main attractions?
kvahth ehrr mahrrk-vehrrt ahth syow? *Hvað er markvert að sjá?*

What is that?
kvahth ehrr theh-dah? *Hvað er þetta?*

How old is it?
kvahth ehrr thahth gahm-ahlt? *Hvað er það gamalt?*

Can I take photographs?
mow yehkh tah-kah mind-irr? *Má ég taka myndir?*

What time does it open/close?
klök-ahn kvahth op-nahrr/ lok-ahrr? *Klukkan hvað opnar/ lokar?*

Going Out

What's there to do in the evenings?
kvahth ehrr haikht ahth gyeh-rra ow kverl-din? *Hvað er hægt að gera á kvöldin?*

Is there a local entertainment guide?
ehrr til baik-leen-görr öm skiehm-tah-nirr hyehrr ow stahth-nöm? *Er til bæklingur um skemmtanir hér á staðnum?*

I feel like	**mig lowngarr**	*Mig langar*
going to a/the ...	**til ahth fahrrah ...**	*til að fara ...*
cinema	**ee bee-oh**	*í bíó*
opera	**ee oh-peh-rrö-nah**	*í óperuna*
theatre	**ee layk-hoo-sith**	*í leikhúsið*
bar	**ow bahrr**	*á bar*
cafe	**ow kahffi-hoos**	*á kaffihús*
concert/gig	**ow tohn-lay-kah**	*á tónleika*
disco	**ow diskoh-tehk**	*á diskótek*
nightclub	**ow nai-törr-kloobb**	*á næturklúbb*
restaurant	**ow vay-teen-gah-hoos**	*á veitingahús*

Sports & Interests

What sports do you play?
kvah-thah ee-thrroh-tirr stön-dahrr thoo? — *Hvaða íþróttir stundar þú?*

What are your interests?
kvehrr eh-rrö theen ow-högah-mowl? — *Hver eru þín áhugamál?*

art	lis-tirr	*listir*
basketball	ker-fö-bol-ti	*körfubolti*
chess	skowk	*skák*
collecting things	ahth sab-nah hlö-töm	*að safna hlutum*
dancing	ahth dahnsah	*að dansa*
food	mah-törr	*matur*
football	fohd-bol-ti	*fótbolti*
hiking	geörn-gö-fehrr-thirr	*gönguferðir*
martial arts	bahrr-dahgah-ee-thrroh-tirr	*bardagaíþróttir*
meeting friends	ahth hih-tah vi-ni	*að hitta vini*
movies	kvik-min-dirr	*kvikmyndir*
music	tohn-list	*tónlist*
nightclubs	nai-törr-kloob-bahrr	*næturklúbbar*
photography	lyohs-min-dön	*ljósmyndun*
reading	lehs-törr	*lestur*
shopping	ahth fah-rrah ee boo-thirr	*að fara í búðir*
skiing	ahth fah-rrah ow skee-thi	*að fara á skíði*
swimming	sönd	*sund*
tennis	tehn-nis	*tennis*
travelling	ahth fehrr-thahst	*að ferðast*
TV/videos	syohn-vahrrp/ mind-bernd	*sjónvarp/ myndbönd*
visiting friends	ahth haym-sai-kyah vi-ni	*að heimsækja vini*

Festivals

During **Þorri**, the fourth month of winter (from mid-January to mid-February), it's common to hold a party called **þorrablót**, where people gather to sing and eat traditional Icelandic food.

Seven weeks before Easter is **bolludagur** 'bun-day', so-called because people are supposed to have all kinds of buns on this day. Children wake their parents in the morning with **bolluvöndur**, a decorated birch-rod. The last day before the beginning of the traditional Lenten fast (Shrove Tuesday) is **sprengidagur**. The name refers to **sprenging** (explosion) because people are supposed to eat as much **saltkjöt og baunir** (salted lamb/mutton, served with split pea soup) as they can, even so much that they may 'explode'.

A very old tradition in Iceland is celebrating the first day of summer, **sumardagurinn fyrsti**. It's an old custom to give **sumargjöf** (a summer gift) to close relatives.

Sautjándi júní, 17 June, is Iceland's National Independence Day. It's celebrated in front of the Parliament where the **fjallkona**, a female symbol of Iceland (usually a young actress in national costume), recites a poem.

The most important day of preparation for **Jólin** (Christmas), is 23 December, called **þorláksmessa** after the only officially canonised Icelandic saint. The main Christmas celebration starts with a Christmas church service on Christmas Eve, **aðfangadagskvöld**, followed by a family dinner. To wish someone a merry Christmas you say **gleðileg jól**

IN THE COUNTRY

Weather

What's the weather like?
kvehrr-dnikh ehrr vehth-rrith?
Hvernig er veðrið?

SIGNS

TJALDSTÆÐI
CAMPING GROUND

It's ... today.	vehth-rrith ehrr ... ee dahkh	*Veðrið er ... í dag.*
Will it be ... tomorrow?	vehrrth-örr ... ow morr-khön?	*Verður ... á morgun?*
cloudy	skee-yahth	*skýjað*
cold	kahlt	*kalt*
hot	hayt	*heitt*
raining	rrikh-neenkh	*rigning*
snowing	snyohrr	*snjór*
sunny	sohl-skin	*sólskin*
windy	kvahst	*hvasst*

Camping

Am I allowed to camp here?
mow yehkh tyahl-dah hyehrr? *Má ég tjalda hér?*

Is there a campsite nearby?
ehrr tyahld-staith-i hyehrr now-laikht? *Er tjaldstæði hér nálægt?*

backpack	bahk-po-ki	*bakpoki*
can opener	doh-sah-op-nah-rri	*dósaopnari*
firewood	ehld-i-vith-örr	*eldiviður*
gas cartridge	gahs-koo-törr	*gaskútur*
mattress	dee-nah	*dýna*
penknife	vah-sah-hneev-örr	*vasahnífur*
rope	snai-rri	*snæri*
tent (pegs)	tyahld(-hai-lahrr)	*tjald(hælar)*
torch/flashlight	vah-sah-lyohs	*vasaljós*
sleeping bag	svehbn-po-ki	*svefnpoki*
stove	ehld-ah-veel	*eldavél*
water bottle	vahs-flahs-ga	*vatnsflaska*

FOOD

breakfast	morr-gön-mah-törr	*morgunmatur*
lunch	how-day-is-maht-örr	*hádegismatur*
dinner	kverld-maht-örr	*kvöldmatur*

Table for ..., please.
gyeht yehkh fayn-gith ... *Get ég fengið ...*
mah-nah borrth? *manna borð?*
Can I see the menu please?
gyeht-yehkh fayn-gith ahth *Get ég fengið að*
syow maht-sehth-il-in? *sjá matseðilinn?*
What does it include?
kvahth ehrr in-i-fahl-ith? *Hvað er innifalið?*
Is service included in the bill?
ehrr thyoh-nös-dah in-i-fahl-in? *Er þjónusta innifalin?*

ashtray	ers-kö-bah-khi	*öskubakki*
the bill	rrayk-ninkh-örr-in	*reikningurinn*
a cup	bod-li	*bolli*
a drink	drrik-örr	*drykkur*
a fork	khahf-adl	*gaffall*
a glass	khlahs	*glas*
a knife	hnee-vörr	*hnífur*
a plate	disk-örr	*diskur*
a spoon	skayth	*skeið*
teaspoon	teh-skayth	*teskeið*

Vegetarian Meals

I'm a vegetarian.
yehkh ehrr grrain-meht-is-ai-tah *Ég er grænmetisæta.*
I don't eat meat.
yehkh borr-thah ehk-i kyert *Ég borða ekki kjöt.*

Staple Foods & Condiments

bread	brreörth	*brauð*
cream	rryoh-mi	*rjómi*
eggs	ehg	*egg*

fish	fis-körr	*fiskur*
fruit	ow-vehg-stirr	*ávextir*
ketchup	toh-mahts-soh-sah	*tómatsósa*
meat	kyert	*kjöt*
mustard	sin-nehp	*sinnep*
pepper	pi-pahrr	*pipar*
potatoes	kahrr-ter-blörr	*kartöflur*
rice	hrrees-grryohn	*hrísgrjón*
salt	sahlt	*salt*
sauce	soh-sah	*sósa*
seasoning	krridd	*krydd*
sugar	si-görr	*sykur*
vegetables	grrain-meh-ti	*grænmeti*

Breakfast Menu

boiled egg	so-thith ehg	*soðið egg*
bread	brreörth	*brauð*
bread roll	rroon-stih-kyi	*rúnstykki*
butter	smyeörrr	*smjör*
cereal	morr-gün-korrdn	*morgunkorn*
cheese	ostörr	*ostur*
coffee	kahf-fi	*kaffi*
fruit juice	ow-vahgs-tah-sah-vi	*ávaxtasafi*
honey	hö-nowng	*hunang*
jam	söl-tah	*sulta*
marmalade	mahrr-meh-lah-thi	*marmelaði*
milk	myohlk	*mjólk*
muesli	müsl	*müsl*
oatmeal	hahv-rrah-grrehü-türr	*hafragrautur*
orange juice	ah-pehl-see-n-sah-vi	*appelsínsafi*
sour milk (type of yoghurt)	soorr-myohlk	*súrmjólk*
sugar	si-görr	*sykur*
tea	teh	*te*
toast	rris-tahth brrehüth	*ristað brauð*
yoghurt	yoh-goorrt	*jógúrt*

Meat & Poultry

beef	neör-tah-kyert	*nautakjöt*
chicken	kyooh-kleen-görr	*kjúklingur*
ham	skin-kah	*skinka*
lamb	lahm-bah-kyert	*lambakjöt*
pork	svee-nah-kyert	*svínakjöt*
reindeer	hrrayn-dee-rrah-kyert	*hreindýrakjöt*
sausage	pil-sah	*pylsa*
turkey	kahl-koodn	*kalkúnn*

Fish

cod	thorr-skörr	*þorskur*
haddock	ee-sah	*ýsa*
halibut	loo-thah	*lúða*
herring	seeld	*síld*
lobster	hö-mahrr	*humar*
(smoked) salmon	(rraykh-dörr) lahks	*(reyktur) lax*
scallop	her-rr-pö-dis-körr	*hörpudiskur*
shrimp	rrai-kyah	*rækja*

Fruit

apples	ehb-li	*epli*
apricots	ah-prree-koh-sörr	*aprikósur*
bananas	bah-nah-nahrr	*bananar*
blueberries	blow-behrr	*bláber*
crowberries	krrai-kyi-behrr	*krækiber*
grapes	veen-behrr	*vínber*
lemon	see-trroh-nah	*sítróna*
oranges	ah-pehl-see-nörr	*appelsínur*
peaches	fehrrs-kyörr	*ferskjur*
pears	peh-rrörr	*perur*
pineapple	ah-nah-nahs	*ananas*
strawberries	yahrr-thahrr-behrr	*jarðarber*

Vegetables

cabbage	kveet-kowl	*hvítkál*
carrots	göl-rrai-törr	*gulrætur*
cauliflower	blohm-kowl	*blómkál*
cucumber	goorr-kah	*gúrka*
garlic	kveet-leör-körr	*hvítlaukur*
green peas	grrai-nahrr beör-nirr	*grænar baunir*
green pepper	grrain pah-prri-kah	*græn paprika*
lettuce	sah-lahd	*salat*
mushrooms	sveh-pirr	*sveppir*
onion	leör-körr	*laukur*
potatoes	kahrr-ter-blörr	*kartöflur*

Desserts

biscuits	smow-ker-körr/kehgs	*smákökur/kex*
cake	kahkah	*kaka*
fruit	ow-vehgs-tirr	*ávextir*
ice cream	ees/rryoh-mah-ees	*ís/rjómaís*
pancakes	per-nö-ker-körr	*pönnukökur*
pudding	boo-theen-görr	*búðingur*
chocolate	sooh-kö-lah-thi	*súkkulaði*
stewed fruit	ow-vahg-stah-grreör-törr	*ávaxtagrautur*

Drinks

coffee	kahf-fi	*kaffi*
(white/black)	(mehth myolk/svahrrt)	*(með mjólk/svart)*
fruit juice	ow-vahgs-tah-sah-vi	*ávaxtasafi*
ice	klah-kyi	*klaki*
soft drinks	gos-drrih-kyirr	*gosdrykkir*
tea	teh	*te*
water	vahdn	*vatn*

DID YOU KNOW ... Alcohol was prohibited in Iceland in 1912. Beer wasn't legalised again until 1 March 1989, now known as Bjórdagurinn, 'beer day'.

MENU DECODER

Starters

flatkökur og hangikjöt	flahd-ker-körr og hown-gyi-kyert	thin unsweet bread made of rye flour, eaten with butter and slices of smoked lamb
grafinn lax	grrahv-inn lahks	grav lax
harðfiskur	harrth-fis-görr	dried fish, stockfish

Main Meals

bjúgu byoo-ö
smoked minced meat sausage. Served hot or cold with potatoes in white sauce.

flatkökur flaht-ker-körr
rye pancakes, also popular with *hangikjöt*

hangikjöt hown-gyi-kyert
smoked lamb, leg or shoulder. Served hot or cold, with potatoes in bechamel sauce and green peas. Also popular as a luncheon meat.

harðfiskur hahrrth-fis-körr
dried fish; haddock, cod or catfish. It does not require cooking but is enjoyed as snack food, often spread with a little butter.

kjötsúpa kyert-soo-pah
soup, made of a small quantity of vegetables and a large quantity of lamb meat and rice. Always served hot.

saltkjöt sahlt-kyert
salted lamb/mutton, served with potatoes or swede turnips and often accompanied by split pea soup

slátur slow-törr
blood and liver puddings. Prepared in the months of September and October, when slaughtering is at its peak. Blood pudding, blóðmör (blohth-mehrr), and liver pudding, lifrarpylsa (liv-rrahrr-pil-sah), are eaten sliced hot or cold. Traditionally, the slátur that could not be eaten fresh was pickled in whey and enjoyed throughout the winter months.

svið svith
singed sheep heads. Eaten hot or cold, with either plain boiled potatoes, mashed potatoes or swede turnips. The pressed and gelled variety is popular for packed lunches.
seytt rúgbrauð saiht rroo-brreörth cooked rye bread, moist and chewy. Popular with hangikjöt.

Desserts

pönnukökur með pern-nö-ker-körr mehth
sykri eða si-grri ehth
með sultu og rjóma mehth söl-tö og rryo-mah
pancakes with sugar or with jam and cream

skyr skyirr
dairy product similar to yoghurt, it's very low in fat. Eaten as dessert with sugar and milk and with fresh berries, when in season.

Alcoholic Drinks

aqua vitae (brandy)	brreh-ni-veen	*brennivín*
beer	byohrr	*bjór*
cognac	ko-nee-ahk	*koníak*
liqueur	lee-kyer	*líkjör*
whisky	vis-kee	*whisky*
red/ white wine	rreörth-veen/ kveet-veen	*rauðvín/ hvítvín*

SHOPPING

general store, shop	**booth**	*búð*
laundry	**thvo-hdah-hoos**	*þvottahús*
market	**mahrr-kahth-örr**	*markaður*
newsagency/ stationers	**blah-thah-sah-lah/ boh-kah-booth**	*blaðasala/ bókabúð*
pharmacy	**ahp-oh-tehk**	*apótek*
shoe shop	**skoh-booth**	*skóbúð*
supermarket	**stohrr-mahrr-kahth-örr**	*stórmarkaður*
vegetable shop	**grrain-meht-is-booth**	*grænmetisbúð*

I'd like to buy ...
mikh lown-khahrr ahth keör-pah ... — *Mig langar að kaupa ...*

Can you write down the price?
gyeht-örr-ö skrri-vahth nith-örr vehrrthith? — *Gætir þú skrifað niður verðið?*

Essential Groceries

batteries	**rrahv-hler-thör**	*rafhlöður*
bread	**brreörth**	*brauð*
butter	**smyer-rr**	*smjör*
cheese	**os-törr**	*ostur*
chocolate	**sooh-kö-lah-thi**	*súkkulaði*
eggs	**ehg**	*egg*
flour	**kvay-ti**	*hveiti*
gas cylinder	**gahs-hihl-kyi**	*gashylki*
honey	**hö-nowng**	*hunang*
marmalade	**mahrr-meh-lah-thi**	*marmelaði*
matches	**ehld-spee-törr**	*eldspýtur*
milk	**myohlk**	*mjólk*
olive oil	**oh-lee-vö-o-lee-ö**	*ólífuolíu*
pepper	**pi-pahrr**	*pipar*
salt	**sahlt**	*salt*
shampoo	**syahm-poh**	*sjampó*

soap	sow-pö	*sápu*
sugar	si-körr	*sykur*
toilet paper	kloh-seht-pah-pirr	*klósettpappír*
toothbrush	tahn-bös-di	*tannbursti*
washing powder	tvoh-tah-dooft	*þottaduft*

Souvenirs

Typically Icelandic souvenirs include **lopapeysur (lo-pah-pay-sör)**, woollen sweaters and all kinds of woollen articles; pieces of jewellery made of icelandic resources, such as chains with a lava cube covered with gold; body lotion and other cosmetics made of the clay from the Blue Lagoon; Icelandic **brennivín (brrehn-ni-veen)**, schnapps, not least **hvannarótar-brennivín (kvahn-nah-rroh-tahrr-brrehn-ni-veen)**, schnapps flavoured with angelica.

Clothing

clothing	fert	*föt*
coat	kow-pah	*kápa*
dress	kyohdl	*kjóll*
jacket	yah-kyi	*jakki*
jumper/sweater	pay-sah	*peysa*
shirt	skyirr-tah	*skyrta*
shoes	skohrr	*skór*
skirt	pils	*pils*
trousers	bög-sörr	*buxur*

Materials

cotton	boh-mödl	*bómull*
handmade	hahnd-gyehrrt	*handgert*
leather	leh-thörr	*leður*
brass	oorr mehs-eeng	*messing*
gold	oorr göd-li	*gulli*
silver	oorr sil-vrri	*silfri*
flax	herrr	*hör*
silk	sil-kyi	*silki*
wool	ödl	*ull*

Colours

black	svahrrt	*svart*
blue	blowt	*blátt*
brown	brroont	*brúnt*
green	grraint	*grænt*
red	rreört	*rautt*
white	kveet	*hvítt*
yellow	gölt	*gult*

Toiletries

comb	grray-thah	*greiða*
condoms	smok-ahrr	*smokkar*
deodorant	svi-tah-likt-ahrr-ay-thirr	*svitalyktareyðir*
razor	rrahk-vyehl	*rakvél*
sanitary napkins	der-mö-bin-di	*dömubindi*
shampoo	syahm-poh	*sjampó*
shaving cream	rrahk-krrehm	*rakkrem*
soap	sow-pah	*sápa*
tampons	vaht-tahp-ahrr/ tahm-poh-nahrr	*vatttappar/ tampónar*
tissues	brryehv-thörr-körr	*bréfþurkur*
toilet paper	kloh-seht-pah-peer	*klósettpappír*
toothpaste	tahn-krrehm	*tannkrem*

Stationery & Publications

map	korrt	*kort*
newspaper	dakh-blahth	*dagblað*
(in English)	(ow ehn-skö)	*(á ensku)*
paper	pah-peer	*pappír*
pen (ballpoint)	pehn-ni/koo-lö-pehn-ni	*penni/kúlupenni*

Photography

How much is it to process this film?

kvahth kos-tahrr ath frrahm-kahdlah thehs-sah fil-mö?	*Hvað kostar að framkalla þessa filmu?*

When will it be ready?

kveh-nairr vehrr- thörr hoon til-boo-in?	*Hvenær verður hún tilbúin?*

I'd like a film for this camera.

mikh vahn-tahrr fil-mö ee thehs-sah min-dah-vyehl	*Mig vantar filmu í þessa myndavél.*

camera	min-dah-vyehl	*myndavél*
develop	frrahm-kad-lah	*framkalla*
film	fil-mah	*filma*
ready	til-boo-ith	*tilbúið*

Smoking

A packet of cigarettes, please.

aydn see-gahrr-eh-dö-pahk-ah tahk	*Einn sígarettupakka, takk.*

Do you have a light?

ow-dö ehld?	*Áttu eld?*

cigarette papers	see-gahrr-eh-dö-brryehv	*sígarettubréf*
cigarettes	see-gahrr-eh-dörr	*sígarettur*
filtered	mehth see-ö/fil-tehrr	*með síu/filter*
lighter	kvay-kyah-rri	*kveikjari*
matches	ehld-speet-örr	*eldspýtur*
menthol	mehnt-ohl	*mentól*
tobacco	toh-bahk	*tóbak*

Sizes & Comparisons

big	stohrrt	*stórt*
small	lee-tith	*lítið*
heavy	thoont	*þungt*
light	lyeht	*létt*
less	mi-nah	*minna*
more	may-rrah	*meira*

HEALTH

Where is a ...?	kvahrr ehrr ...?	*Hvar er ...?*
doctor	laik-nirr	*læknir*
hospital	syook-rrah-hoos	*sjúkrahús*
chemist	ah-poh-tehk	*apótek*
dentist	tahn-laik-nirr	*tannlæknir*

Could I see a female doctor?
gyai-ti yehkh fayn-gith ahth tah-lah vith kvehn layk-ni? — *Gæti ég fengið að tala við kvenlækni?*

What's the matter?
kvahth ehrr ahth? — *Hvað er að?*

Where does it hurt?
kvahrr fin-örr thoo til? — *Hvar finnur þú til?*

It hurts here.
mikh vehrrk-yahrr hyehrr — *Mig verkjar hér.*

Parts of the Body

ankle	erh-kli	*ökkli*
arm	hahnd-lehg-görr	*handleggur*
back	bahk	*bak*
chest	brreeng-gah	*bringa*
ear	ay-rrah	*eyra*
eye	eör-gah	*auga*
finger	feen-görr	*fingur*
feet/legs	fai-törr	*fætur*
hands	hehn-dörr	*hendur*
head	her-vöth	*höfuð*
heart	hyarr-tah	*hjarta*
hips	myath-mirr	*mjaðmir*
mouth	mön-nörr	*munnur*
neck	howls	*háls*
ribs	rriv-bayn	*rifbein*
skin	hooth	*húð*
stomach	mai-i	*magi*
teeth	tehn-nörr	*tennur*
thighs	lai-rri	*læri*

Ailments

I have (a)...	yehkh ehrr mehth ...	*Ég er með ...*
cold	kvehf	*kvef*
constipation	hahrrth-lee-vi	*hægðlífi*
diarrhoea	nith-örr-gowng	*niðurgang*
fever	hi-tah	*hita*
headache	her-vöth-vehrrk	*höfuðverk*
indigestion	mehlt-eeng-ahrr-trröb-lön	*meltingartruflun*
influenza	flehn-sö	*flensu*
low/high blood pressure	low-ahn/how-ahn blohth-thrreest-eeng	*lágan/háan blóðþrýsting*
sore throat	howls-bohl-gö	*hálsbólgu*
sprain	tokh-nön	*tognun*
stomachache	mahkh-ah-vehrrk	*magaverk*
sunburn	sohl-brrö-ni	*sólbruni*
I'm sunburnt.	yehk hehrr sohl-brrön-in	*Ég er sólbrunninn.*

Some Useful Words & Phrases

I'm ...	yehkh ehrr ...	*Ég er ...*
asthmatic	mehth ahs-mah	*með asma*
diabetic	sik-örr-syoo-körr	*sykursjúkur*
epileptic	flokh-ah-vay-körr	*flogaveikur*

I'm allergic to antiobiotics/penicillin.

yehkh ehrr mehth ov-nai-mi firr-irr foo-kah-liv-yöm/ pehn-si-lee-ni	*Ég er með ofnæmi fyrir fúkalyfjum/ pensilíni.*

I'm pregnant.

yehkh ehrr oh-frreesk	*Ég er ófrísk.*

I've been vaccinated.
yehkh fyehk oh-nai-mis-sprreör-tö *Ég fékk ónæmissprautu.*
I feel better/worse.
myehrr leeth-örr beh-törr/vehrr *Mér líður betur/verr.*

antibiotics	foo-kah-lif	*fúkalyf*
antiseptic	soht-hrrayns-ahndi	*sótthreinsandi*
blood pressure	blohth-thrreest-ing-örr	*blóðþrýstingur*
blood test	blohth-prrövah	*blóðprufa*
contraceptive	gyeht-nahth-ahrr-verdn	*getnaðarvörn*
injection	sprreör-tah	*sprauta*
medicine	lif	*lyf*
menstruation	blaith-eeng-ahrr	*blæðingar*
nausea	oh-khleh-thi	*ógleði*
toothache	tahn-pee-nah	*tannpína*

At the Chemist

I need medication for ...
yehkh thahrrf lif vith ... *Ég þarf lyf við ...*
I have a prescription.
yehkh ehrr mehth lif-sehth-il *Ég er með lyfseðil.*

At the Dentist

I have a toothache.
yehkh ehrr mehth tahn-pee-nö *Ég er með tannpínu.*
I've lost a filling.
yehkh hehv misst fid-leen-gö *Ég hef misst fyllingu.*
I've broken a tooth.
yehkh hehv brro-tith tern *Ég hef brotið tönn.*
My gums hurt.
mikh vehrr-kyarr ee tahn-hol-dith *Mig verkjar í tannholdið.*
Please give me an anaesthetic.
gyehrr-thö svo vehl ath day-vah mikh *Gerðu svo vel að deyfa mig.*

TIME & DATES

What date is it today?

kvahth-ah dahkh-örr	*Hvaða dagur*
ehrr ee dahkh?	*er í dag?*

What time is it?

kvahth ehrr klök-ahn?	*Hvað er klukkan?*

It's ... am/pm.

hoon ehrr ... firr-irr how-day-i/	*Hún er ... fyrir hádegi/*
ehf-dirr how-day-i	*eftir hádegi.*

in the morning	**ahth mo-dni**	*að morgni*
in the evening	**ahth kverl-di**	*að kvöldi*

Days of the Week

Monday	**mow-nö-dahkh-örr**	*mánudagur*
Tuesday	**thrrith-yö-dahkh-örr**	*þriðjudagur*
Wednesday	**mith-vik-ö-dahkh-örr**	*miðvikudagur*
Thursday	**fim-tö-dahkh-örr**	*fimmtudagur*
Friday	**fers-dö-dahkh-örr**	*föstudagur*
Saturday	**leörkh-ah-dahkh-örr**	*laugardagur*
Sunday	**sön-ö-dahkh-örr**	*sunnudagur*

Months

January	**yah-noo-ahrr**	*janúar*
February	**fehb-rroo-ahrr**	*febrúar*
March	**mahrrs**	*mars*
April	**ah-prreel**	*apríl*
May	**mai**	*maí*
June	**yoo-nee**	*júní*
July	**yoo-lee**	*júlí*
August	**ow-goost**	*ágúst*
September	**sehft-ehm-behrr**	*september*
October	**okt-oh-behrr**	*október*
November	**noh-vehm-behrr**	*nóvember*
December	**dehs-ehm-behrr**	*desember*

Seasons

summer	sö-mahrr	*sumar*
autumn	heörst	*haust*
winter	veh-törr	*vetur*
spring	vorr	*vor*

Present

today	ee dahkh	*í dag*
this morning	ee morr-gön	*í morgun*
tonight	ee kverld	*í kvöld*
this week	thehs-ah vi-kö	*þessa viku*
this year	theht-ah owrr	*þetta ár*
now	noo-nah	*núna*

Past

yesterday	ee gyairr	*í gær*
two days ago	firr-irr tvay-mörr derkh-öm	*fyrir tveimur dögum*
last night	seeth-öst-ö noht	*síðustu nótt*
last week	(ee) seeth-öst-ö vi-kö	*(í) síðustu viku*
last year	seeth-ast-lith-ith owrr	*síðastliðið ár*

Future

tomorrow	ow morr-gön	*á morgun*
in two days	ehf-dirr tvo dahg-ah	*eftir tvo daga*
next week	(ee) nais-tö vi-kö	*(í) næstu viku*
next month	(ee) nais-tah mown-öthi	*(í) næsta máuði*
next year	(ow) nais-tah ow-rri	*(á) næsta ár*

During the Day

afternoon	ehf-dirr how-day-i	*eftir hádegi*
day	dahkh-örr	*dagur*
midnight	mithnait-i	*miðnætti*
morning	morr-gön	*morgunn*
night	noht	*nótt*
noon	how-day-i	*hádegi*

NUMBERS & AMOUNTS

0	nool	*núll*
1	aydn	*einn*
2	tvayrr	*tveir*
3	thrreer	*þrír*
4	fyoh-rrirr	*fjórir*
5	fimm	*fimm*
6	sehks	*sex*
7	syer	*sjö*
8	owt-dah	*átta*
9	nee-ö	*níu*
10	tee-ö	*tíu*
20	tö-tökh-ö	*tuttugu*
21	tö-tö-gö og aydn	*tuttugu og einn*
30	thrryow-tee-ö	*þrjátíu*
40	fyer-tee-ö	*fjörutíu*
50	fim-tee-ö	*fimmtíu*
60	sehks-tee-ö	*sextíu*
70	syer-tee-ö	*sjötíu*
80	ow-tah-tee-ö	*áttatíu*
90	nee-tee-ö	*níutíu*
100	ayt hön-drrahth	*eitt hundrað*
1000	ayt thoos-önd	*eitt þúsund*
one million	ayn mil-yohn	*ein milljón*

Some Useful Words

a little (amount)	lee-tith	*lítið*
few	fow-irr	*fáir*
more	may-rrah	*meira*
some	nok-rrirr	*nokkrir*
too much/many	ov mi-kith/mahrr-girr	*of mikið/margir*

ABBREVIATIONS

f.h./e.h. – fyrir hádegi/eftir hádegi	am/pm
h.f. – hlutafélag	Ltd./Inc.
S.V.R. – Strætisvagnar Reykjavíkur	Reykjavík Municipal Bus Company
f.kr./e.kr.	BC/AD
frk. – fröken	Miss
frú	Mrs
hr. – herra	Mr/Sir
Rvk. – Reykjavík	Reykjavík
FÍB – Félag íslenskra bifreiðaeigenda	The Icelandic Automobile Association
kl. – klukkan	o'clock
km/klst. – kilómetrar á klukkustund	kilometres per hour
kr. – króna	crown (Icelandic monetary unit)
v. – við	at
vsk. – virðisaukaskattur	tax (included in the price on all goods and services)
t.h. – til hægri	to the right (used in addresses)
hs. – heimasími	telephone at home
vs. – vinnusími	telephone at work
t.v. – til vinstri	to the left (used in addresses)
(1.) h. – hæð	(1st) floor

EMERGENCIES

Help!	**hyowlp!**	*Hjálp!*
Go away!	**fahrr-thö!**	*Farðu!*
Thief!	**thyoh-vörr!**	*þjófur!*

SIGNS

LÖGREGLA
POLICE

LÖGREGLUSTÖÐ
POLICE STATION

There's been an accident!
thahth hehf-örr orrth-ith slis! *Það hefur orðið slys!*

Call a doctor/an ambulance!
now-ith ee laik-ni/ syook-rrah beel! *Náið í lækni/ sjúkrabíl!*

I've been raped.
myehrr vahrr neörth-gahth *Mér var nauðgað.*

I've been robbed!
yehkh vahrr rraind/rrain-dörr! *Ég var rænd/-ur!* (f/m)

Call the police!
nowith ee lerg-rrehgl-ön-ah! *Náið í lögregluna!*

Where is the police station?
kvahrr ehrr lerkh-rrehkh-lö-sterth-in? *Hvar er lögreglustöðin?*

I'm/My friend is ill.
yehkh ehrr/vin-örr min ehrr vay-körr *Ég er/vinur minn er veikur.*

I'm lost.
yehkh ehrr vilt/vilt-örr *Ég er villt/-ur.* (f/m)

Where are the toilets?
kvahrr ehrr snirrt-inkh-in?/ kvahrr ehrr kloh-seht-ith? *Hvar er snyrtingin?/ Hvar er klósettið?*

Could you help me please?
gyai-tirr thoo hyowlp-ahth myehrr? *Gætir þú hjálpað mér?*

Could I please use the telephone?
gyai-ti yehkh fayn-khith ahth hrrin-gyah? *Gæti ég fengið að hringja?*

I'm sorry.
myehrr thik-irr thahth layht *Mér þykir það leitt.*

I didn't realise I was doing anything wrong.	
yehkh vi-si ehk-i ahth yehkh vai-rri ahth gyeh-rrah rrow-nt	*Ég vissi ekki að ég væri að gera rangt.*
I didn't do it.	
yehkh gyehrr-thi thahth ehk-i	*Ég gerði það ekki.*
I wish to contact my embassy/consulate.	
yehkh vil hah-vah sahm-bahnd vith sehndi-rrowth mit/ rraith-is -mahn min	*Ég vil hafa samband við sendiráð mitt/ ræðismann minn.*
I speak English.	
yehkh tah-lah ehn-skö	*Ég tala ensku.*
I have medical insurance.	
yehkh hehf syook-rrah-trrikh-een-gö	*Ég hef sjúkratryggingu.*
My possessions are insured.	
aykh-örr meen-ahrr ehrr-ö trrikhth-arr	*Eigur mínar eru tryggðar.*

My... was stolen.	**... vahrr sto-líth**	*... var stolið.*
I've lost my ...	**yehkh teen-di ...**	*Ég týndi ...*
bags	**ter-skö-nöm mee-nöm**	*töskunum mínum*
handbag	**hahnd-tersk-ön-i mi-ni**	*handtöskunni minni*
money	**pehn-eeng-ön-öm mee-nöm**	*peningunum mínum*
travellers cheques	**fehrrth-ah-tyeh-kö-nöm mee-nöm**	*ferðatékkunum mínum*
passport	**vehg-ah-brryeh-vi-nö mee-nö**	*vegabréfinu mínu*

NORWEGIAN

QUICK REFERENCE

Hello.	gud-*dahg*	*Goddag.*
Goodbye.	*huh*-deh	*Ha det.*
Yes./No.	yah/nay	*Ja./Nei.*
Excuse me.	*un*-shül	*Unnskyld.*
Sorry.	*beh-klah*-gehrr	*Beklager,*
	til-yi mai	*tilgi meg.*
Please.	va sho *snil*	*Vær så snill.*
Thank you.	tuhk	*Takk.*
You're welcome.	*ing*-ön *or*-shahk	*Ingen årsak.*

I'd like a ...	yay vil *ya*-rrnö hah ...	*Jeg vil gjerne ha ...*
one-way ticket	*ehn*-kehlt-bi-*leht*	*enkelt billett*
return ticket	*too*-rrö-*toorr*	*tur-retur*

I (don't) understand.	
yay fosh-*tor-rr* (ik-kö)	*Jeg forstår (ikke).*
Do you speak English?	
snuh-kö du *ehng*-ölsk?	*Snakker du engelsk?*
Where is ...?	
voor arr ...?	*Hvor er ...?*
Go straight ahead.	
deh arr *rreht* frruhm	*Det er rett fram.*
Turn left/right.	
tah til *vehns*-trrö/*höy*-rrö.	*Ta til venstre/høyre.*
Do you have any rooms available?	
hah du *lay*-di-ö *rrum*?	*Har du ledige rom?*
I'm looking for a public toilet.	
yay *leh*-törr eht-törr eht *of*-föntli too-a-*leht*	*Jeg leter etter et offentlig toalett.*

1	ehn	*en*	6	sehks	*seks*
2	too	*to*	7	shu/süv	*sju/syv*
3	trreh	*tre*	8	*ot*-tö	*åtte*
4	*fee*-rrö	*fire*	9	nee	*ni*
5	fehm	*fem*	10	tee	*ti*

NORWEGIAN

Norway has two official written language forms. They are very similar, and every Norwegian learns both at school. **Bokmål** (BM), literally 'book-language', is the urban-Norwegian variety of Danish, the language of the former rulers of Norway. It's the written language of 80 percent of the population. Although many Norwegians speak a local dialect in the private sphere, most of them speak BM in the public sphere. BM is therefore very appropriate for the traveller who wants to communicate with Norwegians all over the country.

The other written language is **Nynorsk** (NN), or 'New Norwegian' – as opposed to Old Norwegian, the language in Norway before 1500 AD, that is, before Danish rule. It's an important part of Norwegian cultural heritage as it's the truly 'Norwegian' language, as opposed to the Danish-based BM. In order to preserve the language, Norway has a NN theatre in Oslo – **Det Norske Teater**. Traditionally, many NN writers also produce their works to be performed in the NN tongue; the language lends itself to theatre and song as it can be very lyrical. By law the national TV and radio channels also broadcast a certain percentage of their text in NN.

In speech the distinction between BM and NN is no problem since Norwegians understand either. Although both are used in the media, BM is predominant in the daily papers, television and radio. Many people are put off trying to speak Norwegian because of the two languages, but in reality, BM is the ruling language. This book uses BM only.

A striking feature of both written languages is that many words have two or more officially authorised forms of spelling in either language. One can choose according to one's speech or social aspirations. In many cases it's possible to choose spellings which are common to either language.

In the rural areas you may come across people who hardly speak a word of English, and if you show an effort to speak Norwegian, it will help a great deal to establish contact. Many Norwegians will answer you in English, as they are only too eager to show off their knowledge. Their use of English is usually very good.

PRONUNCIATION

Vowels

Length, as a distinctive feature of vowels, is very important in the pronunciation of Norwegian. Almost every vowel has a (very) long and a (very) short counterpart, when appearing in a stressed syllable. Generally, it's long when followed by one consonant, and short when followed by two or more consonants.

A few words, mainly function words like pronouns and auxilliaries, are 'mispronounced': the vowel is short in spite of the fact that it's followed by only one consonant.

Pronunciation is given in the pronunciation guide in the front of the book.

PRONOUNS		
SG		
I	yay	*jeg*
you	du	*du*
he/she/it		
PL	hun/hahn/deh	*hun/han/det*
we	vi	*vi*
you (pol)	*deh*-rreh	*Dere*
you (pl)	*deh*-rreh	*dere*
they	dem	*dem*

GREETINGS & CIVILITIES

Top Useful Phrases

Hello.	gud-*dahg*	*Goddag.*
Goodbye.	*hah*-deh	*Ha det.*
Yes.	yah	*Ja.*
No.	nay	*Nei.*
Excuse me.	*un*-shül	*Unnskyld.meg.*
Please.	va sho *snil*	*Vær så snill.*
Thank you.	tuhk	*Takk.*
Many thanks.	*tusn* tuhk	*Tusen takk.*
That's fine.	*ing*-ön *or*-shahk	*Ingen årsak.*
You're welcome.		

May I? Do you mind?	
for-rr yay *lorv*? hah du noo-ö i-*moot* deh?	*Får jeg lov? Har du noe imot det?*
Sorry. (excuse me, forgive me)	
behk-lah-gehrr til-yi mai	*Beklager, tilgi meg.*

Good morning.	gu *morr*-gon	*God morgen.*
Good afternoon.	gud-*dahg*	*Goddag.*
Good evening/night.	gu *kvehl/nuht*	*God kveld/natt.*
How are you?	voorr-duhn *hah* du deh?	*Hvordan har du det?*
Well, thanks.	brrah tuhk	*Bra, takk.*

Forms of Address

Madam/Mrs	frru	*fru*
Sir/Mr	harr	*herr*
Miss	*frrayrr*-kön	*frøken*
companion	kuh-muh-*rraht*	*kamerat*
friend	vehn-*nin*-nö/vehn	*venninne/venn* (f/m)

SMALL TALK

Meeting People

What is your name?	vah *hay*-tö du?	*Hva heter du?*
My name is ...	yay *hay*-törr ...	*Jeg heter ...*

I'd like to introduce you to ...
deh-tö arr ... — *Dette er ...*
I'm pleased to meet you.
hü-gö-li o *trreh*-fö day — *Hyggelig å treffe deg.*

Nationalities

Where are you from?	voorr *arr* du frrah?	*Hvor er du fra?*
I'm from ...	yay *arr* frruh ...	*Jeg er fra ...*
Australia	ow-*strrah*-li-uh	*Australia*
Canada	*kuh*-nuh-duh	*Kanada*
England	*ehng*-luhn	*England*
Ireland	*ee*-rrluhn	*Irland*
New Zealand	nü *say*-luhn	*Ny Zealand*
Norway	*norr*-gö	*Norge*
Scotland	*skot*-luhn	*Skottland*
the USA	a-mehrr-rrik-uha/ ü-wehs-*sah*	*Amerika/ USA*
Wales	vehls	*Wales*

Age

How old are you?
voor *guhm*-muhl arr du? — *Hvor gammel er du?*
I'm ... years old.
yay arr ... — *Jeg er ...*

Occupations

What do you do?

vah *drree-vö* du may? *Hva driver du med?*

I'm a/an ...	yay arr ...	*Jeg er ...*
artist	*kunst*-nörr	*kunstner*
businesswoman/ man	fo-*rreht*-nings-kvin-nö/ fo-*rreht*-nings-muhn	*foretnings kvinne/ forretnings mann*
doctor	*lay*-gö	*lege*
engineer	in-shön-*yayrr-rr*	*ingeniør*
farmer	*gahrr*-brru-körr	*gardbruker*
journalist	shoo-rrnuh-*list*	*journalist*
lawyer	uhd-vo-*kuht*	*advokat*
manual worker	uhrr-*bay*-dörr	*arbeider*
mechanic	meh-*kah*-ni-körr	*mekaniker*
nurse	*sy*-kö-play-örr	*sykepleier*
office worker	koon-*toorr*-uhrr-bay-dörr	*kontor-arbeider*
scientist	*vee*-tön-skahps-muhn	*vitenskapsmann*
student	stu-*deh-nt*	*student*
teacher	*la*-rrörr	*lærer*
waiter	*kehl*-nörr/sehrr-*vay*-rrings-dah-mö	*kelner/ serveringsdame*
writer	fo-rr-*fuht*-törr	*forfatter*

THE LONG AND THE SHORT OF IT

Nearly all vowels in Norwegian have short and long versions. This can affect the meaning, so look at the word carefully.

Religion

What is your religion?
vah arr din rreh-li-*gyoon?* *Hva er din religion?*
I'm not religious.
yay arr *ik*-kö rreh-li-*yers* *Jeg er ikke religiøs.*

I'm ...	yay arr ...	*Jeg er ...*
Buddhist	bud-*dist*	*buddhist*
Catholic	kuh-*tolsk*	*katolsk*
Hindu	*hin*-du	*hindu*
Jewish	*yayrr*-dö	*jøde*
Muslim	*mus*-lim	*muslim*
Protestant	prro-teh-*stuhnt*	*protestant*

Family

Are you married? **arr du *yift*?** *Er du gift?*

I'm...	yay arr ...	*Jeg er ...*
single	ehns-li	*enslig*
married	*yift*	*gift*

How many children do you have?
voor muhng-ö *bah-rrn* hah du? *Hvor mange barn har du?*
I don't have any children.
yay *huh ik*-kö noon bah-rrn *Jeg har ikke noen barn.*
I have a daughter/a son.
yay hahrr ehn *duht-törr/sern* *Jeg har en datter/sønn.*
How many brothers/sisters do you have?
voor muhng-ö *sers*-kön hah du? *Hvor mange søsken har du?*
Is your husband/wife here?
arr *muhn-n* din harr/
arr koo-nuh di harr? *Er mannen din her?/ Er kona di her?*
Do you have a boyfriend/girlfriend?
hah du *fuhst* ferl-lö? *Har du fast følge?*

brother	brroorr	*bror*
children	bah-rrn	*barn*
daughter	*duht*-törr	*datter*
family	fuh-*mee*-li-ö	*familie*
father	fahrr	*far*
grandfather	*behs*-tö-fahrr	*bestefar*
grandmother	*behs*-tö-moorr	*bestemor*
husband	muhn	*mann*
mother	moorr	*mor*
sister	*sers*-törr	*søster*
son	sern	*sønn*
wife	*koo*-nö	*kone*

Kids' Talk

How old are you?
voorr guh-mehl arr du? — *Hvor gammel er du?*

When's your birthday?
norr hahrr du *bush*-dahg? — *Når har du bursdag?*

What do you do after school?
vah *yer* du eh-tehrr skoo-leh-tid? — *Hva gjør du etter skoletid?*

Do you have a pet at home?
hahrr du eht *cha*-leh-dürr yeh-meh? — *Har du et kjæledyr hjemme?*

I have a ...	yay hahrr ehn ...	*Jeg har en ...*
bird	fool	*fugl*
budgerigar	un-du-*luht*	*undulat*
canary	kuh-*nuh*-rri-fool	*kanarifugl*
cat	kuht	*katt*
dog	hun	*hund*
frog	frrorsk	*frosk*

Feelings

I (don't) like ...
yay *lee*-**körr** (*ik*-**kö**) ... — *Jeg liker (ikke) ...*

I feel cold/hot.
yay *frrüs*-**örr**/**yay arr** *vuh-rrm* — *Jeg fryser/Jeg er varm.*

I'm in a hurry.
yay hahrr *huhst*-**varrk** — *Jeg har hastverk.*

You're right.
du hah *rreht* — *Du har rett.*

I'm ...	*yay arr ...*	*Jeg er ...*
angry	*sin*-**nuh**	*sinna*
happy	*lük*-**kö-li**	*lykkelig*
hungry/thirsty	*shul*-**tön**/**ter-sht**	*sulten/tørst*
tired	**trrer-t**	*trøtt*
sad	**oo**-*lük*-**kö-li**/*nay*-**forr**	*ulykkelig/nedfor*
sleepy	*sherv*-**ni**	*søvnig*
well	**brrah**	*bra*
worried	**oo**-*rroo*-**li**	*urolig*

I'm sorry. (condolence)
kon-doo-*lay*-**rrörr** — *Kondolerer.*

I'm grateful.
yay arr *tuhk*-**nehm-li** — *Jeg er takknemlig.*

BREAKING THE LANGUAGE BARRIER

Do you speak English?
snuh-kö du *ehng*-**ölsk?** — *Snakker du engelsk?*

Does anyone speak English?
arr deh noon som snuh-körr *ehng*-**ölsk harr?** — *Er det noen som snakker engelsk her?*

I speak a little ...
yay snuh-kö *lit* ... — *Jeg snakker litt ...*

I don't speak ...
yay snuh-körr *ik*-**kö** ... — *Jeg snakker ikke ...*

I (don't) understand.	
yay fosh-*tor-rr* (*ik*-kö)	*Jeg forstår (ikke).*
Could you speak more slowly please?	
kuhn du snuh-kö luhng-som-mö-rrö?	*Kan du snakke langsommere?*
Could you repeat that?	
kuhn du *yehn*-tuh day?	*Kan du gjenta det?*
How do you say ...?	
vah hay-törr ... por noshk?	*Hva heter ... på norsk?*
What does ... mean?	
vah bö-*türr* ...?	*Hva betyr ...?*

I speak ...	yay snuh-kuhrr ...	*Jeg snakker ...*
English	*ehng*-ehlsk	*engelsk*
French	frruhnsk	*fransk*
German	tüsk	*tysk*
Norwegian	noshk	*norsk*
Spanish	spuhnsk	*spansk*

Some Useful Phrases

Of course./Sure.	*sehl-ferrl-geh-li*/vist	*Selvfølgelig./Visst.*
Just a minute.	vehnt lit; eht öy-eh-blik	*Vent litt; Et øyeblikk.*
It's (not) important.	deh arr (*ik*-kö) *vik*-ti	*Det er (ikke) viktig.*
It's (not) possible.	deh arr (*ik*-kö) *moo*-li	*Det er (ikke) mulig.*
Wait!	vehnt!	*Vent!*
Good luck!	*lük*-kö *til*!	*Lykke til!*

BODY LANGUAGE

It's considered good manners to shake hands with Norwegians when you meet. Remember, this includes both men and women; many Norwegian women feel ignored in English-speaking nations where usually only the men shake hands.

After having met a few times, a friendly hug or a peck on the cheek is common – this includes both women and men.

PAPERWORK

address	uh-*drreh*-sö	*adresse*
age	*uhl*-dörr	*alder*
birth certificate	*ferts*-ls-uht-tehst	*fødselsattest*
border	*grrehn*-sö	*grense*
car owner's title	*vongn*-ko-rt	*vognkort*
car registration	*chehn*-nö-tayn	*kjennetegn*
customs	*tol*	*toll*
date of birth	*fert*-söls-dah-tu	*fødselsdato*
driver's licence	*fayrr*-rrörr-kort	*førerkort*
identification	lay-gay-ti-*muh*-shon	*legitimasjon*
immigration	*in*-vuhn-drring	*innvandring*
marital status	si-*veel*-stuhn	*sivilstand*
name	nuhvn	*navn*
nationality	nuh-shu-nuh-li-*tayt*	*nasjonalitet*
passport (number)	*puhs(*-num-mörr)	*pass(nummer)*
place of birth	*fayrr*-dö-stay	*fødested*
profession	*ürr*-kö	*yrke*
reason for travel	*hehn*-sikt meh *rray*-sn	*hensikt med reisen*
religion	rreh-li-*gyoon*	*religion*
sex	chern	*kjønn*
tourist card	tu-*rrist*-kort	*turistkort*
visa	*vee*-sum	*visum*

GETTING AROUND

What time does ... leave/arrive?	*norr* gor-rr/ kom-mörr ...?	*Når går/ kommer ...?*
the (aero)plane	*flü*-yö	*flyet*
the boat	*bor*-tn	*båten*
the (city) bus	(*bü*-)busn	*(by)bussen*
the (intercity) bus	(*lin*-yö-)busn	*(linje-)bussen*
the train	*tor*-gö	*toget*
the tram	*trrik*-kön	*trikken*

Directions

Where is ...?
voor arr ...? — *Hvor er ...?*

How do I get to ...?
voor-duhn kom-mörr yay til ...? — *Hvordan kommer jeg til ...?*

Is it far from/near here?
arr deh *luhngt harr*-frruh? — *Er det langt herfra?*

SIGNS

BAGASJEINNLEVERING	***CHECK-IN COUNTER***
DAMER/HERRER	***LADIES/GENTLEMEN***
FORBUDT	***PROHIBITED***
GRATIS ADGANG	***FREE ADMISSION***
INFORMASJON/ OPPLYSNINGER	***INFORMATION***
INGEN ADGANG	***NO ENTRY***
INNGANG	***ENTRANCE***
NØDUTGANG	***EMERGENCY EXIT***
REISEGODS	***BAGGAGE COUNTER***
RESERVERT	***RESERVED***
RØYKING FORBUDT	***NO SMOKING***
TELEFON	***TELEPHONE***
TOLL	***CUSTOMS***
UTGANG	***EXIT***
WC/TOALETTER	***TOILETS***
ÅPEN/STENGT	***OPEN/CLOSED***

Can I walk there? **kuhn yay** *gor* **deet?**	*Kan jeg gå dit?*
Can you show me (on the map)? **kuhn du** *vee*-**sö ma (po** *kuh*-**rtö)?**	*Kan du vise meg (på kartet)?*
Are there other means of getting there? **arr deh ehn** *ahn*-**ön mor-tö or kom-mö** *deet* **po?**	*Er det en annen måte å komme dit på?*
I want to go to ... **yay skuhl til ...**	*Jeg skal til ...*
Go straight ahead. **deh arr** *rreht* **frruhm**	*Det er rett fram.*
It's two blocks down. **deh arr** *too* **kvuh-rtahl** *vee*-**dö-rrö**	*Det er to kvartal videre.*

Turn left/right at the ...	*tah* **til** *vehns*-**trrö/** *höy*-**rrö veh ...**	*Ta til venstre/ høyre ved ...*
next corner	*nehs*-**tö** *yayrr*-**nö**	*neste hjørne*
traffic lights	*liüs*-**krrüs-sö**	*lyskrysset*

behind	**bak**	*bak*
in front of	**fo-rruhn**	*foran*
far	**luhngt**	*langt*
near	**narr**	*nær*
opposite	*or*-**vörr**-*forr*	*overfor*
next to	*veh*-**si-dehn**-*uhv*	*ved siden av*

SIGNS

ANKOMST	***ARRIVALS***
AVGANG	***DEPARTURES***
BILLETTKONTOR	***TICKET OFFICE***
JERNBANESTASJON	***TRAIN STATION***
RUTEPLAN	***TIMETABLE***
STASJON	***STATION***
T-BANE	***SUBWAY***

Booking Tickets

Excuse me, where is the ticket office?	
***un*-shül voor *arr* bi-leht-lu-kuh?**	*Unnskyld, hvor er billettluka?*
Where can I buy a ticket?	
***voor* kuhn yay *sher*-peh bi-*leht*?**	*Hvor kan jeg kjøpe billett?*
I want to go to ...	
yay skuhl til ...	*Jeg skal til ...*
Do I need to book?	
arr deh nerd-*vehn*-di o bö-*stil*-lö *pluhs*?	*Er det nødvendig å bestille plass?*
I'd like to book a seat to ...	
yay vil *ya*-rrnö bö-*stil*-lö *si*-tö-pluhs til ...	*Jeg vil gjerne bestille sitte-plass til ...*

I'd like ...	yay vil *ya*-rrnö hah ...	*Jeg vil gjerne ha ...*
a one-way ticket	*ehn*-kehlt-bi-*leht*	*enkelt billett*
a return ticket	*too*-rrö-*toorr*	*tur-retur*
two tickets	*too* bi-*leht*-tehrr	*to billetter*
tickets for all of us	bi-*leh*-tehrr til os *uhl*-lö *suh*-mehn	*billetter til oss alle sammen*
a student's fare	stu-*dehnt*-rruh-buht	*studentrabatt*
a child's fare	*bah*-rrnö-bi-*leht*	*barnebillett*
a pensioner's fare	ho-*nayrr*-bi-*leht*	*honnør-billett*
1st class	*fersh*-tö kluhs-sö	*første klasse*
2nd class	*ahn*-ön kluhs-sö	*annen klasse*

Is it completely full?	
arr deh *halt* fult?	*Er det helt fullt?*
Can I get a stand-by ticket?	
kuhn yay for ehn *shuhn*-sö-bi-*leht*?	*Kan jeg få en sjansebillett?*

Air

Is there a flight to ...?
arr deh eht flü til ...?
Er det et fly til ...?

When is the next flight to ...?
norr gor *nehs*-tö flü-yö til ...?
Når går neste flyet til ...?

How long does the flight take?
voor *luhng*-ö tid tahrr *flüv*-ning-ehn?
Hvor lang tid tar flyvningen?

What is the flight number?
vah arr *flait*-nu-mö-rrö?
Hva er flightnummeret?

You must check in at ...
du mor shehk-kö *in* veh ...
Du må sjekke inn ved ...

SIGNS

BAGASJE
LUGGAGE PICKUP
INNSJEKKING
CHECK-IN

check-in desk	*in*-shehk-*in*-skrruhn-keh	*innsjekking skranke*
airport tax	*luft*-huhvn-*ahv*-yift	*lufthavnavgift*
boarding pass	um-*boorr*-steeg-(n)ing-sko-rt	*ombord-stig(n)ings-kort*
customs	tol	*toll*

Bus

Where is the bus/tram stop?
voor arr *bus*-hol-lö-pluhsn/ *trrik*-hol-lö-pluhsn?
Hvor er bussholdeplassen/ trikkholdeplassen?

Which bus goes to ...?
vil-kön bus gor rtil ...?
Hvilken buss går til ...?

Does this bus go to ...?
gor *rdehn*-nö busn til ...?
Går denne bussen til ...?

How often do buses pass by?
voor muhng-ö *bus*-sörr gor-rdeh?
Hvor mange busser går det?

SIGNS

BUSSHOLDEPLASS
BUS STOP
TRIKKHOLDEPLASS
TRAM STOP

What time is the ... bus?	no-rr kom-mör ... busn?	*Når kommer ... bussen?*
next	*nehs*-tö	*neste*
first	*fer*-shtö	*første*
last	*sis*-tö	*siste*

Train

Is this the right platform for ...?
arr *deht*-tö *rreht*-tö *pluht*-forr-muh forr *tor*-gö til ...?
Er dette rette plattforma for toget til ...?

SIGNS

SPOR
PLATFORM

The train leaves from platform ...
tor-gö gor-rr frra spoorr ... *Toget går fra spor ...*

Passengers must ...	*rray*-sön-dö mor ...	*Reisende må ...*
change trains	*büt*-tö *torg*	*bytte tog*
change platforms	*gor* til spoorr ...	*gå til spor ...*

dining car	*spee*-sö-vongn	*spisevogn*
express	ehks-*prrehs*-torg	*ekspresstog*
local	lu-*kahl*-torg	*lokaltog*
sleeping/ couchette car	*sor*-vö-vongn/ *lig*-gö-vongn	*sovevogn/ ligge-vogn*

Metro

Which line takes me to ...?
vil-kön *lin*-yö/*bah*-nö mor yay tah til ...? — *Hvilken linje/bane må jeg ta til ...?*

What is the next station?
vah arr *nehs*-tö stuh-*shoon?* — *Hva er neste stasjon?*

SIGNS

T-BANE	METRO/UNDERGROUND
UTGANG	WAY OUT
VEKSLING	CHANGE (for coins)

Taxi

Where can I get hold of a taxi?
vorr kuhn yay for *tahk* i ehn drro-shö? — *Hvor kan jeg få tak i en drosje?*

Please take me to ...
vil du *chayrr*-rrö ma teel ...? — *Vil du kjøre meg til ...?*

How much does it cost to go to ...?
vorr *mü*-yö *kos*-törr deh o *chayrr*-rrö til ...? — *Hvor mye koster det å kjøre til ...?*

Here is fine, thank you.
du kuhn *stop*-pö *harr tuhk* — *Du kan stoppe her, takk.*

Continue!
buh-rrö *furrt*-sheht! — *Bare fortsett!*

The next street to the left/right.
nehs-tö gah-teh til *vehn*-strrö/*höy*-rrö — *Neste gate til venstre/høyre.*

Stop here!
stop harr! — *Stopp her!*

Please slow down.
va sho snil o cher-rr lit *suhk*-teh-rreh — *Vær så snill og kjør litt saktere.*

Please wait here.
varr sor snil o *vehn*-tö harr — *Vær så snill å vente her.*

Car

Where can I rent a car?
voor kuhn yay *lay*-ö ehn *beel?* — *Hvor kan jeg leie en bil?*

How much is it daily/weekly?
vorr mü-yö *kos*-törr deh parr *dahg/u*-kö? — *Hvor mye koster det pr. dag/uke?*

Does that include insurance/mileage?
arr deh *in*-kloo-*dehrrt* fo-*shik*-rring/frree *chayrr*-rrö-ah-stuhn? — *Er det inkludert forsikring/fri kjøreavstand?*

Where's the next petrol station?
voor *arr* narr-mös-tö behn-seen-stuh-*shoon?* — *Hvor er nærmeste bensinstasjon?*

How long can I park here?
voor *lehng*-ö kan *beel*-n min *stor* harr? — *Hvor lenge kan bilen min stå her?*

Does this road lead to ...?
arr deh-tö *vay*-yön til ...? — *Er dette veien til ...?*

air (for tyres)	luft	*luft*
battery	buht-tö-*rree*	*batteri*
brakes	*brrehm*-sörr	*bremser*
clutch	klerch	*kløtsj*
driver's licence	*fayrr*-rrörr-kort	*førerkort*
engine	*moo*-turr	*motor*
lights	*liik*-törr	*lykter*
oil	*ul*-yö	*olje*
puncture	pung-*tay*-rring	*punktering*
radiator	rruh-di-*yah*-turr	*radiator*
road map	kuhrt	*kart*
tyres	dehk	*dekk*
windscreen	*frront*-rru-tö	*frontrute*

SIGNS

BILVERKSTED	REPAIRS
BLYFRI	UNLEADED
ENVEISKJØRNING	ONE WAY
GARASJE	GARAGE
INNKJØRNING FORBUDT	NO ENTRY
MEKANIKER	MECHANIC
MOTORVEI	FREEWAY
NORMAL	NORMAL
OMKJØRNING	DETOUR
PARKERING FORBUDT	NO PARKING
SELVBETJENING	SELF SERVICE
STOPP	STOP
SUPER	SUPER
VIKEPLIKT	GIVE WAY

I need a mechanic.
yay *trrehng*-**ehrr ehn**
bil-**meh**-*kah*-**ni**-**körr**
Jeg trenger en bilmekaniker.

The battery is flat.
buht-**tö**-*rree*-**ö arr** *fluht*
Batteriet er flatt.

The radiator is leaking.
rruh-**di**-*ah*-**toorrn arr** *lehk*
Radiatoren er lekk.

I have a flat tyre.
yu-**lö arr pung**-*tayrt*
Hjulet er punktert.

It's overheating.
moo-**toorrn** *koo*-**körr**
Motoren koker.

It's not working.
deh fung-*gay*-**rrörr ik**-**kö**
Det fungerer ikke.

Some Useful Phrases

The train is delayed/cancelled.
tor-gö arr fo-*shing*-keht/*in*-stilt *Toget er forsinket/innstilt.*
How long will it be delayed?
voor *mü*-yö arr deh fo-*shing*-keht? *Hvor mye er det forsinket?*
There is a delay of ... hours.
tor-gö arr ... *tee*-mörr *Toget er ... timer*
eht-törr *rru*-tö *etter rute.*

How long does the trip take?
voor *lehng*-ö tahrr rray-suh? *Hvor lenge tar reisa?*
Is it a direct route?
arr deh eht di-*rrehk*-tö torg? *Er det et direkte tog?*
Is that seat taken?
arr *dehn*-nö *stoo*-ln *up*-tuht? *Er denne stolen opptatt?*
I want to get off at ...
yay vil gor *ahv* i ... *Jeg vil gå av i ...*
Where can I hire a bicycle?
***voor* kuhn yay *lay*-ö** *Hvor kan jeg leie*
ehn *sük*-köl? *en sykkel?*

NORWEGIAN

ACCOMMODATION

Where is a ...?	voor arr eht ...?	*Hvor er et ...?*
cheap hotell	*bil*-li hu-*tehl*	*billig hotell*
good hotel	*got* hu-*tehl*	*godt hotell*
nearby hotel	hu-*tehl* i *narr*-haytn	*hotell i nærheten*
nice/quaint hotel	*koo*-shli/*guhm*-muhl-duhks hu-*tehl*	*koselig/gammeldags hotell*

What is the address?
***vah* arr uh-*drrehs*-ehn?** *Hva er adressen?*
Could you write the address, please?
kuhn du *va*-rrö so snil *Kan du være så snill*
o *skrree*-vö up uh-*drrehs*-ehn? *å skrive opp adressen?*

At the Hotel

Do you have any rooms available?
hah du *lay*-di-ö *rrum*? — *Har du ledige rom?*

I'd like ...	yay vil *ya*-rrnö ...	*Jeg vil gjerne ...*
a single room	hah eht *ehng*-költ-rrum	*ha et enkeltrom*
a double room	hah eht *dob*-ölt-rrum	*ha et dobbeltrom*
to share a dorm	*lig*-gö por *sor*-vö-sah-lön	*ligge på sovesalen*

SIGNS

GJESTGIVERI/PENSJONAT	GUESTHOUSE
HOTELL	HOTEL
VANDRERHJEM	YOUTH HOSTEL

Do you have identification?
hah du lay-gi-ti-muh-*shoon*? — *Har du legitimasjon?*
Your membership card, please.
may-lehms-ko-rtö dit *tuhk* — *Medlemskortet ditt, takk.*
Sorry, we're full.
beh-*klah*-görr deh arr *fült* — *Beklager, det er fullt.*
How long will you be staying?
voor *lehng*-ö *blee-rr* du harr? — *Hvor lenge blir du her?*
How many nights?
voor muhng-ö *neht*-törr? — *Hvor mange netter?*
It's ... per day/per person.
deh arr ... pa *rdahg*/parr pa-*shoon* — *Det er ... pr. dag/pr. person.*
There are (four) of us.
vi arr *(fee*-rrö) *stük*-körr — *Vi er (fire) stykker.*

I want a room with a ...	yay vil *ya*-rrnö hah eht *rrum* meh ...	*Jeg vil gjerne ha et rom med ...*
bathroom	bahd	*bad*
shower	dush	*dusj*
television	*teh-veh*	*tv*
window	*vin*-du	*vindu*

I'm going to stay for ...	yay hah *tehnkt* o blee harr i ...	*Jeg har tenkt å bli her i ...*
one day	*ehn dahg*	*en dag*
two days	*too dah*-gehrr	*to dager*
one week	*an u*-kö	*en uke*

How much is it per night/per person?	
voor *mü*-yö arr deh parr dahg/ parr pa-*shoon*?	*Hvor mye er det pr. dag/ pr. person?*
Can I see it?	
kuhn yay for *se* deh?	*Kan jeg få se det?*
Are there any others?	
hah du *uhn*-drrö?	*Har du andre?*
Are there any cheaper rooms?	
hah du *bil*-li-ö-rrö *rrum?*	*Har du billigere rom?*
Can I see the bathroom?	
kuhn yay fo *se bah*-dö?	*Kan jeg få se badet?*
Is there a reduction for students/children?	
yee du stu-*dehnt*-rruh-*buht*/ *bah*-rrnö-rruh-*buht*?	*Gir du studentrabatt/ barnerabatt?*
Does it include breakfast?	
in-kloo-*deh-rrehrr deh frroo*-kostn?	*Inkluderer det frokosten?*
It's fine, I'll take it.	
brrah yay *tah* rdeh	*Bra, jeg tar det.*
I'm not sure how long I'm staying.	
yay *veht ik*-kö voor *leh-ng*ö yay skuh blee harr	*Jeg vet ikke hvor lenge jeg skal bli her.*
Is there a lift?	
fins deh ehn *hays* harr?	*Finnes det en heis her?*
Where is the bathroom?	
voor arr *bah*-dö?	*Hvor er badet?*
Is there hot water all day?	
arr deh *vuh-rrnt* vuhn *döy*-nö *rrunt*?	*Er det varmt vann døgnet rundt?*

Do you have a safe where I can leave my valuables?
hah du ehn sayf darr yay kan *lehg*-gö va-*rdee*-sah-kö-nö *mee*-nö? — *Har du en safe der jeg kan legge verdisakene mine?*

Is there somewhere to wash clothes?
kuhn yay vuhs-kö *kla*-rrnö mee-nö noo-eh *steh?* — *Kan jeg vaske klærne mine noe sted?*

Can I use the kitchen?
arr deh *lorv* o *brru*-kö *cherk*-kö-nö? — *Er det lov å bruke kjøkkenet?*

Can I use the telephone?
kuhn yay for *lor-nö* tay-lay-*foon*-n? — *Kan jeg få låne telefonen?*

Requests & Complaints

Please wake me up at ...
va sho *snil* o *vehk*-kö ma ... — *Vær så snill å vekke meg ...*

The room needs to be cleaned.
deht-tö *rrum*-mö bayrr yayrr-rrös *rraynt* — *Dette rommet bør gjøres reint.*

Please change the sheets.
va sho snil o *shift*-ö *sehng*-ö-töy — *Vær så snill å skifte sengetøy.*

I can't open/close the window.
yay *grray*-örr ik-kö *orp*-nö/ *luk*-kö *vin*-du-ö — *Jeg greier ikke åpne/ lukke vinduet.*

I've locked myself out of my room.
yay hah *lor-st* ma *oo*-tö ah *rrum*-mö mit — *Jeg har låst meg ute av rommet mitt.*

The toilet won't flush.
yay for-rr *ik*-kö spült *nay* po too-a-*leht*-tö — *Jeg får ikke spylt ned på toalettet.*

I don't like this room.
yay *lee*-körr ik-kö *deht*-tö *rrum*-ö — *Jeg liker ikke dette rommet.*

It's ...	deh arr ...	*Det er ...*
expensive	*dürt*	*dyrt*
noisy	fo mü-yö *brrork*	*for mye bråk*
too dark	forr *mer-rrt*	*for mørkt*
too small	fo *lee*-tö	*for lite*

Some Useful Words & Phrases

I'm leaving now/tomorrow.
yay *rray*-sörr nor/i-*mo*-rn — *Jeg reiser nå/i morgen.*

I'd like to pay the bill.
kuhn yay for *rrehng*-ning-ehn *tuhk?* — *Kan jeg få regningen, takk?*

name	nuhvn	*navn*
surname	*eht*-tö-nuhvn	*etternavn*
address	uh-*drrehs*-sö	*adresse*
room number	*rrum*-num-mörr	*romnummer*
air-conditioning	*klee*-muh-uhn-lehg	*klimaanlegg*
balcony	buhl-*kong*	*balkong*
bathroom	bahd	*bad*
bed	sehng	*seng*
bill	*rray*-ning	*regning*
blanket	*tehp*-pö	*teppe*
chair	stool	*stol*
clean	rrayn	*rein*
cupboard	skahp	*skap*
dirty	*shit*-n	*skitten*
double bed	*dob*-bölt-sehng	*dobbeltseng*
electricity	strrerm	*strøm*
fan	*vif*-tö	*vifte*
key	*nerk*-köl	*nøkkel*
lift (elevator)	hays	*heis*
light bulb	*lüs*-pa-rrö	*lyspære*
a lock	lors	*lås*
mattress	muh-*drruhs*	*madrass*
mirror	spayl	*speil*
padlock	*hehng*-ö-lors	*hengelås*
pillow	*pu*-tö	*pute*

quiet	*stil*-lö	*stille*
room (in hotel)	rrum/*va*-rröl-sö	*rom/værelse*
sheet	*lah*-kön	*laken*
shower	dush	*dusj*
soap	*sor*-pö	*såpe*
suitcase	*kuf*-fört	*koffert*
swimming pool (indoor)	*sverm*-mö-huhl	*svømmehall*
table	boo-rr	*bord*
toilet	doo	*do*
toilet paper	*doo*-puh-*peerr*	*dopapir*
towel	*hong*-klö	*håndkle*
water	vuhn	*vann*
hot/cold water	*vuh-rrnt/kuhlt* vuhn	*varmt/kaldt vann*
window	*vin*-du	*vindu*

AROUND TOWN

I'm looking for ...	yay *leh*-törr eht-törr ...	*Jeg leter etter ...*
the art gallery	*kunst*-guhl-lö-*rree*-ö	*kunstgalleriet*
a bank	*buhng*-kön	*banken*
the church	*chirr*-kehn	*kirken*
the city centre	*sehn*-trrum	*sentrum*
the ... embassy	den ... uhm-buhs-*sah*-dö	*den ... ambassade*
my hotel	hu-*tehl*-lö mit	*hotellet mitt*
the market	*to-rr*-gö	*torget*
the museum	mu-*say*-ö	*museet*
the police	pu-li-*ti*-ö	*politiet*
the post office	*post*-kun-*too*-rrö	*postkontoret*
the chemist	*uh*-po-*tehk*	*apotek*
a public toilet	eht *of*-fönt-li too-a-*leht*	*et offentlig toalett*
the telephone centre	*tay*-lö-*varr*-kö	*televerket*
the tourist information office	tu-*rrist*-in-fo-rr-muh-*shoon*	*turistinformasjon*

What time does it open/close?
norr orp-nö/*stehng*-ö rdehn? *Når åpner/stenger den?*
What street/suburb is this?
vilk-ön *gah*-tö/*forr*-stahd arr deh? *Hvilken gate/forstad er det?*

For directions, see the Getting Around section, page 253.

At the Post Office

I'd like to send a ...	yay skuh *sehn*-nö ...	*Jeg skal sende ...*
letter	eht *brrayv*	*et brev*
postcard	eht *post*-kort	*et postkort*
parcel	ehn *puhk*-kö	*en pakke*
telegram	eht tay-lö-*grruhm*	*et telegram*

I'd like some stamps.
yay vil *ya*-rrnö *hah* noon *frree*-marr-kö *Jeg vil gjerne ha noen frimerker.*
How much does it cost to send this to ...?
voor *mü*-yö kos-törr deh o *sehn*-nö deh-tö til ...? *Hvor mye koster det å sende dette til ...?*

air mail	*luft*-post	*luftpost*
envelope	kon-vu-*lut*	*konvolutt*
mail box	*post*-kuhs-sö	*postkasse*
registered mail	rreh-kom-muhn-*dayrt* post	*rekommandert post*
surface mail	*or*-vörr-flah-tö-*post*	*overflatepost*

Telephone & Internet

I want to ring ...
yay vil *rring*-ö til ... — *Jeg vil ringe til ...*

The number is ...
***num*-mö-rrö arr ...** — *Nummeret er ...*

How much does a three-minute call cost?
voor *mü*-yö *kos*-törr ehn trray mi-*nut*-tehsh *suhm*-tah-lö? — *Hvor mye koster en tre minutters samtale?*

How much does each extra minute cost?
voor *mü-yö kos*-törr *vart* ehks-trruh mi-*nut*? — *Hvor mye koster hvert ekstra minutt?*

I'd like to speak to (Mr Olsen).
yay skul-lö *ya*-rrnö for *snuhk*-kö may (harr *ol*-sehn) — *Jeg skulle gjerne få snakke med (herr Olsen).*

I want to make a reverse-charges phone call.
yay vil bö-*stil*-lö ehn *suhm*-tah-lö meh noo-*tay*-rrings-*or*-vörr-*fay*-rring — *Jeg vil bestille en samtale med noteringsoverføring.*

It's engaged.
deh arr *upp*-tuht — *Det er opptatt.*

I've been cut off.
suhm*-tah-lön blay *brrut — *Samtalen ble brutt.*

Where can I get Internet access?
voor kuhn yay for *ahd*-gang til *in*-tehrr-neht? — *Hvor kan jeg få adgang til Internet?*

I'd like to send an email.
yay vil *ya*-rrnö sehn-deh ehn *ee*-mayl — *Jeg vil gjerne sende en email.*

At the Bank

I want to exchange some money/ travellers cheques.
yay vil *ya*-**rrnö** *vehks*-**lö** *pehng*-**örr/***heh-vö* **noon** *rray*-**sö-shehk-körr**
Jeg vil gjerne veksle penger/heve noen reisesjekker.

What is the exchange rate?
vah arr vuh-*loo*-**tuh-ku-shön?**
Hva er valutakursen?

How many Norwegian kroner per dollar?
voor *muhng*-**ö** *krroo*-**nörr forr** *ehn dol*-**luhrr?**
Hvor mange kroner for en dollar?

Can I have money transferred here from my bank?
kuhn yay for or-vörr-fayrr-rt pehng-örr *heet* **frrah** *buhng*-**kön min?**
Kan jeg få overført penger hit fra banken min?

How long will it take to arrive?
voor *lehng*-**ö vil deh** *tah?*
Hvor lenge vil det ta?

Has my money arrived yet?
hahrr *pehng*-**ö-nö mee-nö** *kom*-**möt nor?**
Har pengene mine kommet nå?

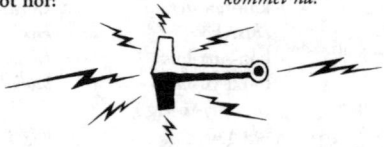

autobank	*mi*-**ni-buhnk**	*minibank*
bank draft	*vehk*-**sl/rreh-***mis*-**sö**	*veksel/remisse*
bank notes	*pehng*-**ö-sehd-lörr**	*pengesedler*
cashier	**kuh-***say*-**rrörr**	*kasserer*
coins	*miin*-**törr**	*mynter*
credit card	**krreh-***dit*-**kort**	*kredittkort*
exchange	*vehk*-**sling**	*veksling*
loose change	*vehk*-**slö-pehng-örr**	*vekslepenger*
signature	*un*-**nörr-skrrift**	*underskrift*

INTERESTS & ENTERTAINMENT

Sightseeing

Do you have a guidebook/local map?

hah du ehn *gaid*/**eht** *lo-kuhl*-**kuhrt?**	*Har du en guide/et lokalkart?*

What are the main attractions?

vah **arr di** *vik*-**ti-stö say-***varr*-**di-hay-törr?**	*Hva er de viktigste severdigheter?*

What is that?

vah arr *deh*?	*Hva er det?*

How old is it?

voor *guhm*-**mölt arr deh?**	*Hvor gammelt er det?*

Can I take photographs?

kuhn **yay tah** *bil*-**dörr?**	*Kan jeg ta bilder?*

What time does it open/close?

norr orp-nö/*stehng*-**ö dehn?**	*Når åpner/stenger den?*

ancient	*guhm*-mehl	*gammel*
beach	strruhn	*strand*
castle	slot	*slott*
cathedral	kuh-teh-*drrahl*	*katedral*
church	*chirr*-kö	*kirke*
concert hall	kon-*sart*-hus	*konserthus*
library	bi-bli-yu-*tayk*	*bibliotek*
main square	(*stoo-rr*)-to-rrgö	*(stor)torget*
market	*to-rr*gö	*torget*
town hall	*rrord*-hus	*rådhus*
monastery	*klos*-törr	*kloster*
monument	his-*too*-rrisk *büg*-ning	*historisk bygning*
mosque	mos-*kay*	*moské*
old town	guhm-möl *bü*	*gammel by*
the old city	*guhm*-lö-bü-yön	*gamlebyen*
opera house	*oo*-pö-rruh-hus	*operahus*
palace	slot	*slott*
ruins	rroo-*ee*-nörr	*ruiner*

stadium	*stah*-di-on	*stadion*
statues	*bil*-löd-ster-törr	*billedstøtter*
synagogue	sü-nuh-*goo*-gö	*synagoge*
temple	*hor-v/tehm*-pöl	*hov/tempel*
university	u-ni-va-shi-*tayt*	*universitet*

Going Out

What's there to do in the evenings?
vah kuhn muhn *yer*-rrö
om *kvehl*-n?
Hva kan man gjøre om kvelden?

Are there any discos?
arr deh noon dis-ku-*tayk***?**
Er det noen diskotek?

Are there places where you can hear local folk music?
arr deh noo-ön stay-dörr darr ehn kuhn *her*-rrö **po noshk** *fol*-kö-mu-*sik***?**
Er det noen steder der en kan høre på norsk folkemusikk?

How much does it cost to get in?
voor *mü*-yö **kost-örr deh forr o ko-mö** *in***?**
Hvor mye koster det for å komme inn?

cinema	*chee*-nu	*kino*
concert	kon-*sart*	*konsert*
discotheque	dis-ku-*tayk*	*diskotek*
theatre	tay-*ah*-törr	*teater*

Sports & Interests

What do you do in your spare time?

vah yer rdu i frree-ti-dehn? *Hva gjør du i fritiden?*

What sport do you play?

vah shluhgs id-rreht drri-vehrr du? *Hva slags idrett driver du?*

art	**kunst**	*kunst*
basketball	***buh*-skeht-*buhl***	*basketball*
boxing	***buk*-sing**	*boksing*
cooking	***muht-luhg*-ing**	*matlaging*
fishing	***fee*-sking**	*fisking*
football/soccer	***fut*-buhl**	*fotball*
going out	**gor *ut***	*gå ut*
going to the cinema	**gor por *chee*-nu**	*gå på kino*
music	**mu-*sik***	*musikk*
photography	**foo-too-grruh-*fee*-rring**	*fotografering*
reading	***lehs*-ning**	*lesning*
shopping	***huhn*-dlay**	*handle*
sport	**sport/*i*-drreht**	*sport/idrett*
the theatre	**ti-*uh*-tehrr**	*teater*
travelling	***rray*-sehrr**	*reiser*
writing	***skrri*-vehrr**	*skriver*

Festivals

Santa Lucia is celebrated on 13 December. Children dressed in white, the boys wearing cone-shaped hats and the girls with tinsel and glitter in their hair, take part in candlelight processions.

Jul (Christmas) is celebrated on the evening of 24 December, when gifts are exchanged. In the countryside, people mount sheaves of oats, **julenek**, on poles for the birds, and many people leave a bowl of porridge out for the **nisse**, a type of Christmas gnome traditionally thought to bring good luck to farmers.

At Easter, **påske**, the Sami people hold colourful celebrations in Karasjok and Kautokeino with concerts, **joik** (traditional chanting), reindeer races and other festivities.

Syttende maj (17 May) is Norway's Constitution Day. Everybody celebrates, and many wear traditional costume. In every city and town there are marching bands and parades of school children. The biggest celebrations take place in Oslo where you'll see thousands of school children march up Karl Johans gate to the palace, where they're greeted by the royal family.

Midsummer's Eve (**Jonsok**), is celebrated throughout the country, with bonfires and parties.

IN THE COUNTRY

Weather

What's the weather forecast?

vah arr *varr*-**mehl-ling-uh?**		*Hva er værmeldinga?*

The weather is ...	*va*-**rrö arr ...**	*Været er ...*
today.	**i-dahg**	*i dag.*
Will it be ...	**blee rdeh ...**	*Blir det ...*
tomorrow?	**i**-*mo-rrn*?	*i morgen?*
cloudy	*or*-**vö-shü-yeht**	*overskyet*
cold	**kuhlt**	*kaldt*
foggy	*tor*-**kö**	*tåke*
frosty	*frrost*-**va-rr**	*frostvær*
hot	**vuh-rnt**	*varmt*
raining	**rrayn**	*regn*
snowing	**sner**	*snø*
sunny	**mü-yö** *sool*	*mye sol*
windy	**mü-yö** *vin*	*mye vind*

Camping

SIGNS	
KAMPING/LEIRPLASS	CAMPING GROUND

Am I allowed to camp here?
for-rr yay lorv til o *shlor* op *tehl*-tö mit harr?
Får jeg lov til å slå opp teltet mitt her?

Is there a campsite nearby?
fins deh ehn *kam*-ping plass i *narr-hay*-tön?
Finnes det en camping-plass i nærheten?

backpack	*rrüg*-sehk	*ryggsekk*
can opener	*boks*-or-pnörr	*boksåpner*
compass	kom-*puhs*	*kompass*
crampons	*brrod*-dör	*brodder*
firewood	veh	*ved*
gas cartridge	prru-*pahn*-bö-*hol*-lörr	*propanbeholder*
ice axe	*ees*-erks	*isøks*
mattress	muh-*drruhs*	*madrass*
penknife	*lum*-mö-kneev	*lommekniv*
rope	tohv	*tau*
tent	tehlt	*telt*
tent pegs	*tehlt-plug*-görr	*teltplugger*
torch (flashlight)	*lum*-mö-lükt	*lommelykt*
sleeping bag	*sor*-vö-poo-sö	*sovepose*
stove	*koo*-kö-uhp-puh-*rraht*	*kokeapparat*
water bottle	*vuhn*-fluhs-kö	*vannflaske*

FOOD

Some Useful Words & Phrases

breakfast	*frroo*-kost	*frokost*
lunch	lernsh	*lunsj*
dinner	*mid*-dahg	*middag*

Table for ..., please. eht *boo-rr* til ... tuhk	*Et bord til ..., takk.*
Can I see the menu please? kuhn yay for meh-*nü*-yön tuhk	*Kan jeg få menyen, takk.*
I'd like today's special, please. yay vil *ya*-rrnö hah *dah*-göns rreht takk	*Jeg vil gjerne ha dagens rett, takk.*
What does it include? vah in-kloo-*deh*-rreh rdeh?	*Hva inkluderer det?*
Is service included in the bill? arr bö-*vart*-ning-uh *ee*-bö-rray-nöt?	*Er bevertninga iberegnet?*
Not too spicy please. *ik*-kö fo *shtarrkt* krrüd-drruh tuhk	*Ikke for sterkt krydra, takk.*

ashtray	*uhs*-kö-bay-görr	*askebeger*
the bill	*rray*-ning-ön	*regningen*
a cup	ehn *kop*	*en kopp*
dessert	deh-*sehrr*	*dessert*
a drink	ehn *drringk*	*en drink*
a fork	ehn *guhf*-föl	*en gaffel*
a glass	eht *gluhs*	*et glass*
a knife	ehn *kneev*	*en kniv*
a plate	ehn tuhl-larr-kön	*en tallerken*
spicy	starrkt (*krrüd*-rruh)	*sterkt (krydra)*
a spoon	ehn *shay*	*en skje*
stale	*dor*-vönt	*dovent*
starter	*for*r-reht	*forrett*
sweet	sayrr-t	*søt*
teaspoon	*tay*-sheh	*teskjed*
toothpick	*tuhn*-pirr-körr	*tannpirker*

Vegetarian Meals

I'm a vegetarian.

yay arr veh-geh-tuh-rri-*ah-nörr* — *Jeg er vegetarianer.*

I don't eat meat.

yay *spi*-sörr ik-kö *cher-t* — *Jeg spiser ikke kjøtt.*

I don't eat chicken or fish or ham.

yay spee-sörr *varr*-kön *chül*-ling ehl-lörr *fisk* ehl-lö *shing*-kö — *Jeg spiser verken kylling eller fisk eller skinke.*

Breakfasts & Breads

biscuit	chehks	*kjeks*
brown bread	*grrorv*-brrer	*grovbrød*
crisp-bread	*kneh*-keh-brrer	*knekkebrød*
cured ham	*speh*-keh-shin-keh	*spekeskinke*
food on top of a sandwich, like cold cuts	*por*-lehg	*pålegg*
fried egg (sunny side up)	*spayl*-ehg	*speilegg*
hard-boiled	*hahrr*-kukt	*hardkokt*
honey	*hun-ning*	*honning*
jam	*sül*-teh-töy	*syltetøy*
oatmeal biscuits	*huh*-vrreh-*chehks*	*havrekjeks*
oatmeal porridge	*huh*-vrreh-*grrert*	*havregrøt*
open sandwich	smer-brrer	*smørbrød*
peanut butter	*pi-a*-nert-smer-rr	*peanøttsmør*
porridge, cereal	grrert	*grøt*
roll	*rrun*-stü-keh	*rundstykke*
rusk	*kuh*-vrring	*kavring*
scrambled eggs	*ehg*-eh-*rreh*-rreh	*eggerøre*
slice	*shi*-veh	*skive*
soft-boiled	*blert*-kukt	*bløtkokt*
white bread	loof	*loff*
wholemeal bread	*hehl*-koorrn-brrer	*helkornbrød*

MENU DECODER

Dairy Products

gammalost	*guh*-muhl-ust	semi-hard brown cheese with strong flavour
geitost	*yayt*-ust	sweet brown goat cheese
gudbrands dalsost	*gud*-brruhns-duhls-ust	cheese similar to **geitost**
mysost	*müs*-ust	brown whey cheese
normannaost	nor-*man*-nuh-ust	Danish Blue
pultost	*pült*-ust	soft fermented cheese, often with caraway seeds
riddarost	*rrid*-ehrr-ust	Munster cheese
remuladesaus	*rrehm*-u-luh-deh-sows	cream mayonnaise with chopped gherkins and parsley

Soups & Mixed Dishes

dagens rett	dah-gehns-*rreht*	today's special
fårikål	*forr*-ih-*korl*	lamb in cabbage stew
flatbrød	*fluht*-brrer	thin wafer of rye/barley
gryte(rett)	*grrü*-teh-(reht)	casserole
italiensk salat	it-uhl-i-*ehnsk*-sah-*luht*	salad of diced cold meat, potatoes, apples and vegetables in mayonnaise
lapskaus	*luhp*-skows	thick stew of diced meat, potatoes, onions and other vegetables
koldtbord	*korlt*-boorr	buffet of cold dishes (fish, meat, cheese, salad and a sweet)
pyttipanne	*püt*-i-*puh*-nö	chunks of meat and potatoes, fried with onions, etc
suppe	*su*-pö	soup
surkål	*surr*-korl	boiled cabbage flavoured with caraway seeds, sugar and vinegar

Meat

bankebiff	*ban*-keh-*bif*	slices/chunks of beef simmered in gravy
benløse fugler	*behn*-lor-sö-*foo*-lehrr	rolled slices of veal stuffed with minced meat
blodpudding	*bloo*-pud-ing	black pudding
bris/brissel	brris/*brri*-söl	sweetbread
dyrestek	*dü*-rreh-stayk	roast venison
fenalår	*feh*-nuh-lor-rr	cured leg of lamb
fleske pannekake	*fleh*-skeh-*puh*-neh *kah*-keh	thick pancake with bacon, baked in the oven
fleskepølse	*fleh*-skeh-*perl*-seh	pork sandwich spread
fyll	fül	stuffing, forcemeat
kålruletter	*korl*-rru-*leht*-ehrr	minced meat in cabbage leaves
kalvetunge	*kuhl*-veh-tung-eh	calf's tongue
kjøttdeig	*chert-day*	minced meat
kjøttkake	*chert*-kah-keh	small hamburger steak
kjøttpålegg	*chert*-por-lehg	cold meat cuts
kjøttpudding	*chert*-pud-ing	meat loaf
lam(mebog)	*luh*-meh-*boog*	(shoulder of) lamb
lever(postei)	*leh*-vehrr pu-*stay*	liver (pate)
medaljong	mehd-uhl-*yong*	small round fillet
pai	pai	pie
pinnekjøtt	*pi*-neh-*chert*	salted and fried lamb ribs
postei	pu-*stay*	meat pie
spekemat	*speh*-keh-maht	cured meat (lamb, beef, pork, reindeer, often served with scrambled eggs)
spekepølse	*speh*-keh-*perl*-seh	air-dried sausage
syltelabb	*sül*-teh-*lahb*	boiled, salt-cured pig's trotter

Seafood

fiskebolle	*fis*-keh-*bol*-eh	fish ball
fiskegrateng	*fis*-keh-grruh-*teng*	fish casserole
fiskekake	*fis*-keh-*kah*-keh	fried fishball

fiskepudding	*fis*-keh-pud-ing	fish pate fried in a pan
gaffelbitar	*guh*-fehl-*bee*-tehrr	salt- and sugar-cured sprat/herring fillets
gravlaks	*grrahv-luhks*	salt- and sugar-cured salmon with dill and a creamy sauce
kaviar	kuh-vi-*uhrr*	smoked cod-roe spread
klippfisk	*klip*-fisk	salted and dried cod
lutefisk	*lu*-teh-*fisk*	stockfish treated in lye solution, boiled
plukkfisk	*pluk*-fisk	poached fish in white sauce
rakefisk	*rrahk*-fisk	cured and fermented fish (often trout)
sildesalat	*sil*-deh-suh-*laht*	salad with slices of herring, cucumber, onions, etc
spekesild	*speh*-keh-*sild*	salted herring, often served with pickled beetroot, potatoes and cabbage
Desserts		
arme riddere	*uhrr*-meh-*rri*-deh-rreh	slices of bread dipped in batter, fried and served with jam
bløtkake	*blert-kah*-keh	rich sponge layer cake with whipped cream
fløteis	*fler*-teh-*ees*	ice cream made of cream
fløtevaffel	*fler*-teh-*vuh*-fehl	cream-enriched waffle with jam
fromasj	frroo-*muhsh*	mousse/blancmange
fruktis	*frrukt*-ees/sorr-*beh*	sorbet/water ice
julekake	*yu*-leh-*kah*-keh	rich fruit cake
hvetebolle	*veh*-teh-*bor*-leh	bun; sweet roll
kransekake	*krruhn*-seh-*kah*-keh	pile of almond-macaroon rings
kringle	*krring*-leh	ring-twisted bread with raisins
lefse	*lehf*-seh	thin pancake (without eggs)
napoleonskake	*nuh*-pool-eh-uns-*kah*-keh	custard slice

riskrem	*rrees*-krrehm	boiled rice with whipped cream and raspberry jam
rislapp	*rrees*-luhp	small sweet rice cake
rødgrøt	*rrer-grrert*	fruit pudding with vanilla cream
rømmegrøt	*rrer*-meh-grrert	boiled sour cream porridge with cinnamon and sugar
rørte tyttebær	*rreh*-teh-*tü*-teh-*barr*	mashed uncooked cranberries
sirupsnipp	*si*-rrup-*snip*	ginger cookie
tilslørte bonde-piker	*til*-sler-teh-bon-deh-*pee*-kehrr	layers of apple sauce and breadcrumbs, topped with whipped cream
vannbakkels	*vuhn-buh*-kehls	cream puff
vørterkake	*ver-rr*-teh-*kah*-keh	spiced malt bread
wienerbrød	*wee*-nehrr-*brrer*	Danish pastry

Non-Alcoholic Drinks

brus	brrus	fizzy fruit drink
kefir	*keh*-firr	fermented milk
kulturmelk	kul-*turr-mehlk*	cultured thick milk
vørterøl	*ver*-tehrr-*erl*	non-alcoholic beer

Alcoholic Drinks

akevitt	uh-*keh*-vit	kind of gin flavoured with spices
bokkøl	*buk*-erl	bock beer
dram	drrahm	drink/tot/shot
exportøl	ehks-*purt*-erl	strong, light-coloured beer
gløgg	glerg	kind of mulled wine, with schnapps and spices
hjemmebrent	*yeh*-meh-*brrehnt*	home-made brandy
lett-	leht	with little/less alcohol or sugar
pils	pils	lager
pjolter	*pyorl*-tehrr	long drink of whisky and soda water
toddi	to-di	mulled wine

Dairy Products

butter	smer-rr	*smør*
cheese	ust	*ost*
cream	*fler*-teh	*fløte*
cream cheese	*fler*-teh-ust	*fløteost*
sour cream	*rrer*-mö	*rømme*
whipped cream	krrehm; *pis*-keht-krrehm	*krem; pisket krem*

Meat

beef	*uk*-seh-*chert*	*oksekjøtt*
fillet of beef	*uk*-seh-fi-*leh*	*oksefilet*
game	vilt	*vilt*
ham	*shin*-keh	*skinke*
kidney	*nü*-rreh	*nyre*
lamb/mutton	sow-eh-chert	*sauekjøtt*
meat	chert	*kjøtt*
meatball	*chert-bor*-leh	*kjøttbolle*
pork	*svi*-neh-*chert*	*svinekjøtt*
pork chop	*svi*-neh-kort-eh-*leht*	*svinekotelett*
roast beef	*uk*-seh-stayk	*oksestek*
roast pork	*svi*-neh-stayk	*svinestek*
roast reindeer	*rrayns*-dürr-stayk	*reinsdyrstek*
rump steak	*mer*-brrahd	*mørbrad*
sausage	*perl*-seh	*pølse*
spare rib	*svi*-neh-*rri*-beh	*svineribbe*
veal	*kuhl*-veh-*chert*	*kalvekjøtt*

Seafood

anchovy	uhn-*shoos*	*ansjos*
catfish	*stayn*-bit	*steinbit*
coalfish	say	*sei*
cod	torshk	*torsk*
crab	*krruh*-beh	*krabbe*
crayfish	krrehps	*kreps*
eel	orl	*ål*

fish	fisk	*fisk*
flounder	*flün*-drreh	*flyndre*
frog fish/ angler fish	*brray*-fluhb	*breiflabb*
haddock	*hü*-seh/*korl*-yeh	*hyse/kolje*
herring	sil	*sild*
lobster	*hu*-mehrr	*hummer*
mackerel	muh-*krrel*	*makrell*
mussel	*blor*-shehl	*blåskjel(l)*
pickled/ marinated herring	*krrüd*-ehrr-sil/*sürr*-sil	*kryddersild/sursild*
plaice	*rrer-speh*-teh	*rødspette*
(rainbow) trout	(*rrayng*-büeh-)*er*-eht	*(regnbue)ørret*
roe	rrorrngn	*rogn*
sea trout	*sher-er*-rreht	*sjøørret*
shellfish	*skuhl*-dürr	*skaldyr*
shrimps	*rray*-kehrr	*reker*
(smoked) salmon	(*rrer*-keh-)*luhks*	*(røyke)laks*
sole	*sher-tun*-geh	*sjøtunge*
sprat/sardine	*brris*-ling	*brisling*
tuna	*tun*-fisk	*tunfisk*
whale steak	*vahl*-bif	*hvalbiff*

Poultry & Wildfowl

black grouse	*orr*-fool	*orrfugl*
chicken	*chül*-ling	*kylling*
chicken fricassee	*hern*-seh-frri-kuh-*seh*	*hønsefrikasse*
duck	uhn	*and*
goose	gors	*gås*
partridge	*rrap-hern*-eh	*rapphøne*
ptarmigan	*rrü*-peh	*rype*
quail	*vuhk*-tehl	*vaktel*
turkey	kuhl-*kun*	*kalkun*

Vegetables

beans	*bern-nehrr*	*bønner*
beetroot	rrrr-*beh*-tehrr	*rødbeter*
Brussels sprouts	*rroo*-sehn-*korl*	*rosenkål*
button mushroom	sham-pin-*yong*	*sjampinjong*
cabbage	korl	*kål*
carrots	*gu*-leh-rrer-tehrr	*gulrøtter*
cauliflower	*blorm-korl*	*blomkål*
chives	*grrehs*-lerk	*gressløk*
cucumber	uh-*gurrk*	*agurk*
horseradish	*peh*-pehrr-*rroot*	*pepperrot*
leek	*pu*-rreh	*purre*
lentils	*lin*-sehrr	*linser*
marrow/squash	*grrehs*-kahrr	*gresskar*
mashed potatoes	por-*teht*-mos	*potetmos*
mushroom	sop	*sopp*
onion	lerk	*løk*
peas	*at*-tehrr	*erter*
pickled gherkin	*sül*-teh-uh-*gurrk*	*sylteagurk*
potato dumplings	rruh-speh-*buh*-lehrr	*raspeballer*
potato pancake	*lum*-peh	*lompe*
radish	rreh-*dik*	*reddik*
red cabbage	*rror*-korl	*rødkål*
spinach	spi-*naht*	*spinat*
sugar peas	*su*-kehrr-at-tehrr	*sukkererter*
swede	korl-rah-*bi*	*kålrabi*
tomato	too-*maht*	*tomat*
vegetables	*grrern*-suh-kehrr	*grøn(n)saker*

Spices, Herbs & Condiments

caraway seeds	*kuhrr*-veh	*karve*
cardamom	kuhrr-deh-*mum*-meh	*kardemomme*
cinnamon	kuh-*nehl*	*kanel*
curry	*kuh*-rri	*karri*
garlic	*veet*-lerk	*hvitløk*

mustard	*sehn*-ehp	*sennep*
parsley	pa-*shi*-leh	*persille*
pepper	*peh*-pehrr	*pepper*
spices/herbs	krrü-*dehrr*	*krydder*
sugar	*su*-kehrr	*sukker*
tarragon	ehs-trruh-*gon*	*estragon*
thyme	*ti*-mi-uhn	*timian*
vinegar	*eh*-dik	*eddik*

Fruit

apple	*ehp*-leh	*eple*
apricot	uh-prri-*kus*	*aprikos*
banana	buh-*nahn*	*banan*
bilberries	*blor-barr*	*blåbær*
blackberries	*byer*-neh-*barr*	*bjørnebær*
blackcurrants	*sool-barr*	*solbær*
cherry	*shi*-sheh-*barr*	*kirsebær*
cranberries	*tü*-teh-*barr*	*tyttebær*
currant	kor-int	*korint*
fruit	frrukt	*frukt*
fruit salad	frrukt-suh-*laht*	*fruktsalat*
gooseberries	*sti*-kehls-*barr*	*stikkelsbær*
grapes	*drroo*-ehrr	*druer*
lemon	si-*trroon*	*sitron*
orange	uh-pehl-*seen*	*appelsin*
peach	*fa*-shkehn	*fersken*
pear	*pah*-rreh	*pære*
pineapple	*uh*-nuh-*nuhs*	*ananas*
plum	*plu*-meh	*plomme*
raisin	rroo-*sin*	*rosin*
raspberries	*brring*-eh-*barr*	*bringebær*
redcurrants	rrips	*rips*
rhubarb	rruh-*buhrr*-brruh	*rabarbra*
stewed plums	*plu*-meh-*grrert*	*plommegrøt*
stewed prunes	*svi*-skeh-*grrert*	*sviskegrøt*
strawberries	*yoorr*-barr	*jordbær*

Desserts, Cakes & Cookies

apple cake	*eh*-pleh-*kah*-keh	*eplekake*
biscuit/cookie	*smor*-*kah*-keh	*småkake*
cake	*kah*-keh	*kake*
chocolate	shoo-kor-*luh*-deh	*sjokolade*
ice cream	ees	*is*
meringue	muh-*rrehngs*	*marengs*
pancake	*puh*-neh-*kah*-keh	*pannekake*
sponge cake	*suk*-kehrr-*brrer*	*sukkerbrød*
tart	*tahrr*-teh	*terte*

Non-Alcoholic Drinks

apple juice	*eh*-pleh-*must*	*eplemost*
cocoa	kuh-*kuh*-oo	*kakao*
coffee	*kuh*-feh	*kaffe*
fruit juice	yoos	*jus*
ice	ees	*is*
milk	mehlk	*melk*
mineral water	*fuhrr*-is	*farris*
non-alcoholic	*uhl*-ku-hool-*frri*	*alkoholfri*
orangeade	*uh*-pehl-*seen*-*brrus*	*appelsinbrus*
squash	suhft	*saft*
tea	teh	*te*
water	vuhn	*vann*

Alcoholic Drinks

beer	erl	*øl*
brandy	*brrehn*-eh-vin	*brennevin*
cognac	*kon*-yuhk	*konjakk*
dark beer	*bah*-yehrr	*bayer*
double	*dor*-behl	*dobbel*
dry	ter-rr	*tørr*
liqueur	li-*ker*-rr	*likør*
port	*purrt*-vin	*portvin*
red/white wine	*rrer*-vin/*veet*-vin	*rødvin/hvitvin*
rum	rroom	*rom*
sparkling	mus-*sehrr*-ehn-deh	*musserende*

AT THE MARKET

Basics

bread	brrer	*brød*
butter	smer-rr	*smør*
cheese	ust	*ost*
chocolate	shoo-kor-*luh*-deh	*sjokolade*
cooking oil	*ol*-yeh	*olje*
eggs	ehg	*egg*
flour (plain)	mehl	*mel*
jam	*sül*-teh-töy	*syltetøy*
milk	mehlk	*melk*
rice	rrees	*ris*
sugar	*su*-kehrr	*sukker*
mineral water	*fuhrr*-is	*farris*

Meat & Poultry

beef	*uk*-seh-*chert*	*oksekjøtt*
chicken	*chül*-ling	*kylling*
duck	uhn	*and*
ham	*shin*-keh	*skinke*
lamb/mutton	sow-eh-chert	*sauekjøtt*
meat	chert	*kjøtt*
pork	*svi*-neh-*chert*	*svinekjøtt*
sausage	*perl*-seh	*pølse*
turkey	kuhl-*kun*	*kalkun*
veal	*kuhl*-veh-*chert*	*kalvekjøtt*

Vegetables

beans	*bern-nehrr*	*bønner*
beetroot	rrrr-*beh*-tehrr	*rødbeter*
Brussels sprouts	*rroo*-sehn-*korl*	*rosenkål*
cabbage	korl	*kål*
carrots	*gu*-leh-rrer-tehrr	*gulrøtter*
cauliflower	*blorm-korl*	*blomkål*
cucumber	uh-*gurrk*	*agurk*
mushroom	sop	*sopp*

AT THE MARKET

onion	lerk	*løk*
peas	*at*-tehrr	*erter*
potato	por-*teht*	*potet*
red cabbage	*rror*-korl	*rødkål*
spinach	spi-*naht*	*spinat*
tomato	too-*maht*	*tomat*
vegetables	*grrern*-suh-kehrr	*grøn(n)saker*

Seafood

cod	torshk	*torsk*
crab	*krruh*-beh	*krabbe*
crayfish	krrehps	*kreps*
fish	fisk	*fisk*
herring	sil	*sild*
lobster	*hu*-mehrr	*hummer*
mackerel	muh-*krrel*	*makrell*
mussel	*blor*-shehl	*blåskjel(l)*
salmon	*luhks*	*laks*
shrimps	*rray*-kehrr	*reker*
whale steak	*vahl*-bif	*hvalbiff*

Fruit

apple	*ehp*-leh	*eple*
apricot	uh-prri-*kus*	*aprikos*
banana	buh-*nahn*	*banan*
bilberries	*blor-barr*	*blåbær*
fruit	frrukt	*frukt*
grapes	*drroo*-ehrr	*druer*
lemon	si-*trroon*	*sitron*
orange	uh-pehl-*seen*	*appelsin*
peach	*fa*-shkehn	*fersken*
pear	*pah*-rreh	*pære*
plum	*plu*-meh	plomme
strawberries	*yoorr*-barr	jordbær

SHOPPING

How much is it ...?
vorr mü-yö ***kos-törr*** **deh ...?** *Hvor mye koster det ...?*

bookshop	***book***-huhn-dl	*bokhandel*
camera shop	***foo***-tu-fo-***rreht***-ning	*fotoforretning*
clothing store	***klays***-bu-***tik***	*klesbutikk*
delicatessen	deh-li-kuh-***tehs***-sö-fo-***rreht***-ning	*delikatesse-forretning*
general store; shop	***dah***-lig-vah-rrö-fo-***rreht***-ning	*dagligvare-forretning*
green grocer	***grrern***-sahks-***huhn***-dlörr	*grøn(n)sakshandler*
laundry	rrehn-sö-***rree***	*renseri*
market	***muhrr***-köd	*marked*
newsagency/ stationers	chyosk	*kiosk*
pharmacy	uh-pu-***tayk***	*apotek*
shoeshop	***skoo***-töy-fo-***rreht***-ning	*skotøyforretning*
souvenir shop	su-vö-***neerr***-shuhp	*suvenirsjapp*
supermarket	***snahrr***-cherp(s-bu-***tik***)	*snarkjøp(sbutikk)*

I'd like to buy ...
yay kuhn ***for*** ... *Jeg kan få ...*
Do you have others?
hah du uhn-drreh? *Har du andre?*
I don't like it.
deh ***lee***-**körr yay** ***ik***-**kö** *Det liker jeg ikke.*
Can I look at it?
kuhn yay for ***say*** **po deh?** *Kan jeg få se på det?*
I'm just looking.
yay bah-rrö ***sayrr*** **ma rrünt** *Jeg bare ser meg rundt.*
Can you write down the price?
kuhn du ***skrree***-**vö** ***up prree***-**sn?** *Kan du skrive opp prisen?*
Do you accept credit cards?
tah **du i-*moot* krray-*dit*-kort?** *Tar du imot kredittkort?*

Could you lower the price?
kun-nö du seht-tö *ned prree*-sn? *Kunne du sette ned prisen?*
I don't have much money.
yay *hahrr* ik-kö mü-yö *pehng*-örr *Jeg har ikke mye penger.*

Can I help you?
kuhn yay *yehl*-pö day? *Kan jeg hjelpe deg?*
Will that be all?
vah rdeh sor noo *ahnt*? *Var det så noe annet?*
Would you like it wrapped?
skuhl yay puhk-kö deh *in* forr *day?* *Skal jeg pakke det inn for deg?*
Sorry, this is the only one.
bö-*klah*-görr deht-tö arr dehn *ay*-nehs-tö *Beklager, dette er den eneste.*
How much/many do you want?
voor *mü*-yö/*muhng*-ö vil du *hah*? *Hvor mye/mange veel du ha?*

Essential Groceries

batteries	buh-teh-*ri*	*batteri*
bread	brrer	*brød*
butter	smer-rr	*smør*
cheese	ust	*ost*
chocolate	shoo-kor-*luh*-deh	*sjokolade*
cooking oil	*ol*-yeh	*olje*
eggs	ehg	*egg*
flour (plain)	mehl	*mel*
ham	*shin*-keh	*skinke*
honey	*hun-ning*	*honning*
jam	*sül*-teh-töy	*syltetøy*
matches	*für*-sti-kehr	*fyrstikker*
milk	mehlk	*melk*
pepper	*peh*-pehrr	*pepper*
rice	rrees	*ris*
salt	suhlt	*salt*

shampoo	*shuhm*-poo	*sjampo*
soap	*sor*-pö	*såpe*
sugar	*su*-kehrr	*sukker*
toilet paper	*doo*-puh-pee-rr	*dopapir*
toothbrush	*tuhn*-ber-shtö	*tannbørste*

Souvenirs

earrings	*ohrr*-rrö-*dob*-börr	*øredobber*
glasswork	*gluhs*-töy	*glasstøy*
handicraft	*kunst*-huhn-varrk	*kunsthandverk*
necklace	*huhls*-chay-dö	*halskjede*
Norwegian vest	*kuf*-tö	*kofte*
pottery	*stayn-töy*	*steintøy*
ring	*rring*	*ring*
rug	*rrü*-yö	*rye*

Clothing

clothing	klarr	*klær*
coat	frruhk	*frakk*
dress	*choo*-lö	*kjole*
jacket	*yuhk*-kö	*jakke*
jumper (sweater, jersey)	*gehn*-sörr	*genser*
shirt	*shu*-rtö	*skjorte*
shoes	skoo	*sko*
skirt	sher-rt	*skjørt*
trousers	*buk*-sörr	*bukser*

It doesn't fit.	deh *puhs*-sörr ik-kö	*Det passer ikke.*
It's too ...	deh arr forr ...	*Det er for ...*
big	*shtoort*	*stort*
small	*lee*-tö	*lite*
short	*kort*	*kort*
long	*luhngt*	*langt*
tight	*teht*-sit-tuhn-nö	*tettsittande*
loose	lowst	*laust*

Materials

cotton	*bum*-ul	*bomull*
handmade	*hon-lah*-göt	*håndlaget*
leather	larr	*lær*
brass	*mehs*-sing	*messing*
gold	gul	*gull*
silver	serlv	*sølv*
silk	sil-kö	*silke*
wool	ul	*ull*

Toiletries

comb	kuhm	*kam*
condoms	kun-*doom*	*kondom*
deodorant	day-yu-du-*rruhnt*	*deodorant*
hairbrush	*hor-rr*-ber-shteh	*hårbørste*
razor	buhrr-*bayrr*-her-völ	*barberhøvel*
sanitary napkins	*dah*-mö-bin	*damebind*
shampoo	*shuhm*-poo	*sjampo*
shaving cream	buhrr-*bayrr*-krraym	*barberkrem*
soap	*sor*-pö	*såpe*
sunblock cream	*sern*-blok-ul-yö	*sunblock-olje*
tampons	tuhm-*pong*-örr	*tamponger*
tissues	puh-*peerr*-lum-mö-ter-rr-klö	*papirlommetørkle*
toilet paper	*doo*-puh-peerr	*dopapir*
toothpaste	*tuhn*-krraym	*tannkrem*

Stationery & Publications

map	kuhrt	*kart*
newspaper	uh-*vees*	*avis*
newspaper in English	*ehng*-ölsk-sprror-kli uh-*vees*	*engelskspråklig avis*
novels in English	*ehng*-öl-skö rru-*mah*-nörr	*engelske romaner*
paper	puh-*peerr*	*papir*
pen (ballpoint)	pehn (*kü*-lö-pehn)	*penn (kulepenn)*
scissors	suhks	*saks*

Photography

How much is it to process this film?

voor mü-yö *kos*-törr deh o *fruhm*-kuhl-lö dehn-nö *fil*-mön?	*Hvor mye koster det å framkalle denne filmen?*

When will it be ready?

***norr* arr dehn *fa*-rdi?**	*Når er den ferdig?*

I'd like a film for this camera.

yay vil *ya*-rrnö hah ehn film til dehn-nö *kah*-mö-rruhn	*Jeg vil gjerne ha en film til denne kameraen.*

B&W (film)	**svuhrt-vit**	*svart-hvitt*
camera	***kah*-mö-rruh**	*kamera*
colour (film)	***fuhrr*-gö(-film)**	*farge(film)*
film	**film**	*film*
flash	**blits**	*blitz*
lens	***lin*-sö**	*linse*
light meter	***lüs*-mor-lörr**	*lysmåler*

Smoking

A packet of cigarettes, please.

***ehn* puhk-kö si-guh-*rreht*-törr tuhk**	*En pakke sigaretter, takk.*

Are these cigarettes strong/mild?

arr dis-sö si-guh-rreht-tö-neh krruhf-ti-yö/*mil*-lö?	*Er disse sigarettene kraftige/milde?*

Do you have a light?

hah du *fürr*?	*Har du fyr?*

cigarette papers	*rrul*-lö-puh-*pee-rr*	*rullepapir*
cigarettes	si-guh-*rreht*-törr	*sigaretter*
filtered	*fil*-törr	*filter*
lighter	*lai*-törr	*lighter*
matches	*für*-stik-körr	*fyrstikker*
menthol	*mehn*-tol	*mentol*
pipe	*pee*-pö	*pipe*
tobacco (pipe)	(*pee*-pö)-tu-*buhk*	*(pipe)tobakk*

Colours

black	svuhrt	*svart*
blue	blor	*blå*
brown	brrun	*brun*
green	grrern	*grønn*
pink	*rroo*-suh	*rosa*
red	rrer	*rød*
white	veet	*hvit*
yellow	gul	*gul*

Sizes & Comparisons

small	*lee*-tn	*liten*
big	stoorr	*stor*
heavy	tung	*tung*
light	leht	*lett*
more	mehrr	*mer*
less	*min*-drrö	*mindre*
too much/many	fort *mü*-yö/*muhng*-ö	*for mye/mange*
many	*muhng*-ö	*mange*
enough	nok	*nok*
also	*os*-so	*også*
a little bit	lit	*litt*

HEALTH

Where is the ...?	*voor* arr ...?	*Hvor er ...?*
chemist	uh-pu-*tay*-kö	*apoteket*
dentist	*tuhn*-lay-gön	*tannlegen*
doctor	*lay*-gön	*legen*
hospital	*sü*-kö-hu-sö	*sykehuset*

I'm/My friend is sick.	
yay art/*vehn*-n min arr *sük*	*Jeg er/ Vennen min er syk.*
Could I see a female doctor?	
kuhn yay for *snuhk*-kö mayn *kvin*-nö-li *lay*-gö?	*Kan jeg få snakke med en kvinnelig lege?*
What's the matter?	
vah arr i *vay*-ön?	*Hva er i veien?*
Where does it hurt?	
voor yer rdeh *vunt?*	*Hvor gjør det vondt?*
It hurts here.	
deh yer-rr *vunt harr*	*Dette gjør vondt.*
My ... hurts.	
deh yer-rr *vunt* i ...	*Det gjør vondt i ...*

Parts of the Body

ankle	*uhng*-kö-lön	*ankelen*
arm	*uhrr*-mön	*armen*
back	*rrüg*-gön	*ryggen*
chest	*brrüst*-kuhs-suh	*brystkassa*
ear	*ohrr*-rreh	*øret*
eye	*öy*-eh	*øyet*
finger	*fing*-ö-rrön	*fingeren*
foot	*foo*-tn	*foten*
hand	*hon*-nuh	*hånda*
head	*hoo*-deh	*hodet*
heart	*ya*-rteh	*hjertet*
leg	*bay*-neh	*beinet*
mouth	*mun*-n	*munnen*
nose	*nay*-suh	*nesa*
teeth	*tehn*-n-neh	*tennene*
throat	*strru*-pön	*strupen*

Ailments

I have (a/an) ...	yay hahr ...	*Jeg har ...*
allergy	ehn uhl-lehrr-*gee*	*en allergi*
anaemia	*bloo*-muhng-öl	*blodmangel*
burn	eht *brrehn*-sor-rr	*et brennsår*
cold	*snu*-ö	*snue*
constipation	fo-*shtop*-pölsö	*forstoppelse*
cough	*hoos*-tö	*hoste*
diarrhoea	*mah*-gö-show	*magesjau*
fever	*fay*-börr	*feber*
headache	*vunt* i *hoo*-dö	*vondt i hodet*
hepatitis	*gul*-sot	*gulsott*
indigestion	*dor*-rrli fo-*rdöy*-öl-sö	*dårlig fordøyelse*
infection	ehn beh-*tehn*-öl-sö	*en betennelse*
influenza	in-flu-*ehn*-suh	*influensa*
low/high blood pressure	*lahft/höyt* *bloo*-trrük	*lavt/høyt* *blodtrykk*
pain	*sma*-rtö	*smerte*
sore throat	*vunt* i *huhl*-sn	*vondt i halsen*
sprain	ehn fo*shtu*-ing	*en forstuing*
sunburn	*sool*-brrehnt-hayt	*solbrenthet*
venereal disease	*chern*-sük-dom	*kjønnssykdom*
worms	*in*-vols-muhrrk	*innvollsmark*

Some Useful Words & Phrases

I'm ...	yay hahr ...	*Jeg har ...*
asthmatic	*uhst*-muh	*astma*
diabetic	*suk*-kö-sük-eh	*sukkersyke*
epileptic	*fuhl*-lö-sük-eh	*fallesyke*

I'm allergic to antibiotics/penicillin.
yay arr uh-*lehrr*-gisk moot uhn-ti-bi-*yoo*-ti-kuh/ pehn-ni-si-*leen*
Jeg er allergisk mot antibiotika/ penicillin

I'm pregnant.
yay arr grruh-*veed*
Jeg er gravid.

I'm on the pill.
yay tahrr *pay*-pil-lön
Jeg tar P-pillen.

I haven't had my period for ... months.
yay hahrr *ik*-kö huht mehns por ... *mor*-ntörr
Jeg har ikke hatt mens på ... måneder.

I have been vaccinated.
yay arr vuhk-si-*nay-rt*
Jeg er vaksinert.

I have my own syringe.
yay hahrr min *eh*-gön *sprröy*-tö-spis
Jeg har min egen sprøytespiss.

I feel better/worse.
yay *fayrr*-lörr meh *bay*-drrö/*varr*-ö
Jeg føler meg bedre/verre.

accident	*oo*-lük-kö	*ulykke*
addiction	ahv-*hehng*-i-hayt	*avhengighet*
aspirin	dis-*prril*	*dispril*
bandage	buhn-*dah*-shö	*bandasje*
blood test	*bloo*-prrer-vö	*blodprøve*
contraceptive	prray-vehn-*shoons*-midl	*prevensjonsmiddel*
injection	*sprröy*-tö	*sprøyte*
menstruation	mehns-trroo-uh-*shoon*/ mens	*menstruasjon/ mens*

At the Chemist

I need medication for ...
yay trrehng-örr eht midl moot ...
Jeg trenger et middel mot ...

I have a prescription.
yay hahrr ehn rrö-sehpt
Jeg har en resept.

TIME & DATES

What time is it?	vah arr *klok-kuh*?	*Hva er klokka?*
It's ... (am/pm)	*klok*-kuh arr ...	*Klokka er ...*
in the morning	um *fo-rr*-mid-dah-gön	*om formiddagen*
in the afternoon	um *eht*-törr-mid-dah-gön	*om ettermiddagen*
in the evening	um *kvehl*-n	*om kvelden*

What date is it today?
vah *dah*-tu arr deh i-*dahg*? *Hva dato er det i dag?*

Days of the Week

Monday	*muhn*-dah(g)	*mandag*
Tuesday	*teesh*-dah(g)	*tirsdag*
Wednesday	*uns*-dah(g)	*onsdag*
Thursday	*toosh*-dah(g)	*torsdag*
Friday	*frreh*-dah(g)	*fredag*
Saturday	*ler*-rdah(g)	*lørdag*
Sunday	*sern*-dah(g)	*søndag*

NUTS ABOUT KNUT

Knut Hamsun is probably the best-known Norwegian writer since Henrik Ibsen. Often characterised as one of the most influential European writers of the 20th century, he is credited with inventing a new literary style. He was awarded the Nobel Prize for Literature in 1920 but is often shunned in Norway because of his support for Hitler and the Norwegian Nazi Party during WWII.

Months

January	yuh-noo-*wahrr*	*januar*
February	feh-brroo-*wahrr*	*februar*
March	mahsh	*mars*
April	uh-*prril*	*april*
May	*mah*-i	*mai*
June	*yoo*-ni	*juni*
July	*yoo*-li	*juli*
August	ow-*gust*	*august*
September	sehp-*tehm*-börr	*september*
October	uk-*too*-börr	*oktober*
November	no-*vehm*-börr	*november*
December	deh-*sehm*-börr	*desember*

Seasons

summer	*som*-mörr	*sommer*
autumn	herst	*høst*
winter	*vin*-törr	*vinter*
spring	vor-rr	*vår*

Present

today	i-*dahg*	*i dag*
this morning	i-*morr*-ös	*i morges*
tonight (evening)	i-*kvehl*	*i kveld*
this week	dehn-nö *u*-kuh	*denne uka*
this year	i-*yor-rr*	*i år*
now	nor	*nå*

Past

yesterday	i-*gor-rr*	*i går*
day before yesterday	i *forr*-gor-sh	*i forgårs*
yesterday morning	i-*gor-rr forr*-mid-dahg	*i går formiddag*
last night	i-*nuht*	*i natt*
last week/month	*sis*-tö *u*-kö/*mor-nt*	*siste uke/måned*
last year	i-*fyoorr*	*i fjor*

Future

tomorrow (morning)	i-*mor-rrn*	*i morgen*
day after tomorrow	i-*or*-vörr-mor-rrn	*i overmorgen*
next week/year	*nehs*-tö *u*-kö/*or-rr*	*neste uke/år*

During the Day

afternoon	*eht*-törr-mid-dahg	*ettermiddag*
dawn, very early morning	*dahg*-grrü	*daggry*
day	dahg	*dag*
early	*tee*-li	*tidlig*
midnight	*mit*-nuht	*midtnatt*
morning	*forr*-mid-dahg	*formiddag*
night	nuht	*natt*
noon	klok-kuh *tol*	*klokka tolv*

NUMBERS & AMOUNTS

0	nul	*null*
1	ehn	*en*
2	too	*to*
3	trreh	*tre*
4	*fee*-rrö	*fire*
5	fehm	*fem*
6	sehks	*seks*
7	shu/süv	*sju/syv*
8	*ot*-tö	*åtte*
9	nee	*ni*
10	tee	*ti*

11	*el*-vö	*elleve*
12	tol	*tolv*
13	*trreh*-tehn	*tretten*
14	*fyor*-tehn	*fjorten*
15	*fehm*-tehn	*femten*
16	*sehks*-tehn	*seksten*
17	*sü*-tehn	*sytten*
18	*at*-tehn	*atten*
19	*ni*-tehn	*nitten*
20	*chu*-ö	*tjue*
21	*chu*-ehn	*tjueen*
30	*trreht*-te/*trrehd*-vö	*trettil tredve*
40	*fer*-rti	*førti*
50	*fem*-ti	*femti*
60	*sehks*-ti	*seksti*
70	*ser*-ti	*sytti*
80	*ot*-ti	*åtti*
90	*nit*-ti	*nitti*
100	*hun*-drrö	*hundre*
1000	*tus*-ön	*tusen*
one million	ehn mi-li-*yoon*	*en million*

1/4	ehn *kvuh-rt*	*en kvart*
1/3	ehn *trray*-dayl	*en tredel*
1/2	ehn *huhl*	*en halv*
3/4	*trreh*-kvuh-rt	*trekvart*
1st	*fersh*-tö	*første*
2nd	*ahn*-drreh	*andre*
3rd	*trreh*-dyö	*tredje*

Some Useful Words

Enough!	nok!	*Nok!*
a little (amount)	lit	*litt*
double	*dob*-bölt	*dobbelt*
a dozen	tol	*tolv*
few	for	*få*
less	*min*-drrö	*mindre*
many	*muhng*-ö	*mange*
more	may-rr/*flay*-rrö	*mer/flere*
once	ehn guhng	*en gang*
a pair	eht puhrr	*et par*
percent	prru-*sehnt*	*prosent*
some	*noo*-n	*noen*
too much	forr *mü*-yö	*for mye*
twice	*too* guhng-örr	*to ganger*

ABBREVIATIONS

AS	company
EF	EC
e.Kr./f.Kr.	AD/BC
FN	UN
f.o.m.	from (eg. today)
gt./vn.	St/Rd
hovudpostkontor	GPO
Herr/Fru	Mr/Mrs/MS
m.o.h.	metres above sea level
NAF	AA (Automobile Association)
nord/sør	Nth/Sth
NSB	Norwegian Railway Company
postnummer	ZIP-code
Storbritannia	UK

EMERGENCIES

Help!
yehlp! *Hjelp!*

It's an emergency!
deht-tö arr eht uh-*kut*-til-fehl-lö! *Dette er et akutt-tilfelle!*

There's been an accident!
deh hah shehd ehn *oo*-lük-kö! *Det har skjedd en ulykke!*

Call a doctor!
***rring* ehn *lay*-gö!** *Ring en lege!*

Call an ambulance!
***rring* eht-törr ehn *sü*-kö-beel!** *Ring etter en sykebil!*

I've been raped.
yay arr *vol*-tuht *Jeg er voldtatt.*

I've been robbed.
yay arr *rrah*-nuh *Jeg er rana.*

Call the police!
rring pu-li-*tee*-ö! *Ring politiet!*

Where is the police station?
***voor* arr pu-li-*tee*-stuh-shoon-n?** *Hvor er politistasjonen?*

Go away!/Buzz off!
fo-*shvin!*/stik-*ahv!* *Forsvinn!/Stikk av!*

I'll call the police!
ya *til*-kuhl-lörr pu-li-*tee*-ö! *Jeg tilkaller politiet!*

SIGNS

POLITI	**POLICE**
POLITISTASJON/ LENSMANNSKONTOR	**POLICE STATION**

Thief! *tiiv!*	*Tyv!*
I'm ill. yay arr *sük*	*Jeg er syk.*
I'm lost. yay hahrr got meh *vil*	*Jeg har gått meg vill.*
Where are the toilets? voor arr too-uh-*leht-tö*-nö/veh-seh?	*Hvor er toalettene/wc?*
Could you help me please? kuhn du *yehl*-pö meh *kuhn*-shö?	*Kan du hjelpe meg kanskje?*
Could I please use the telephone? kuhn yay for *lor*-nö teh-leh-*foon*-n?	*Kan jeg få låne telefonen?*
I'm sorry. yay arr *lay* fo *rdeh*	*Jeg er lei for det.*
I didn't realise I was doing anything wrong. yay vahrr ik-kö *klahrr* or-vörr uht yay yoo-rrö noo-ö *gahlt*	*Jeg var ikke klar over at jeg gjorde noe galt.*
I didn't do it. yay hahrr *ik*-kö yurt deh	*Jeg har ikke gjort det.*
I wish to contact my embassy/consulate. va-sho-*snil* o lah meh for kon-*tuhk*-tö min uhm-buh-*sab*-dö/mit kon-su-*laht*	*Vær så snill å la meg få kontakte min ambassade/mitt konsulat.*
I speak English. yay snuh-körr *ehng*-ölsk	*Jeg snakker engelsk.*
I have medical insurance. yay hah *sü*-kö-fo-*shik*-rring	*Jeg har sykeforsikring.*
My possessions are insured. *ay*-ön-day-lö-nö mee-nö arr fo-*shik*-rröt	*Eiendelene mine er forsikret.*

My ... was stolen.	... arr styor-löt	*... er stjålet.*
I've lost my ...	yay hahrr *mis*-teht ...	*Jeg har mistet ...*
bags	buh-*gah*-shön min	*bagasjen min*
handbag	*vehs*-kuh mee	*vesken min*
money	*pehng*-eh-nö mee-nö	*pengene mine*
travellers cheques	*rray*-sö-shehk-kuh-neh mee-nö	*reisesjekkene mine*
passport	*puhs*-sö mit	*passet mitt*

SWEDISH

QUICK REFERENCE

Hello.	hay	*Hej.*
Goodbye.	uh-*yer!/hay dor!*	*Adjö!/Hej då!*
Yes./No.	yah/nay	*Ja./Nej.*
Excuse me.	ü-*shehk*-tuh *may*	*Ursäkta mig.*
Sorry.	fer-*lort*	*Förlåt.*
Please.	*tuhk*	*Tack.*
Thank you.	tuhk	*Tack.*
You're welcome.	*vuh*-sho-*goo*	*Varsågod.*
I'd like a...	yuh *skul*-leh	*Jag skulle*
	vil-yuh *hah* ehn ...	*vilja ha en ...*
one-way ticket	*ehn*-kehl-bil-*yeht*	*enkelbiljett*
return ticket	rreh-*türr*-bil-*yeht*	*returbiljett*
I (don't) understand.		
yuh fer-*shtor-rr* (*in*-teh)		*Jag förstår (inte).*
Do you speak English?		
tah-luhrr du *ehng*-ehls-kuh?		*Talar du engelska?*
Where is ...?		
vahrr *air/lig*-gehrr ...?		*Var är/ligger ...?*
Go straight ahead.		
gor *rrahkt frruhm*		*Gå rakt fram.*
Turn left/right.		
svehng til *vehns*-tehrr/ *her*-gehrr.		*Sväng till vänster/ höger.*
Do you have any rooms available?		
fins deh nor-grruh *lea*-di-guh *rrum*?		*Finns det några lediga rum?*
I'm looking for a public toilet.		
yuh *lea*-tuhrr ehf-tehrr ehn oo-*fehnt*-li too-uh-*leht*		*Jag letar efter en offentlig toalett.*

1	eht	*ett*	6	sehx	*sex*
2	tvor	*två*	7	fhü	*sju*
3	trrea	*tre*	8	*ot-tuh*	*åtta*
4	*fü-rruh*	*fyra*	9	*nee-oo*	*nio*
5	fehm	*fem*	10	*tee-oo*	*tio*

SWEDISH

Swedish belongs to the Nordic branch of the Germanic languages. It's spoken by the Swedes, who number close to nine million, and by the Finnish-Swedish minority in southern Finland, including the island of Åland. The language is very closely related to Danish and Norwegian. In fact, Scandinavians can usually make themselves understood in their sister countries. Outside this northern outpost, however, it's a different matter, so most Swedes speak at least some English, which is a compulsory subject on school curriculums. Many Swedes actually enjoy practising their English on tourists.

Since English and Swedish have common roots in ancient Germanic, there are many similarities between the languages. Many words were also borrowed from Old Norse into the English language during the Viking period, which ended about a thousand years ago, making the language connection even stronger. In modern times the borrowing is going in the opposite direction, with Swedish borrowing mainly from American English.

There are also quite a few differences between English and Swedish. For a start, you will notice that there are three extra letters in Swedish: å, ä and ö. These are the last three letters of the alphabet, so if you want to look up Åkesson in the telephone directory, you have to look near the end.

Even though you won't have too much difficulty getting around with English, making the effort to learn a few common phrases in Swedish will definitely pay off, as it will be greatly appreciated by the Swedes, who are not used to foreign visitors speaking their language.

PRONUNCIATION

There's a great variety of dialects in Sweden. The pronunciation guide in this book reflects a neutral Swedish, rikssvenska, but don't be surprised if you're given a slightly different pronunciation from a Swede. It all depends on where they come from!

It's important to get the stress right in words. Swedish can have a single or a double accent on a word, giving it its sing-song quality, and sometimes the difference of meaning between two identical-looking words can be huge depending on which accent is used. A good example is **anden** '*uhn*-**dehn**' and **anden** '*uhn-dehn*' where the former is 'the duck' and the latter is 'the spirit/ghost'. In this guide we have used italic letters to denote stressed syllables.

Pronunciation is given in the pronunciation guide in the front of this book, with the following exceptions:

Vowels

Most Swedish vowels have a long and a short variant. In a stressed syllable, a vowel is short if it's followed by two consonants and (generally) long when followed by only one consonant. The unstressed syllables have short vowel sounds.

The letter **e** is always pronounced in Swedish, even at the end of words, and the letter **y** is always a vowel.

The vowels are divided into two groups, the hard vowels are **a, o, u, å** and the soft vowels are **e, i, y, ä, ö**. They help determine the pronunciation of certain preceding consonants.

Diphthongs

SWEDISH	GUIDE	SOUNDS
e	ea	as in British English 'fear'

Consonants

Some consonants have different sounds depending on whether the following vowel is hard or soft (see *Vowels* above).

SWEDISH	GUIDE	SOUNDS
g	g	as in 'get' in front of hard vowels and consonants
	y	as in 'yet' in front of soft vowels
j	y	as in 'yet'. This sound can be spelled *dj, gj, hj, lj* at the beginning of words.
k	k	as 'c' in 'cap' in front of hard vowels and consonants
	ch	as *tj* in front of soft vowels
tj	ch	as the 'ch' in 'cheap' but without the slight 't' sound initially. Can also be spelled *ch, k, kj*.
sj	fh	not unlike 'sh' in 'ship' but try touching the inside of your lower lip with your front teeth while saying it. Can be spelled *ch sch, skj, stj*.
sk	fh	in front of soft vowels as *sj*, in other positions each letter is pronounced separately

PRONOUNS		
SG		
I	yahg	*jag*
you	dü/nee	*du/ni*
he/she/it	huhn/hoon/dea	*han/hon/det*
PL		
we	vee	*vi*
you	nee	*ni*
they	dom	*de*

GREETINGS & CIVILITIES

Top Useful Phrases

Hello.	hay	*Hej.*
Goodbye.	uh-*yer!/hay dor!*	*Adjö!/Hej då!*
Yes./No.	yah/nay	*Ja./Nej.*
Excuse me.	ü-*shehk*-tuh *may*	*Ursäkta mig.*
May I?	*for* yuh?	*Får jag?*
Do you mind?	*yer-rr* deh *nor*-got?	*Gör det något?*
Sorry.	fer-*lort*	*Förlåt.*
Please.	*tuhk*	*Tack.* (at the end of a request)
	snehl-luh!	*Snälla!* (when pleading)
Thank you.	tuhk	*Tack.*
Many thanks.	*tuhk* sor *mü*-keh	*Tack så mycket.*
That's fine.	dea air *brrah*	*Det är bra.*
You're welcome.	*vuh*-sho-*goo*	*Varsågod.*

Greetings

Good morning.	goo-*mo-rr-on*	*Godmorgon.*
Good afternoon.	goo-*mid*-duh	*Godmiddag.*
Good evening/ night.	goo-*kvehl/* goo-*nuht*	*Godkväll/ Godnatt.*
How are you?	*hürr* stor rde *til?*	*Hur står det till?*
Well, thanks.	*brrah* tuhk	*Bra, tack.*

Forms of Address

you (sg)	dü	*du*
you (pol sg & pl)	nee	*ni*
Mrs	frrü	*fru*
Mr	harr	*herr*
Miss	*frrer*-kehn	*fröken*
companion	kuhm-*rraht/kom*-pis	*kamrat/kompis*
friend	veh-*nin-nuh*/vehn	*väninna/vän* (f/m)

SMALL TALK

Meeting People

What is your name?
vuh *hea*-tehrr du? — *Vad heter du?*

My name is ...
yuh *hea*-tehrr ... — *Jag heter ...*

I'd like to introduce you to ...
for-rr yuh prreh-sehn-*tea*-rra ... — *Får jag presentera ...*

I'm pleased to meet you.
trreav-lit uht *trrehf*-fuhs/ *uhn*-yeh-*nairmt* — *Trevligt att träffas./ Angenämt.* (pol)

Nationalities

Where are you from?
vahrr-i-frrorn *kom*-mehrr doo? — *Varifrån kommer du?*

I'm from ...	yuh *kom*-mehrr frrorn ...	*Jag kommer från ...*
Australia	uh-u-*strrah*-lee-ehn	*Australien*
Canada	*kuh*-nuh-duh	*Kanada*
England	*ehng*-luhnd	*England*
Ireland	*eer*-luhnd	*Irland*
New Zealand	nü-uh *sea*-luhnd	*Nya Zealand*
Scotland	*skot*-luhnd	*Skottland*
Sweden	*svarr*-yeh	*Sverige*
the USA	*ü*-ehs-*ah*	*USA*
Wales	wayls	*Wales*

Age

How old are you?
hürr *guh*-muhl *air* du? *Hur gammal är du?*
I'm ... years old.
yuh air ... *or-rr guh*-mal *Jag är ... år gammal.*

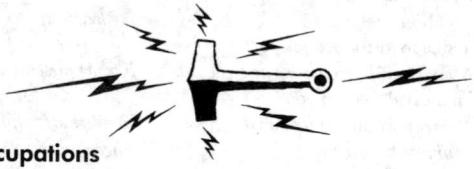

Occupations

What is your profession?
vuh *hahrr* du fer-rr *ürr-keh?* *Vad har du för yrke?*

I'm (a/an) ...	yuh air ...	*Jag är ...*
artist	*konst-naer*	*konstnär*
business person	uh-*faesh-muhn*	*affärsman*
computer expert	*dah*-to-rr-ehks-*part*	*datorexpert*
doctor	*lair*-kuh-*rreh*	*läkare*
engineer	in-fhehn-*yer-rr*	*ingenjör*
farmer	*boon-deh*	*bonde*
handyman	*huhnt-varr*-kuh-rreh	*hantverkare*
journalist	fhoo-nuh-*list*	*journalist*
lawyer	uhd-voo-*kaht*	*advokat*
manual worker	*krrops*-uhrr-*bea*-tuh-rreh	*kroppsarbetare*
mechanic	meh-*kahn*-i-kehrr	*mekaniker*
nurse	*fhük-fher*-tehsh-kuh	*sjuksköterska*
office worker	kon-too-*rrist*	*kontorist*
scientist	nuh-*türr-vea*-tuh-rreh	*naturvetare*
student	stoo-*dea*-rruhn-deh	*studerande*
teacher	*laer*-uhrr-*eh*	*lärare*
waiter	sehrr-vi-*trrees*/ sehrr-vi-*ter-rr*	*servitris*/ *servitör* (f/m)
writer	fer-rr-*fuht*-tuh-rreh	*författare*

Religion

What is your religion?
vil-kehn rreh-li-*yoon* *til*-her-rr *du?* — *Vilken religion tillhör du?*

I'm not religious.
yuh air *in*-teh rreh-li-*fhers* — *Jag är inte religös.*

I'm ...	yuh air ...	*Jag är ...*
Buddhist	bu-*dist*	*buddist*
Catholic	kuh-too-*leek*	*katolik*
Christian	*krris-tehn*	*kristen*
Hindu	hin-*dü*	*hindu*
Jewish	*yü-deh*	*jude*
Muslim	mus-*leem*	*muslim*
Protestant	prroo-tehs-*tuhnt*	*protestant*

Family

Are you married? air du *yift?* — *Är du gift?*

I'm ...	yuh air ...	*Jag är ...*
married	*yift*	*gift*
single	*ü-yift*	*ogift*

How many children do you have?
hürr mong-uh *bahrn hahrr* du? — *Hur många barn har du?*

I don't have any children.
yuh *hahrr* ing-uh *bahrn* — *Jag har inga barn.*

I have a daughter/son.
yuh hahrr ehn *dot-ehrr/sorn* — *Jag har en dotter/son.*

How many brothers/sisters do you have?
hürr mong-uh *brrer*-dehrr/*süs-trruhrr* hahrr du? — *Hur många bröder/systrar har du?*

Do you have a ...?	harr doo non ...?	*Har du någon ...?*
boyfriend	*poyk-vehn/kil*-leh	*pojkvän/kille* (col)
girlfriend	*flik-vehn/cheby*	*flickvän/tjej* (col)
brother/s	brroorr/*brrer*-dehrr	*bror/bröder*
children	bahrn	*barn*
daughter/s	*dot-tehrr/dert-rruhrr*	*dotter/döttrar*
de facto husband/wife	*suhm-boo*	*sambo*
family	fuh-*mily*	*familj*
father	fahrr/*puh-puh*	*far/pappa*
grandparents	*moorr-moorr* o	*mormor och*
(maternal)	*moorr-fuhrr*	*morfar*
grandparents	*fuhrr-moorr* o	*farmor och*
(paternal)	*fuhrr-fuhrr*	*farfar*
husband	muhn	*man*
mother	moorr/*muh-muh*	*mor/mamma*
sister/s	*süs-tehrr/süs-trruhrr*	*syster/systrar*
son/s	sorn/*ser-nehrr*	*son/söner*
wife	frrü	*fru*

Kids' Talk

How old are you?
hürr *guh*-**muhl** *air* **du?** — *Hur gammal är du?*

When's your birthday?
naer fül-ler du *or-rr?* — *När fyller du år?*

What do you do after school?
vuh *yer-rr* **du ehf-tehrr** *skoo-luhn?* — *Vad gör du efter skolan?*

Do you have a pet at home?
hahrr du nor-rruh *hüs-yürr?* — *Har du några husdjur?*

I have a ...	yuh hahrr ...	*Jag har ...*
bird	ehn *for*-gehl	*en fågel*
budgerigar	ehn un-du-*laht*	*en undulat*
canary	ehn kuh-*nah*-rree-eh-*for*-gehl	*en kanariefågel*
cat/pussycat	ehn *kuht/kis*-seh-*kuht*	*en katt/kissekatt*
dog/bow-wow	ehn *hund/voov-veh*	*en hund/vovve*
fish	*fis-kuhrr*	*fiskar*
frog	ehn *grroo-duh*	*en groda*
guinea pig	eht *mah-shveen*	*ett marsvin*
hamster	ehn *huhm*-stehrr	*en hamster*
horse	ehn *hehst*	*en häst*

Feelings

I (don't) like ...
yuh tük-kehrr (*in*-teh) *om ...* *Jag tycker (inte) om ...*

I'm ...	yuh hahrr ...	*Jag har ...*
in a hurry	*brrot-tom*	*bråttom*
right/wrong	*rreht/feal*	*rätt/fel*
I'm ...	yuh air ...	*Jag är ...*
grateful	*tuhk-suhm*	*tacksam*
hot	vuhrrm	*varm*
hungry/thirsty	*hung-rri/ter-shti*	*hungrig/törstig*
angry	uhrry	*arg*
happy/sad	glahd/*leh-sehn*	*glad/ledsen*
tired	trrert	*trött*
worried	*oo-rroo*-li	*orolig*
I'm cold.	yuh *frrü*-sehrr	*Jag fryser.*
I'm well.	yuh mor-rr *brrah*	*Jag mår bra.*
I'm sorry. (condolence)	yuh beh-*klah*-guhrr	*Jag beklagar.*

BREAKING THE LANGUAGE BARRIER

Do you speak English? *tah*-luhrr du *ehng*-ehls-kuh?	*Talar du engelska?*
Does anyone speak English? fins deh *non hair* som tah-luhrr *ehng*-ehls-kuh?	*Finns det någon här som talar engelska?*
I speak a little ... yuh *tah*-luhrr *lee*-teh ...	*Jag talar lite ...*
I don't speak ... yuh *tah*-luhrr *in*-teh ...	*Jag talar inte ...*
I (don't) understand. yuh fer-*shtor-rr* (*in*-teh)	*Jag förstår (inte).*
Could you speak more slowly please? kuhn du vuh *snehl* o *tah*-luh lee-teh *long-suhm*-muh-rreh?	*Kan du vara snäll och tala lite långsammare?*
Could you repeat that? kuhn doo *up-rrea*-puh *deh?*	*Kan du upprepa det?*
How do you say ...? hürr *say*-ehrr muhn ...?	*Hur säger man ...?*
What does that mean? vuh beh-*tü*-dehrr *dea?*	*Vad betyder det?*

I speak ...	yuh *tah*-luhrr ...	*Jag talar ...*
Danish	*duhn-skuh*	*danska*
Dutch	*hol-lehn*-skuh	*holländska*
English	*ehng*-ehl-skuh	*engelska*
Finnish	*fin-skuh*	*finska*
French	*frruhn-skuh*	*franska*
German	*tüs-kuh*	*tyska*
Italian	i-tuhl-*yean*-skuh	*italienska*
Norwegian	*nosh-kuh*	*norska*
Swedish	*svehn-skuh*	*svenska*

Some Useful Phrases

Sure.	yuh-*vist*	*Javisst.*
Just a minute.	eht *er*-gon-*blik!*	*Ett ögonblick!*
It's (not) important.	deh air (*in*-teh) *vik-tit*	*Det är (inte) viktigt.*
It's (not) possible.	deh air (*oo-*)*mey-lit*	*Det är (o-)möjligt.*
Good luck!	*lük*-kuh *til!*	*Lycka till!*

BODY LANGUAGE

Swedes aren't very different from other westerners when it comes to body language. They nod their head for yes and shake it for no. An unarticulated little **uhuh** or **umh** always means 'yes' and is often accompanied by nodding. 'No' is **nej** or **nähä** or a plain shake of the head without a sound.

You'll find that the Swedes will want to shake hands with you every time you meet, men and women alike. Kissing on the cheek is becoming more common among close friends, but the old hand shake is still the most common form of greeting.

SIGNS

BAGAGEINLÄMNING	BAGGAGE COUNTER
DAMER/HERRAR	LADIES/GENTLEMEN
EJ INGÅNG	NO ENTRY
FÖRBJUDET	PROHIBITED
GRATIS INTRÄDE	FREE ADMISSION
INCHECKNING	CHECK-IN COUNTER
INFORMATION/UPPLYSNINGAR	INFORMATION
INGÅNG	ENTRANCE
NÖDUTGÅNG	EMERGENCY EXIT
RESERVERAD	RESERVED
RÖKNING FÖRBJUDEN	NO SMOKING
TELEFON	TELEPHONE
TOALETTER	TOILETS
TULL	CUSTOMS
UTGÅNG	EXIT
VARM/KALL	HOT/COLD
ÖPPET/STÄNGT	OPEN/CLOSED

PAPERWORK

address	uh-*drrehs*	*adress*
age	*ol*-dehrr	*ålder*
birth certificate	pa-*shoon*-beh-*vees*	*personbevis*
border	grrehns	*gräns*
date of birth	*fer*-dehl-seh-*dah*-tum	*födelsedatum*
driver's licence	*cher-rr-koort*	*körkort*
identification	leh-gi-ti-muh-*fhoon*	*legitimation*
immigration	*puhs*-kont-*rrol*	*passkontroll*
marital status	si-*veel-stond*	*civilstånd*
name	nuhmn	*namn*
nationality	nuht-fhoo-nuh-li-*teat*	*nationalitet*
passport (number)	*puhs*(-*num*-mehrr)	*pass(nummer)*
place of birth	*fer*-dehl-seh-*oort*	*födelseort*
profession	*ürr-keh*	*yrke*
reason for travel	*rrea*-suhns	*resans*
	ehn-duh-*morl*	*ändamål*
religion	rreh-li-*yoon*	*religon*
sex	chern	*kön*
tourist card	tu-*rrist-koort*	*turistkort*
visa	*vee-sum*	*visum*

GETTING AROUND

What time does the ... leave/arrive?	hürr duhks *gor-rr*/ *kom*-mehrr ...?	*Hur dags går/ kommer ...?*
(aero)plane	*(flüg-)plah*-neht	*(flyg)planet*
boat	*bor*-tehn	*båten*
bus	*bu*-sehn	*bussen*
ferry	*farr-yuhn*	*färjan*
train	*tor*-geht	*tåget*
tram	*spor-rr-vuhng*-nehn	*spårvagnen*

Directions

Where is ...?
vahrr *air/lig*-**gehrr** ...? — *Var är/ligger ...?*

How do I get to ...?
hürr *kom*-**mehrr muhn til** ...? — *Hur kommer man till ...?*

Is it near here?
air deh *longt* **haer-i**-*frrorn?* — *Är det långt härifrån?*

Can I walk there?
kuhn muhn *gor deet?* — *Kan man gå dit?*

Can you show me (on the map)?
kuhn du *vee*-**suh may** (**po** *kah-rtuhn)?* — *Kan du visa mig (på kartan)?*

Are there other means of getting there?
kuhn muhn kom-muh *deet* **po** *uhn*-**nuht** *seht?* — *Kan jag komma dit på annat sätt?*

Go straight ahead.
gor *rrahkt frruhm* — *Gå rakt fram.*

SIGNS

ANKOMST	ARRIVALS
AVGÅNG	DEPARTURES
BAGAGEUTLÄMNING	LUGGAGE PICKUP
BILJETTKONTOR	TICKET OFFICE
BUSSHÅLLPLATS	BUS STOP
FLYGBUSS	AIRPORT BUS
GÅNGTUNNEL	SUBWAY (pedestrian)
JÄRNVÄGSSTATION	TRAIN STATION
PASSKONTROLL	IMMIGRATION
SPÅR	PLATFORM
SPÅRVAGNSHÅLLPLATS	TRAM STOP
TIDTABELL	TIMETABLE
TUNNELBANA	SUBWAY (metro)
VÄXEL	CHANGE (for coins)

Turn left/ right at the ...	*svehng* til *vehns*-tehrr/ *her*-gehrr veed ...	*Sväng till vänster/ höger vid ...*
next	*nehst*-uh	*nästa*
corner	*her-rn*	*hörn*
traffic lights	trruh-*feek-yü*-seht	*trafikljuset*
behind	*bah-kom*	*bakom*
in front of	*frruhm-fer-rr*	*framför*
far	longt	*långt*
near	*nae-rruh*	*nära*
opposite	*mit* eh-*moot*	*mitt emot*

Booking Tickets

Where can I buy a ticket?	
vahrr kuhn yuh *ker*-puh ehn bil-*yeht?*	*Var kan jag köpa en biljett?*
I want to go to ...	
yuh vil *or*-kuh til ...	*Jag vill åka till ...*
Do I need to book?	
mos-teh muhn *boo-kuh?*	*Måste man boka?*
I'd like to book a seat to ...	
yuh *skul*-leh vil-yuh *boo*-kuh ehn *pluhts* til ...	*Jag skulle vilja boka en plats till ...*

I'd like (a) ...	yuh *skul*-leh vil-yuh *hah* ...	*Jag skulle vilja ha ...*
one-way ticket	ehn *ehn*-kehl-bil-*yeht*	*en enkelbiljett*
return ticket	ehn rreh-*türr*-bil-*yeht*	*en returbiljett*
two tickets	*tvor* bil-*yeht*-ehrr	*två biljetter*
student's fare	ehn stu-*dehnt*-bil-*yeht*	*en studentbiljett*
child's fare	ehn *bahrn*-bil-*yeht*	*en barnbiljett*
pensioner's fare	puhn-fhoo-*naesh*-bil-*yeht*	*en pensionärs-biljett*
1st class	*fersh*-tuh *kluhs*	*första klass*
2nd class	*uhn*-drruh *kluhs*	*andra klass*

Is it completely full?
arr deat *uhl*-**deh-lehs** *fult?* — *Är det alldeles fullt?*
Can I get a stand-by ticket?
fins deh non *vehn*-**teh-**_lis_-**tuh?** — *Finns det någon väntelista?*

Air

Is there a flight to ...?
fins deh not *flüg* **til ...?** — *Finns det något flyg till ...?*
How long does the flight take?
hürr long teed *tahrr flü*-**geht?** — *Hur lång tid tar flyget?*
What is the flight number?
vil-keht *flight-num*-**mehrr** *air* **deh?** — *Vilket flightnummer är det?*

airport tax	*flüg*-**pluhts**-*skuht*	*flygplatsskatt*
boarding pass	*boo*-**rding**-*kahrd*	*boardingcard*
customs	**tul**	*tull*

Bus

Where is the bus/tram stop?
vahrr air *bus*-**hol**-*pluht*-**sehn/** *spor-rr*-**vuhngns-hol**-*pluht*-**sehn?** — *Var är busshållplatsen/ spårvagnshållplatsen?*
Which bus goes to ...?
vil-kehn *bus* **gor-rr til ...?** — *Vilken buss går till ...?*
Could you let me know when we get to ...?
kuhn du seh-ya *til* **naer vi** *kom*-**mehrr til ...?** — *Kan du säga till när vi kommer till ...?*
I want to get off!
yuh vil gor *ahv!* — *Jag vill gå av!*

What time is the ... bus?	**naer gor-rr ...?**	*När går ...?*
next	*nehs*-**ta** *bus*	*nästa buss*
first	*fersh*-**tuh** *bu*-**sehn**	*första bussen*
last	*sis*-**tuh** *bu*-**sehn**	*sista bussen*

Metro

Which line takes me to ...?
vil-kehn *leen*-**yeh gor-rr til** ...? — *Vilken linje går till ...?*

What is the next station?
vil-kehn air *nehs*-**tuh stuh-***fhoon?* — *Vilken är nästa station?*

Train

Is this the right platform for the train to/from ...?
air deh *haer rreht* **pa-***rrong* **fer-rr** *tor*-**geht til/frrorn** ...? — *Är det här rätt perrong för tåget till/från ...?*

Passengers for ... must change trains in ...
rrea-**suhn-deh moot** ... — *Resande mot ...*
mos-teh *bü*- **tuh** *torg* **i** ... — *måste byta tåg i ...*

The train leaves from platform ...
torg-**eht** *ahv-gor-rr* **frrorn** *spor-rr* ... — *Tåget avgår från spår ...*

dining car	**rrehs-tu-***rruhng-vuhngn*	*resturangvagn*
express	**ehx-***prrehs-torg*	*expresståg*
local	**loo-***kahl-torg*	*lokaltåg*
sleeping car	*sorv-vuhngn*	*sovvagn*

SWEDISH

Taxi

Can you take me to ...?
kuhn doo *cher*-**rruh may til** ...? — *Kan du köra mig till ...?*

How much does it cost to go to ...?
vuh *kos*-**tuhrr deh til** ...? — *Vad kostar det till ...?*

Here is fine, thank you.
haer **bleer** *brrah* **tuhk** — *Här blir bra, tack.*

The next corner, please.
nehs-**tuh** *her-rn* **tuhk** — *Nästa hörn, tack.*

Continue!
foort-sheht! — *Fortsätt!*

Stop here!
stuhn-uh *haer!* — *Stanna här!*

Please slow down.
kuhn du suhk-tuh *nearr?* — *Kan du sakta ner?*

Please wait here.
kuhn du *vehn*-**tuh** *haer?* — *Kan du vänta här?*

Some Useful Phrases

The train is delayed/cancelled.
tor-**geht air fer-***shea*-**nuht/** *in-stehlt* — *Tåget är försenat/ inställt.*

How long will it be delayed?
hurr *mük-keh* **air deh fer-***shea*-**nuht?** — *Hur mycket är det försenat?*

How long does the trip take?
hurr long *teed tuhrr rrea*-**suhn?** — *Hur lång tid tar resan?*

Is it a direct route?
air deh ehn di-*rrehkt*-**fer-rr-***bin*-**dehl-seh?** — *Är det en direktförbindelse?*

Is that seat taken?
air deh *up-tah*-**geht** *haer?* — *Är det upptaget här?*

I want to get off at ...
yuh vil gor *ahv* **ee ...** — *Jag vill gå av i ...*

Where can I hire a bicycle?
vahrr kuhn yuh *hü*-**rruh ehn** *sük*-**kehl?** — *Var kan jag hyra en cykel?*

SWEDISH

HOW FAR?

In Sweden, all road signs show distance in kilometres, but the Swedes prefer to use the term mil (meel) for 10 km when they talk about how far away a place is, eg. 50 km is fem mil

Car

Where can I rent a car?
vahrr kuhn yuh *hü*-rruh ehn beel?
Var kan jag hyra en bil?

How much is it daily/weekly?
hurr mük-keh kos-tuhrr deh parr *dahg*/parr *vehk-kuh?*
Hur mycket kostar det per dag/per vecka?

Does that include insurance/mileage?
in-gor-rr fer-*shaek*-rring/ *free*-uh *meel?*
Ingår försäkring/ fria mil?

Where's the next petrol station?
vahrr air *nehs*-tuh behn-*seen*-stuh-*fhoon?*
Var är nästa bensinstation?

How long can I park here?
hurr *lehng*-eh for-rr muhn puhrr-*kea*-rruh *haer?*
Hur länge får man parkera här?

Does this road lead to?
gor-rr dehn *haer vair*-gehn til ...?
Går den här vägen till ...?

SWEDISH

SIGNS

BILMEKANIKER	MECHANIC
BILUTHYRNING	CAR RENTAL
BILVERKSTAD/GARAGE	GARAGE
BLYFRI BENSIN	UNLEADED
EJ INFART	NO ENTRY
ENKELRIKTAT	ONE WAY
FÖRBJUDET ATT STANNA	NO STANDING
MOTORVÄG	FREEWAY
PARKERING FÖRBJUDEN	NO PARKING
REPARATIONER	REPAIRS
SJÄLVBETJÄNING	SELF SERVICE
STOPP	STOP
SUPER/HÖGOKTANIG BENSIN	SUPER
VÄJNINGSPLIKT	GIVE WAY

air (for tyres)	**luft**	*luft*
battery	**buh-teh-***rree*	*batteri*
brakes	*brrom-suhrr*	*bromsar*
clutch	*kop-ling*	*koppling*
driver's licence	*cher-rr-koort*	*körkort*
engine	*moo-to-rr*	*motor*
fan belt	*flehkt-rrehm*	*fläktrem*
lights	*lü-seh*	*lyse*
oil	*ol-yuh*	*olja*
puncture	**punk-***tea***-rring**	*punktering*
radiator	*chü***-luh-rreh**	*kylare*
road map	*vairg-kah***-rtuh**	*vägkarta*
studded winter tyres	*dub-dehk*	*dubbdäck*
tyres	**dehk**	*däck*
windscreen	**vind-rrü-tuh**	*vindruta*
windscreen wipers	*vind***-rrü-teh-***to-rr***-kuh-rreh**	*vindrutetorkare*
windscreen washer fluid	*spoo***-luhrr-***vehts***-kuh**	*spolarvätska*

SWEDISH

I need a mechanic.
yuh beh-*her***-vehrr ehn meh-***kah***-ni-kehrr** — *Jag behöver en mekaniker.*

The battery is flat.
buh-teh-*rree***-eht air** *slüt* — *Batteriet är slut.*

The radiator is leaking.
*chü***-luh-rrehn** *lehk***-kehrr** — *Kylaren läcker.*

I have a flat tyre.
yuh hahrr fot punk-*tea***-rring** — *Jag har fått punktering.*

It's overheating.
*moo***-to-rn** *koo-kuhrr* — *Motorn kokar.*

It's not working.
dehn *gor-rr* **in-teh** — *Den går inte.*

ACCOMMODATION

Where is	vahrr *fins* deh	*Var finns det*
a ... hotel?	eht ... hoo-*tehl?*	*ett ... hotell?*
cheap	*bil*-lit	*billigt*
good	*brrah*	*bra*
nearby	*naer*-lig-guhn-deh	*närliggande*

What is the address?
vil-kehn uh-*drrehs air* deh? *Vilken adress är det?*
Could you write the address, please?
kuhn du skrree-vuh *Kan du skriva*
nearr uh-*drrehs*-sehn? *ner adressen?*

At the Hotel

Do you have any rooms available?
fins deh nor-grruh *Finns det några*
lea-di-guh *rrum?* *lediga rum?*
I'd like to share a dorm.
yuh *skul*-leh vil-yuh *Jag skulle vilja*
boo ee *sorv-sahl* *bo i sovsal.*

I'd like a ...	yuh *skul*-leh vil-yuh *hah* ...	*Jag skulle vilja ha ...*
single room	eht *ehn*-kehl-*rrum*	*ett enkelrum*
double room	eht *dub*-behl-*rrum*	*ett dubbelrum*
bed	ehn *sehng*	*en säng*

I want a room	yuh vil *hah*	*Jag vill ha*
with a ...	eht *rrum* meh ...	*ett rum med ...*
balcony	buhl-*kong*	*balkong*
bathroom	*bahd*	*bad*
shower	dufh	*dusch*
television	*tea-vea*	*teve*
window	*fern*-stehrr	*fönster*

SWEDISH

I'm going to stay for ...	yuh tehn-kehrr *stuhn-nuh* ...	*Jag tänker stanna ...*
one day	*ehn dah*	*en dag*
two days	*tvor dah-guhrr*	*två dagar*
one week	*ehn veh-kuh*	*en vecka*

Do you have identification?
hahrr du leh-gi-ti-muh-*fhoon?* — *Har du legitimation?*

Your membership card, please.
dit *mead*-lehms-*koort tuhk* — *Ditt medlemskort, tack.*

Sorry, we're full.
tü-*varr* air deh *ful*-beh-*luhkt* — *Tyvärr är det fullbelagt.*

How long will you be staying?
hurr lehng-eh *stuhn*-nuhrr *ni?* — *Hur länge stannar ni?*

It's ... per day/per person.
deh *kos-tuhrr* ... parr *dahg*/ parr pa-*shoon* — *Det kostar ... per dag/ per person.*

How much is it per night/ per person?
hurr mük-keh *kos*-tuhrr deh parr *nuht*/parr pa-*shoon?* — *Hur mycket kostar det per natt/per person?*

Can I see the room?
kuhn yuh for *sea rrum*-meht? — *Kan jag få se rummet?*

Are there any other/cheaper rooms?
fins deh nor-grruh *uhnd*-rruh/ *bil*-li-guh-rreh *rrum?* — *Finns det några andra/ billigare rum?*

Is there a reduction for students/ children?
fins deh stu-*dehnt*-rruh-*buht*/ *bahrn*-rruh-*buht?* — *Finns det studentrabatt/ barnrabatt?*

Does it include breakfast?
***in-gor-rr frru*-kost i *prree*-seht?** — *Ingår frukost i priset?*

It's fine, I'll take it.
deht bleer *brrah* yuh *tahrr* deh — *Det blir bra, jag tar det.*

I'm not sure how long I'm staying.
yuh *veat* in-teh hurr *lehng*-eh yuh *stuhn*-uhrr
Jag vet inte hur länge jag stannar.

Is there a lift?
fins deh *his*?
Finns det hiss?

Where is the bathroom?
vahrr air *bahd-rrum*-meht?
Var är badrummet?

Do you have a safe where I can leave my valuables?
hahrr ni non fer-rr-*vah*-rrings-*boks* daer yuh kuhn *lehm*-nuh mee-nuh *vaer*-deh-*sah*-kehrr?
Har ni någon förvaringsbox där jag kan lämna mina värdesaker?

Is there somewhere to wash clothes?
fins deh non *tveht-stü*-guh?
Finns det någon tvättstuga?

Can I use the kitchen?
kuhn yuh *uhn-vehn*-duh *ker*-keht?
Kan jag använda köket?

May I use the telephone?
for-rr yuh *lor*-nuh teh-leh-*for*-nehn?
Får jag låna telefonen?

Requests & Complaints

Please wake me up at ...
kuhn ni *vehk*-kuh may klok-kuhn ...?
Kan ni väcka mig klockan ...?

The room needs to be cleaned.
rrum-meht beh-her-vehrr *stair-duhs*
Rummet behöver städas.

I can't open/close the window.
yuh kuhn in-teh *erp-nuh*/ *stehng-uh fernst*-rreht
Jag kan inte öppna/ stänga fönstret.

I've locked myself out of my room.
yuh hahrr lorst may *ü-teh*
Jag har låst mig ute.

The toilet won't flush.
too-uh-*leht*-tehn *spoo*-luhrr *in*-teh
Toaletten spolar inte.

I (don't) like this room.

yuh tük-kehrr (*in*-teh) *om* deh *haer rrum*-meht	*Jag tycker inte om det här rummet.*

It's too ...	deh air fer-rr ...	*Det är för ...*
dark	*mer-rrkt*	*mörkt*
expensive	*dürt*	*dyrt*
noisy	*bul-rrit*	*bullrigt*
small	*lee-teht*	*litet*

Some Useful Words & Phrases

I'm/We're leaving now.

yah/vee skuh *or*-kuh *nü*	*Jag/Vi ska åka nu.*

I'd like to pay the bill.

yuh *skul*-leh vil-yuh beh-*tah*-luh *rrairk*-ning-*ehn*	*Jag skulle vilja betala räkningen.*

name	nuhmn	*namn*
surname	*ehf*-tehrr-*nuhmn*	*efternamn*
address	uh-*drrehs*	*adress*
room number	*rrums-num*-mehrr	*rumsnummer*
air-conditioning	*luft*-kon-di-fhoo-*nea*-rring	*lufikonditionering*
balcony	buhl-*kong*	*balkong*
bathroom	*bahd-rrum*	*badrum*
bed	sehng	*säng*
blanket	filt	*filt*
chair	stool	*stol*
clean (adj)	rreant	*rent*
cot	*bahrn-sehng*	*barnsäng*
cupboard	skorp	*skåp*
dirty	*smut-sit*	*smutsigt*
double bed	*dub*-behl-*sehng*	*dubbelsäng*
electricity	ehl-ehk-trri-si-*teat*	*elektricitet*
excluded	*in*-gor-rr *ay*	*ingår ej*
fan	flehkt	*fläkt*
heater	*varr*-meh-eh-leh-*mehnt*	*värmeelement*

included	*in*-beh-*rraek*-nuht/ *in-gor-rr*	*inberäknat/ ingår*
key	*nük-kehl*	*nyckel*
lift (elevator)	hiss	*hiss*
light bulb	*glerd-luhm*-puh	*glödlampa*
a lock	lors	*lås*
mattress	muh-*drruhs*	*madrass*
mirror	*spea-gehl*	*spegel*
padlock	*hehng-lors*	*hänglås*
pillow	*kud-deh*	*kudde*
quiet	tüst	*tyst*
quilt	*teh-keh*	*täcke*
refrigerator	*chül-skorp*	*kylskåp*
room (in hotel)	rrum	*rum*
sauna	*buhs-tu*	*bastu*
sheet	*lah-kuhn*	*lakan*
shower	dufh	*dusch*
soap	tvorl	*tvål*
suitcase	*rreas-vehs*-kuh	*resväska*
swimming pool	*sim*-buh-*sehng*	*simbassäng*
table	boord	*bord*
toilet (paper)	too-uh-*leht*(-*puhp*-pehrr)	*toalett(papper)*
towel	*huhn-dook*	*handduk*
(hot/cold) water	*(vuhrrm-/kuhl-)vuht*-ehn	*(varm/kall)vatten*
window	*fern*-stehrr	*fönster*

SIGNS

CAMPINGPLATS	CAMPING GROUND
FULLBELAGT/ INGA LEDIGA RUM	FULL/ NO VACANCIES
GÄSTGIVERI/PENSIONAT	GUESTHOUSE
HOTELL	HOTEL
MOTELL	MOTEL
LEDIGA RUM/RUM ATT HYRA	ROOMS AVAILABLE
VANDRARHEM	YOUTH HOSTEL

AROUND TOWN

I'm looking for	yuh *lea*-tuhrr	*Jag letar*
(the/a) ...	ehf-tehrr ...	*efter ...*
art gallery	*konst*-mu-*sea*-eht	*konstmuséet*
bank	ehn *buhnk*	*en bank*
cathedral	*doom-chürr*-kuhn	*domkyrkan*
church	*chürr-kuhn*	*kyrkan*
city centre	*sehnt*-rrum	*centrum*
... embassy	... uhm-buh-*sah*-dehn	*... ambassaden*
hotel	mit hoo-*tehl*	*mitt hotell*
market (outdoor)	*sah*-lu-*to-rr*-yeht	*salutorget*
market (indoor)	*sah*-lu-*huhl*-lehn	*saluhallen*
museum	mu-*sea*-eht	*muséet*
police	poo-*lee*-sehn	*polisen*
post office	*pos*-tehn	*posten*
public toilet	ehn oo-*fehnt*-li too-uh-*leht*	*en offentlig toalett*
public telephone	ehn teh-leh-*forn-chosk*	*en telefonkiosk*
tourist information office	tu-*rrist*-in-for-muh-*fhoon*-ehn	*turist-informationen*

What time does it open/close?	narr *erp*-nuhrr/ *stehng*-ehrr *dom?*	*När öppnar/ stänger de?*
What ... is this?	vuh air deh *haer* fer-rr ...	*Vad är det här för ...?*
road	*vairg*	*väg*
street	*gah-tuh*	*gata*
suburb	*stuhts-deal/ fer-rr-oort*	*stadsdel/ förort*

For directions, see the Getting Around section, page 319.

At the Post Office

I'd like	yuh *skul*-leh vil-yuh	*Jag skulle vilja*
to send a ...	*fhik*-kuh eht ...	*skicka ett ...*
letter	*brreav*	*brev*
postcard	*vü-koort*	*vykort*
parcel	puh-*keat*	*paket*
telegram	teh-leh-*grruhm*	*telegram*

I'd like some stamps.
yuh skul-leh vil-yuh *hah* **nor-grruh** *fhree-marr*-kehn
Jag skulle vilja ha några frimärken.

How much does it cost to send this to ...?
hurr mük-keh *kos*-**tuhrr deh uht** *fhik*-**uh deh** *haer* **til ...?**
Hur mycket kostar det att skicka det här till ...?

an aerogram	eht ae-rroo-*grruhm*	*ett aerogram*
airmail	*flüg-post*	*flygpost*
envelope	ku-*vaer*	*kuvert*
mailbox	*brreav-lor* -duh	*brevlåda*
registered mail	rreh-kom-mehn-*dea*-rruht	*rekommenderat*
	brreav	*brev*
surface mail	*üt-post*	*ytpost*

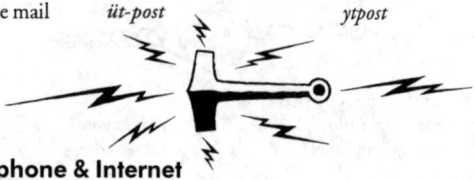

Telephone & Internet

Can I use the telephone, please?
kuhn *yah* **fo** *lor*-**nuh teh-leh-***for***-nehn?**
Kan jag få låna telefonen?

I want to ring ...
yuh vil *rring*-**uh til ...**
Jag vill ringa till ...

The number is ...
num-**rreht air ...**
Numret är ...

How much does a three-minute call cost?
hurr mük-keh *kos*-**tuhrr eht** *trrea*-**mi**-*nü*-**tehsh-suhm**-*tahl?*
Hur mycket kostar ett treminuterssamtal?

How much does each extra minute cost?
hurr mük-keh *kos*-**tuhrr** *vuhrr*-**yeh** *ehks*-**trruh mi**-*nüt?*
Hur mycket kostar varje extra minut?

I'd like to speak to (Göran Persson).
yuh *skul*-**leh vil-yuh** *tah*-**luh meh (yer-rruhn** *pae*-**shon)**
Jag skulle vilja tala med (Göran Persson).

I want to make a reverse-charges phone call.
yuh *skul*-**leh vil-yuh** *yer*-**rruh eht** *bea-ah*-**suhm**-*tahl*
Jag skulle vilja göra ett ba-samtal.

What is the area code for ...?
vuh air *rrikt-num*-**rreht til ...?**
Vad är riktnumret till ...?

It's engaged.
deh air *up-tah*-**geht**
Det är upptaget.

I've been cut off.
suhm-tahl-**eht** *brrerts*
Samtalet bröts.

Is there an Internet cafe nearby?
fihns **deh not** *in*-**tehrr-neht-kuh**-*fea* **i** *naer-hea*-**tehn?**
Finns det något Internet-kafé i närheten?

Can I access the Internet from here?
kuhn **yuh kop-luh** *up* **may por** *in*-**tehrr-neht** *haer*-**i**-*frrorn?*
Kan jag koppla upp mig på Internet härifrån?

I'd like to check my e-mail.
yuh *skul*-**leh vil-yuh**-*kol*-**luh min** *ea-mail*
Jag skulle vilja kolla min e-mail.

computer	*dah-to*-**rr**	*dator*
public telephone	**teh-leh**-*forn-chosk*	*telefonkiosk*
telephone directory	**teh-leh**-*forn-kuh-tuh-lorg*	*telefonkatalog*

At the Bank

I want to exchange some money/ travellers cheques.
yuh *skul*-**leh vil-yuh** *vehks*-**luh** *pehng*-**uhrr/** *rrea*-**seh-** *chehk*-**kuhrr** — *Jag skulle vilja växla pengar/resecheckar.*

What is the exchange rate?
vuh air *vehks*-**ehl-** *ku*-**shehn?** — *Vad är växelkursen?*

How many kronor per dollar?
hurr mong-uh *krroo*-**ner parr** *dol*-**luhrr?** — *Hur många kronor per dollar?*

automatic teller machine	**buhn-koo-***maht*	*bankomat*
bank draft	*post-vehk*-**sehl**	*postväxel*
bank notes	*sead-luhrr*	*sedlar*
cashier	*kuhs-suh*/**kuh-***ser*	*kassa/kassör*
coins	**münt**	*mynt*
credit card	**krreh-***deet-koort*	*kreditkort*
to exchange	*vehks-luh*	*växla*
foreign exchange	*üt-lehnsk* **vuh-***lü-tuh*	*utländsk valuta*
loose change	*smor-pehng*-**uhrr**	*småpengar*
signature	*un*-**dehrr-***skrrift*	*underskrift*

SWEDISH

INTERESTS & ENTERTAINMENT

Sightseeing

Do you have a guidebook/map of ...?
hahrr ni ehn *rrea*-**seh-huhnd-***book/* *kah-rtuh* **er-vehrr ...?** — *Har ni en resehandbok/ karta över ...?*

What are the main attractions?
vilk-**uh air** *hü*-**vud-uht-rruhk-***fhoon***-**ehrr-nuh?** — *Vilka är huvudattraktionerna?*

What is that?
vuh air *dea?* — *Vad är det?*

How old is it?
hurr *guhm*-**muhl** *air* **dehn?** — *Hur gammal är den?*

May I take photographs?
for-rr yuh foo-too-grruh-*fea*-rruh? *Får jag fotografera?*
What time does it open/close?
hurr *duhks erp*-nuhrr/ *stehng*-ehrr dom? *Hur dags öppnar/ stänger de?*

ancient	*foo-rn-tee*-duh	*forntida*
archaeological	uhrr-keh-o-*lor*-gisk	*arkeologisk*
beach	strruhnd	*strand*
bridge	brroo	*bro*
building	*büg-nuhd*	*byggnad*
castle	slot	*slott*
cathedral	*doom-chürr*-kuh	*domkyrka*
church	*chürr-kuh*	*kyrka*
concert hall	kon-*saer-hüs*	*konserthus*
island	er	*ö*
lake	fher	*sjö*
library	bib-lee-oo-*teak*	*bibliotek*
the main square	*stoorr-to-rr*-yeht	*stortorget*
market (outdoor)	*to-rry-huhn*-dehl	*torghandel*
market (indoor)	*sah*-lu-*huhl*	*saluhall*
monastery	*klos*-tehrr	*kloster*
monument	mo-nu-*mehnt*	*monument*
mosque	mos-*kea*	*moské*
the old city	guhm-luh *stahn*	*gamla stan*
palace	puh-*luhts*/slot	*palats/slott*
opera house	*oo*-peh-rruh-*hüs*	*operahus*
river	or/ehlv	*å/älv*
ruins	rru-*ee*-nehrr	*ruiner*
the sea	*hah*-veht	*havet*
square	*to*-rry	*torg*
stadium	*ee*-drrots-*pluhts*	*idrottsplats*
statues	stuh-*tü*-ehrr	*statyer*
synagogue	*sü*-nuh-*goo*-guh	*synagoga*
temple	*tehm*-pehl	*tempel*
university	u-ni-va-shi-*teat*	*universitet*

Going Out

What's there to do in the evenings?

vuh fins deh uht *yer*-rruh po *kvehl*-luhrr-*nuh?*	*Vad finns det att göra på kvällarna?*

Are there places where you can hear Swedish folk music?

fins* deh not *stehl-leh* daer muhn kuhn *her*-rruh *svehnsk folk*-mu-*seek?	*Finns det något ställe där man kan höra svensk folkmusik?*

How much does it cost to get in?

hurr mük-keh *kos*-tuhrr deh ee *in-trrair*-deh?	*Hur mycket kostar det i inträde?*

cinema	*bee*-oo	*bio*
concert	kon-*saer*	*konsert*
discotheque	dis-koo-*teak*	*diskotek*
nightclub	*nuht-klub*	*nattklubb*
theatre	teh-*ah*-tehrr	*teater*

Sports & Interests

What sports do you play?

vil-kuh *spo-rtehrr üt*-er-vuhrr du?	*Vilka sporter utövar du?*

What are your interests?

vuh hahrr du fer-rr in-*trrehs-sehn?*	*Vad har du för intressen?*

art	konst	*konst*
bandy (team sport on ice)	*buhn*-dü	*bandy*
basketball	*bahs*-keht	*basket*
canoeing	uht *puh*-dluh kuh-*noot*	*att paddla kanot*
chess	fhuhk	*schack*
collecting ...	yuh *suhm*-luhrr ...	*Jag samlar ...*
computer games	*dah*-to-rr-*speal*	*datorspel*
dancing	duhns	*dans*
fishing	uht *fis-kuh*	*att fiska*
football	*foot-boll*	*fotboll*
hiking/trekking	uht *vuhn-drruh*	*att vandra*
horse riding	uht *rree-duh*	*att rida*
icehockey	*ees-hok*-kü	*ishockey*
martial arts	*kuhmp-spo*-rtehrr	*kampsporter*
meeting	uht trrehf-fuh	*att träffa*
(new) friends	(*nü*-uh) *vehn-nehrr*	*(nya) vänner*
movies	film	*film*
music	mu-*seek*	*musik*
photography	foo-too-grruh-*fea*-rring	*fotografering*
reading	uht *lair-suh*	*att läsa*
running	uht *sprring-uh/yog-guh*	*att springa/jogga*
sailing	uht *seag-luh*	*att segla*
shopping	uht *shop-puh*	*att shoppa*
skating	uht or-kuh *skrri*-sker	*att åka skridskor*
(downhill) skiing	uht or-kuh (*slah*-lom)/*fhee-der*	*att åka (slalom)/skidor*
swimming	uht *sim-muh/bah-duh*	*att simma/bada*
tennis	*tehn*-nis	*tennis*
travelling	uht *rrea-suh*	*att resa*
visiting friends	uht gor *hehm* til *kom*-pi-suhrr	*att gå hem till kompisar*
walking	uht gor *üt* o *gor*	*att gå ut och gå*

Festivals

Lucia is celebrated 13 December, which was the longest night in the old calendar. During the dark ages it was vital to make sure the evil forces of darkness didn't get a foothold, so people feasted with lots of food and bright lights. These days, **Lucia**, a young woman wearing a crown of candles, and her followers all dressed in white and carrying candles, sing traditional songs and serve golden saffron buns in the early morning hours.

On the first Sunday of Advent the first of four candles, one for every Sunday of Advent, is lit in every home. The big Christmas celebrations take place on **julafton**, the evening of 24 December. The tree, **julgranen**, is decorated with candles, tinsel, home-made crackers, hearts and a star on top and the Christmas table is laden with food.

On Christmas Day morning, the churches are lit with candles for the pre-dawn service, **Julottan**. In central Sweden you may see people arrive at church in a horse drawn sleigh. To wish someone a merry Christimas, you say **God Jul**!

In some cultures Lent (**Fastan**) is observed as a time of fasting, but not in Sweden! Instead the Swedes indulge in traditional Shrove Tuesday fare of delicious **fastlagsbullar** or **semlor** (sweet buns with almond paste and cream) after a meal of **bruna bönor och fläsk** (brown beans and pork). The home is decorated with **fastlagsris**, small birch or willow branches with coloured feathers tied to them.

Easter, **Påsk**, is in the beginning of spring – daffodils are called **påskliljor** (Easter lilies) in Swedish. Eggs are painted in delicate patterns before being served and some are blown empty and hung in the **påskris**, small birch branches decorated with fluffy chickens, eggs and feathers.

The **påskkärringar**, Easter hags, are said to fly off to **Blåkulla** (the Blue Hill) on Maundy Thursday to party with the devil and on **påskafton**, Easter Saturday, they return home. To prevent the witches landing in their community, people light bonfires and shoot firecrackers to scare them off. Children dress up as **påskkärringar** and go around with Easter letters to their neighbours calling out **Glad Påsk**!

On 30 April, **Valborgsmässoafton** (Walpurgis Night), Sweden celebrates the coming of spring with predominantly male choirs singing traditional songs by huge bonfires.

Perhaps the most exotic of all Swedish festivals, **Midsommar** (Midsummer) is celebrated all over the country. The maypole, **majstången**, decorated with leaves and flowers, is erected in an open space. People who have a traditional costume wear it, and girls wear wreaths of flowers in their hair. Everyone dances around the maypole and sings traditional songs until late into the night that never really goes beyond dusk.

Throughout the year there are also many local cultural festivals and events all over Sweden. To mention but a few:

Jokkmokk Winter Market in Lapland since 1602. Meet the Same people and their reindeer at this unique cultural event.

Vasaloppet is 85 km of skiing from Sälen to Mora in Dalecarlia, following the tracks of King Gustav Vasa in the 1520s.

Himlaspelet in Leksand, Dalecarlia is an open air theatre performance in traditional costumes which has been on stage since 1941.

Stockholm Water Festival is a huge event with all sorts of activities including sports, music and fireworks.

Medieval Week, Visby, Gotland. The medieval city goes back to the 1300s with historical re-enactments, markets and a medieval banquet.

IN THE COUNTRY

Sweden offers unique possibilities for trekking, canoeing and camping as **Allemansrätten** 'Everyman's right' allows you to use all land, regardless of ownership, as long as you are careful and don't cause any damage or bother the owner. You can even pitch a tent for one night without permission, but for a caravan or a longer stay, ask the land owner first. And remember to clean up before you leave!

Weather

What's the weather like?

hürr air *vaird*-**rreht?**	*Hur är vädret?*

It's ...	**deh air ...**	*Det är ...*
cloudy	*mol-nit*	*molnigt*
cold	*kuhlt*	*kallt*
foggy	*dim-mit*	*dimmigt*
frosty	*frrost ü*-**teh**	*frost ute*
warm	*vuhrrmt*	*varmt*

It's raining.	**deh** *rrehng-nuhrr*	*Det regnar.*
It's snowing.	**deh** *sner-uhrr*	*Det snöar.*
It's sunny.	*soo*-**lehn** *fhee*-**nehrr**	*Solen skiner.*
It's windy.	**deh** *blor*-**sehrr**	*Det blåser.*

Camping

Am I allowed to camp here?

for-rr yuh *kuhm*-**puh** *haer?*	*Får jag campa här?*

Is there a campsite nearby?

fins **deh non** *kuhm*-**ping**-*pluhts* **ee** *naer-hea*-**tehn?**	*Finns det någon campingplats i närheten?*

backpack	*rrüg-sehk*	*ryggsäck*
can opener	**kon**-*sehrrv-erp*-**nuh-rreh**	*konservöppnare*
compass	**kom**-*puhs*	*kompass*
crampons	*ees-brrod*-**duhrr**	*isbroddar*
firewood	**vead**	*ved*
gas cartridge	**guh**-*sorl-fluhs*-**kuh**	*gasolflaska*

gas cylinder	guh-*sol-tüb*	*gasoltub*
hammock	*hehng-muht*-tuh	*hängmatta*
ice axe	*ees-ük*-suh	*isyxa*
mattress	muh-*drruhs*	*madrass*
mosquito repellent	*müg-ol*-yuh	*myggolja*
padlock	*hehng-lors*	*hänglås*
penknife	*fik-kneev*	*fickkniv*
rope	rreap	*rep*
tent (pegs)	*tehlt(-pin*-nuhrr)	*tält(pinnar)*
torch/flashlight	*fik-luhm*-puh	*ficklampa*
sleeping bag	*sorv-sehk*	*sovsäck*
stove (for camping)	guh-*sorl-cherk*	*gasolkök*
water bottle	*vuht*-ehn-*fluhs*-kuh	*vattenflaska*

FOOD

The Swedish **smörgåsbord** is famous throughout the world for its great variety of cold and hot dishes, but there's more to Swedish food than that. Many dishes are associated with different seasons and may be difficult to find at other times.

Spring

The first sign of spring is the **semla**, a sweet bun filled with almond paste and whipped cream, traditionally served on Tuesdays during Lent. Some prefer it in a bowl with hot milk and then it's called **hetvägg**. Following Lent is Easter with its tradition of brightly painted Easter eggs which are eaten with ham or fish dishes like **gravad lax** (cured salmon).

Summer

During summer the Swedes eat light food, with many cold meals like salads and smoked ham, lots of fish and for dessert a variety of berries (**bär**) with cream (**grädde**) or ice cream (**glass**).

During the Midsummer celebrations, **inlagd sill** (pickled herring) with sour cream and chives and new potatoes boiled with dill is a must and it's accompanied by a cold beer and a **snaps** (shot of akvavit) or two. **Jordgubbar** (strawberries) are most likely served as dessert. Ideally, this meal should be eaten outdoors.

Autumn

Towards the end of August the crayfish season is in full swing with **kräftskivor** (crayfish parties) all over the country. People wearing bibs and party hats, get together to eat **kräftor** (crayfish) boiled with dill, and drink quite a few glasses of **snaps** in between singing well-known drinking songs, **snapsvisor**.

If you're in the north, you might try their autumn specialty, **surströmming** (fermented herring), which tastes somewhat better than it smells. It's eaten with raw onion on **tunnbröd** (thin bread) or **knäckebröd** (crisp bread), and quite a few **snapsar**.

Autumn also sees an abundance of funghi, **svamp**, in the woods. Try **kantareller**, which should be available at markets and well-stocked grocery stores throughout the season.

More berries appear in autumn such as **lingon** (lingonberries) and the northern delicacy **hjortron** (cloudberries), and apples, pears and plums are ripe on the trees.

Winter

The cold weather requires substantial meals. The traditional Thursday dinner is **ärter med fläsk** (yellow peasoup with pork) and for dessert **pannkakor med lingonsylt** (pancakes with lingonberry jam).

December 13 is **Lucia** when **lussekatter** (saffron-flavoured sweet buns), **pepparkakor** (ginger snaps) and **glögg** (mulled wine) are served by **Lucia**, and her followers.

At Christmas, a special **smörgåsbord** called **julbord** is the tradition. On the **julbord** you will find ham, different sorts of pickled herring, sausages, **kalvsylta** (brawn), patés, red cabbage, **vörtbröd** (rye bread flavoured with wort, a kind of herb) **lutfisk** (dried ling soaked in lye before being boiled), mustard, cheese, **risgrynsgröt** (sweet rice pudding) and more. A special Christmas beer, **julöl**, is served and the children get **julmust**, a sweet dark-brown soft drink which forms a head like beer when poured.

Some Useful Words & Phrases

breakfast	*frroo*-kost	*frukost*
lunch	lunfh	*lunch*
dinner	*mid*-duh	*middag*
supper	su-*peal/kvehls-morl*	*supé/kvällsmål*

Table for ..., please.
eht *boord* fer-rr ... tuhk — *Ett bord för ..., tack!*

Can I see the menu, please?
kuhn yuh for *sea* meh-*nün?* — *Kan jag få se menyn?*

What does it include?
vuh *in-gor-rr* i *dea?* — *Vad ingår i det?*

Is service included in the bill?
air sehrr-*vea*-rrings-ahv-*yif-tehn* *in-rraek*-nuhd? — *Är serveringsavgiften inräknad?*

ashtray	eht *uhsk-faht*	*ett askfat*
the bill	*noo-tuhn*	*notan*
a cup	ehn *kop*	*en kopp*
dessert	dehs-*saer*	*dessert*
a drink	*nor*-got uht *drrik-kuh*	*något att dricka*
a fork	ehn *guhf*-fehl	*en gaffel*
fresh	faeshk	*färsk*
a glass	eht *glahs*	*ett glas*
a knife	ehn *kneev*	*en kniv*
a plate	ehn *tuhl-rrik*	*en tallrik*
spicy	*vairl-krrüd*-duht	*välkryddat*
a spoon	ehn *fhead*	*en sked*
stale (bread)	tort	*torrt*
sweet	sert	*söt*
teaspoon	ehn *tea-fhead*	*en tesked*
toothpick	ehn *tuhnd-pea*-tuh-rreh	*en tandpetare*

Vegetarian Meals

I'm a vegetarian.

yuh air veh-geh-tuh-rri-*ahn*	*Jag är vegetarian.*

I don't eat meat.

yuh *ae*-tehrr *in*-teh *chert*	*Jag äter inte kött.*

I don't eat chicken, or fish, or ham.

yuh *ae*-tehrr *vuhrr*-kehn *chük*-ling ehl-lehrr *fisk* ehl-lehrr *fhing-kuh*	*Jag äter varken kyckling eller fisk eller skinka*

Spices, Herbs & Condiments

allspice	*krrüd-pehp*-puhrr	*kryddpeppar*
chives	*grraes-lerk*	*gräslök*
dill	dil	*dill*
garlic	*veet-lerk*	*vitlök*
herbs	*errt-krrü*-der	*örtkryddor*
mustard	*sea-nuhp*	*senap*
parsley	*pa-shil*-yuh	*persilja*
pepper	*pehp-puhrr*	*peppar*
salt	suhlt	*salt*
soy sauce	*soh-yuh*	*soja*
spices	*krrüd-der*	*kryddor*
sugar	*sok*-kehrr	*socker*
tomato sauce	*keht*-chup	*ketchup*
vinegar	vi-*nae*-gehrr/ *veen-eh*-ti-kuh	*vinäger/ vinättika*

Vegetables

asparagus	*spuhrr*-rris	*sparris*
beans	*ber-ner*; huh-rri-koo-*vaer*	*bönor; haricot vert*
beetroot	*rrerd-beht*-ter	*rödbetor*
Brussels sprouts	*brrüs*-sehl-*korl*	*brysselkål*
cabbage	*veet-korl*	*vitkål*
capsicum	*puhp*-rri-*kuh*	*paprika*
carrot	*moo-rroot*	*morot*
cauliflower	*bloom-korl*	*blomkål*
cucumber	*gurr-kuh*	*gurka*
leek	*purr*-yoo-*lerk*	*purjolök*

lettuce	*suhl*-luhd	*sallad*
mushrooms	svuhmp/ fham-pin-*yoo*-nehrr	*svamp/ champinjoner*
onion	lerk	*lök*
parsnip	*puhls*-tehrr-*nuhk*-kuh	*palsternacka*
peas	*a-rtehrr*	*ärter*
potato	poo-*tah*-tis	*potatis*
spinach	speh-*naht*	*spenat*
tomato	too-*maht*	*tomat*
turnip	*korl-rroot*	*kålrot*

Fruit & Berries

apple	*ehp-leh*	*äpple*
banana	buh-*nahn*	*banan*
blackberries	*bjer-rn*-baer	*björnbär*
black/ red currants	*svuh*-rtuh/ *rrer*-duh *veen*-baer	*svarta/ röda vinbär*
blueberries	*blor*-baer	*blåbär*
cherries	*chersh*-baer/ bi-guh-*rror*-ehrr	*körsbär/ bigarråer*
cloudberries	*yoort-rron*	*hjortron*
cranberries	*trrahn*-baer	*tranbär*
gooseberries	*krrüs*-baer	*krusbär*
grapefruit	*grreyp*-frrukt	*grapefrukt*
grapes	*veen-drrü*-ver	*vindruvor*
lemon	sit-*rroon*	*citron*
lingonberries	*ling-on*	*lingon*
orange	uh-pehl-*seen*	*apelsin*
peach	*pa*-shi-*kuh*	*persika*
pear	*pae-rron*	*päron*
pineapple	*uh*-nuh-nuhs	*ananas*
plum	*ploo-mon*	*plommon*
raspberries	*huhl-lon*	*hallon*
rhubarb	rruh-*buhrr*-behrr	*rabarber*
strawberries	*yoord-gub*-buhrr	*jordgubbar*
wild strawberries	*smult-rron*	*smultron*

Breakfast

bread	brrerd	*bröd*
bread roll	*smor-frruhns*-kuh/ *frru*-kost-*bul*-leh	*småfranska/ frukostbulle*
butter	smer-rr	*smör*
boiled egg	*kookt ehg*	*kokt ägg*
cereal	*fling-er/müs*-li	*flingor/müsli*
cheese	oost	*ost*
coffee	*kuh-feh*	*kaffe*
fried egg	*steakt ehg*	*stekt ägg*
jam/marmalade	sült/muhrr-meh-*lahd*	*sylt/marmelad*
milk	mjerlk	*mjölk*
orange juice	uh-pehl-*seen-yoos*	*apelsinjuice*
scrambled eggs	oo-meh-*leht*	*omelett*
sugar	*sok*-kehrr	*socker*
tea	tea	*te*
toast	rros-tuht *brrerd*	*rostat bröd*
yoghurt	*yorg*-urt	*yoghurt*

Soup

broth	bul-*yong*	*buljong*
chicken soup	*herns-sop*-puh	*hönssoppa*
fish soup	*fisk-sop*-puh	*fisksoppa*
mushroom soup	*svuhmp-sop*-puh	*svampsoppa*
vegetable soup	*grrern*-sahks-*sop*-puh	*grönsakssoppa*

Meat

beef	*nert-chert*	*nötkött*
casserole	*grrü-tuh*	*gryta*
chicken	*chük-ling*	*kyckling/broiler*
fillet of beef	*ooks*-fi-*lea*	*oxfilé*
ham	*fhing-kuh*	*skinka*
lamb chops	*luhm*-kot-*leht*-tehrr	*lammkotletter*
liver paté	*lea*-vehrr-puhs-*tehy*	*leverpastej*
meatballs	*chert-bul*-luhrr	*köttbullar*
minced beef	*chert-fash*	*köttfärs*
minced beef and pork	*bluhnd-fash*	*blandfärs*

pork (lean)	*grrees-chert*	*griskött*
pork (with fat)	*flehsk*	*fläsk*
pork chops	*flehsk*-kot-*leht*-tehrr	*fläskkotletter*
roast beef	*ooks-steak/rrost-bif*	*oxstek/rostbiff*
roast lamb	*luhm-steak*	*lammstek*
sausage/salami	ko-rrv/suh-*lah*-mi	*korv/salami*
spare ribs	*rreav*-beans-*spyehl*	*revbensspjäll*
steak	bif/uhn-trreh-*kor*	*biffentrecote*
turkey	kuhl-*koon*	*kalkon*
veal	*kuhlv-chert*	*kalvkött*

Fish & Seafood

baltic herring	*strrer-ming*	*strömming*
caviar	*rrüsk kuhv*-yuhrr	*rysk kaviar*
cod (roe)	*toshk(-rrom)*	*torsk(rom)*
cod roe cream	*kuhv*-yuhrr	*kaviar*
crab	*krruhb-buh*	*krabba*
crayfish	*krrehf-ter*	*kräftor*
eel	orl	*ål*
fish	*fisk*	*fisk*
haddock	*kol-yuh*	*kolja*
halibut	*hehl*-leh-*flund*-rruh	*hälleflundra/ helgeflundra*
herring	sil	*sill*
lobster	*hum*-mehrr	*hummer*
mackerel	*muhk-rril*	*makrill*
mussels	*mus-ler*	*musslor*
oysters	*oost-rron*	*ostron*
perch	*uhb-bor*-rreh	*abborre*
pike	*yehd-duh*	*gädda*
plaice	*rrerd-speht*-tuh	*rödspätta*
prawns	*huhfs-krrehf*-ter	*havskräftor*
salmon	luhks	*lax*
shrimps	*rrair-ker*	*räkor*
sole	*fher-tung*-uh	*sjötunga*
trout	fo-*rrehl*	*forell*
whiting	*vit-ling*	*vitling*

Desserts & Pastries

apple pie	*ehp*-pehl-*puhy*	*äppelpaj*
cake (with cream)	*tor-rtuh*	*tårta*
cake (no cream)	*myük kah*-kuh	*mjuk kaka*
cheese cake	*oost-kah*-kuh	*ostkaka*
mousse	frroo-*mahsh*	*fromage*
custard	vuh-*nily-krrairm*/ muhy-*sea-nuh*	*vaniljkräm*/ *maizena*
fruit salad	*frrukt-suhl*-luhd	*fruktsallad*
ginger snaps	*pehp*-puhrr-*kah*-ker	*pepparkakor*
ice cream	gluhs	*glass*
pancakes	*puhn-kah*-ker/ *pleht-tuhrr*	*pannkakor*/ *plättar*
whipped cream	*visp-grrehd*-deh	*vispgrädde*

Non-Alcoholic Drinks

apple juice	*ehp*-pehl-*must*	*äppelmust*
coffee	*kuhf-feh*	*kaffe*
herbal tea	*errt-tea*	*örtte*
hot chocolate	*vuhrrm* fhook-*lahd*	*varm choklad*
milk	myerlk	*mjölk*
orange juice	uh-pehl-*seen-yoos*	*apelsinjuice*
punch	*frrukt-borl*	*fruktbål*
soft drink (carbonated)	lehsk	*läsk*
cordial	suhft	*saft*
tea	tea	*te*
water	*vuht*-tehn	*vatten*

Alcoholic Drinks

beer	erl/*pils*-nehrr	*öl/pilsner*
fortified wine	*stuhrrk-veen*	*starkvin*
liqueur	li-*ker-rr*	*likör*
red/white wine	*rrerd-veen*; *vit veen*	*rödvin; vitt vin*

MENU DECODER

Breakfast

filmjölk	*feel-myerlk*	cultured milk, similar to buttermilk, eaten with cereal and a sprinkle of sugar
gröt	grrert	porridge made of rolled oats
knäckebröd	*knehk*-keh-*brrerd*	crisp bread, usually rye
välling	*vehl-ling*	gruel (Try it, you'll like it!)

Breads and Sandwiches

tunnbröd *tun-brrerd*
very thin crisp or soft bread made from barley

vörtbröd *verrt-brrerd*
rye bread flavoured with wort (a kind of herb)

franskbröd	*frruhnsk-brrerd*	white French loaf
fullkornsbröd	*ful*-koonsh-*brrerd*	whole grain loaf
grahamsbulle	*grrah*-huhms-*bul*-leh	brown bread roll
kavring	*kahv-rring*	dark sweetened rye bread
limpa	*lim-puh*	loaf of bread
rågbröd	*rrorg-brrerd*	rye bread
sötlimpa	*sert-lim*-puh	sweetened brown loaf

Swedish sandwiches are always open and if they're very elaborate you eat them with a knife and fork. In winter you may be served grilled open sandwiches, varma smörgåsar, for an evening snack. You can make a smörgås with any sort of bread, a thin spread of butter and some pålägg (any kind of sandwich topping).

landgång	'gangplank' – long gourmet sandwich with a variety of pålägg
räksmörgås	shrimps on lettuce, hardboiled egg, mayonnaise and lemon
sillsmörgås	pickled herring on cold boiled potato
smörgåstårta	a large layered sandwich with lots of different fillings, cut like a cake

Soup

kålsoppa — *korl-sohp*-puh
med frikadeller — meh frri-kuh-*dehl*-lehrr
cabbage soup with boiled meatballs (usually pork)

köttsoppa — *chert-sop*-puh
beef broth with meat and vegetables

nässelsoppa — *neh*-sehl-*sop*-puh
nettle soup with a hardboiled egg (spring only)

ärtsoppa — *art-sop*-puh
yellow pea soup with pork

Meat

Meat is quite expensive in Sweden and the Swedes have come up with a host of different ways of making a little meat go a long way. Casseroles are common, as are dishes made with minced meat like köttbullar (Swedish meatballs), but perhaps the most famous Swedish meat product is the sausage, korv, which comes in all shapes and forms.

biff á la Lindström — *bif* uh-luh *lin-strrerm*
patties of minced meat mixed with beetroot and served with a fried egg

blodpudding med lingon — *blood-pud*-ding meh *ling-on*
black pudding with lingonberry jam

bruna bönor och fläsk — brrü-nuh *ber*-ner o *flehsk*
brown beans in a sweet sauce with bacon

falukorv — *fah*-lu-*ko-rrv*
a lean sausage cut in thick slices and fried

isterband *is*-tehrr-*buhnd*
sausage of pork, beef and barley grains

kalops kuh-*lops*
meat casserole with onions and allspice

pannbiff med lök *puhn-bif* meh *lerk*
minced beef patties with lots of fried onion

pytt i panna püt-i-*puhn-nuh*
diced meat, boiled potatoes and onion fried and served with beetroot and a fried egg

rotmos och fläskkorv *rroot-moos o flehsk-ko-rrv*
boiled pork sausage with mashed turnips

varm korv *vuhrrm ko-rrv*
hot dog on a breadroll, the special comes with mashed potatoes – Swedish fast food!

viltgryta *vilt-grrü*-tuh
game casserole – try älg, elk, in October

kåldolmar	*korl-dol*-muhrr	stuffed cabbage leaves
lövbiff	*lerv-bif*	very thinly sliced beef
renskav	*rrean-skahv*	thinly sliced reindeer meat

Fish & Seafood

Sweden has an enormous coastline and thousands of lakes and fish is an important part of the diet. Kräftor (crayfish) are caught in creeks and lakes from late August and many other types of seafood are brought ashore all year round.

inlagd sill *in*-luhgd *sil*
pickled herring which comes in a great number of varieties

lutfisk *lüt-fisk*
dried ling soaked in lye before being boiled. Served with a white sauce with allspice. (Christmas only)

sotare *soo*-tuh-*rreh*
'chimney sweep' – lightly salted herring grilled over an open fire

böckling	*berk-ling*	smoked herring
gravad lax	*grrah*-vuhd *luhks*	cured salmon

Potatoes

Swedes eat potatoes with just about everything and there's a great number of ways to prepare them for the table.

Janssons frestelse — *yahn*-sons *frrehs*-tehl-*seh*
'Jansson's Temptation' – potato, onion and anchovy, oven-baked with lots of cream

raggmunkar/rårakor — *rruhg-mung*-kuhrr/*rror-rrah*-ker
pancakes made from grated potatoes

råstekt potatis — *rror-steakt* poo-*tah*-tis
raw potato slices fried in oil

skalpotatis — *skahl*-poo-*tah*-tis
potatoes boiled in their jackets

stekt potatis — *steakt* poo-*tah*-tis
fried pre-boiled potatoes

stuvad potatis — *stü*-vuhd poo-*tah*-tis
potatoes in white sauce

potatismos	poo-*tah*-tis-*moos*	mashed potatoes
potatissallad	poo-*tah*-tis-*suhl*-luhd	potato salad
färskpotatis	*fashk*-poo-*tah*-tis	new potatoes

Desserts & Pastries

chokladpudding — fhook-*lahd-pud*-ding
chocolate mousse

kanelbulle — kuh-*neal-bul*-leh
sweet roll with cinnamon and cardamon

kräm och mjölk — krrairm-o-*myerlk*
thickened berry juice with milk

mazarin — muh-suh-*rreen*
pastry with almond paste filling

nyponsoppa *nü*-pon-*sop*-puh
rose hip soup, eaten with a dollop of cream
prinsesstårta prrin-*sehs-tor*-rtuh
layered sponge cake with jam, cream and custard filling covered with green marzipan
ris á la malta *rrees* uh-luh *muhl-tuh*
rice with whipped cream and orange
schwartzwaldstårta *shvuhrtsh*-vuhlds-*tor*-rtuh
meringue, cream and chocolate cake
småländsk ostkaka *smor*-lehnsk *oost-kah*-kuh
baked curd cake with almonds
sockerkaka *sok*-kehrr-*kah*-kuh
sponge cake, usually flavoured with lemon

skorpor	*skohrr-per*	rusks
småkakor	*smor-kah*-ker	biscuits/cookies
wienerbröd	*vee*-nehrr-*brrerd*	Danish pastries

Alcoholic Drinks

Alcohol can only be purchased by those over 20 at special shops called Systembolaget. If a Swede asks you if you would like 'a drink', they probably have alcohol in mind as the word drink in Swedish denotes an alcoholic drink, usually a cocktail.

brännvin *brrehn-veen*
spirit distilled from potatoes, may be flavoured with herbs and berries or plain
glögg glerg
mulled wine with raisins and almonds, served in winter
punsch punfh
a sweet liqueur flavoured with arrack
snaps snuhps
a shot of *brännvin*. With the word Skål! a shot glass is emptied in one go.
vinbål *veen-borl*
a punch based on wine

SHOPPING

bookshop	*book-huhn*-dehl	*bokhandel*
camera shop	*foo*-too-uh-*faer*	*fotoaffär*
clothing store	*moo*-deh-bu-*teek*	*modebutik*
delicatessen	deh-li-kuh-*tehs*-uh-*faer*	*delikatessaffär*
general store	di-*veh*-sheh-*huhn*-dehl	*diversehandel*
laundry/laundrette	tveht/tveh-too-*maht*	*tvätt/tvättomat*
market (indoor)	*sah*-lu-*huhl*	*saluhall*
market (outdoor)	*to*-rry-*huhn*-dehl	*torghandel*
newsagency	*prrehs-bü*-rro/ *too*-buhks-uh-*faer*	*pressbyrå/ tobaksaffär*
pharmacy	uh-poo-*teak*	*apotek*
shoeshop	*skoo*-uh-*faer*	*skoaffär*
shop	uh-*faer*	*affär*
souvenir shop	soo-veh-*neer*-uh-*faer*	*souveniraffär*
stationers	*puhp*-pehsh-*huhn*-dehl	*pappershandel*
supermarket	*snuhb-cherp*	*snabbköp*
vegetable shop	*grrern*-sahks-uh-*faer*	*grönsaksaffär*

I'd like to buy ...
yuh *sku*-leh vil-yuh *hah* ... — *Jag skulle vilja ha ...*

Do you have others?
hahrr* ni nor-rruh *uhn-drruh? — *Har ni några andra andra?*

I (don't) like it.
yuh tük-kehrr (*in*-teh) *om* dehn/deh — *Jag tycker (inte) om den/det.*

I'm just looking.
yuh *tit*-tuhrr *bah*-rruh — *Jag tittar bara.*

How much is it?
hurr *mük*-keh *kos*-tuhrr deh? — *Hur mycket kostar det?*

Can you write down the price?
kuhn doo skrree-vuh *nearr prree*-seht? — *Kan du skriva ner priset?*

Do you accept credit cards?
tahrr* ni krreh-*deet-koort? — *Tar ni kreditkort?*

Could you lower the price?
kuhn du gor *nearr* i *prrees?* — *Kan du gå ner i pris?*

Can I help you?	
kuhn yuh *yehl*-**puh** *day?*	*Kan jag hjälpa dig?*
Will that be all?	
vahrr deh *uhlt?*	*Var det allt?*
Sorry, this is the only one.	
tü-*varr* **deh** *haer* **air**	*Tyvärr, det här är*
dehn *ehn-duh*	*den enda.*
How much/many do you want?	
hurr *mük*-**keh/**	*Hur mycket/*
mong-uh **vil du** *hah?*	*många vill du ha?*

Essential Groceries

batteries	**buh-teh-rree-ehrr**	*batterier*
bread	**brrerd**	*bröd*
butter	**smer-rr**	*smör*
cheese	**oost**	*ost*
chocolate	**fhook**-*lahd*	*choklad*
cooking oil	*maht-ol*-**yuh**	*matolja*
dishwashing liquid	*disk-mea*-**dehl**	*diskmedel*
eggs	**ehg**	*ägg*
flour (plain)	*vea*-**teh**-*myerl*	*vetemjöl*
ham	*fhing-kuh*	*skinka*
honey	*hor-nung*	*honung*
marmalade	**muhrr-meh**-*lahd*	*marmelad*
matches	*tehnd-stik*-**korr**	*tändstickor*
milk	**myerlk**	*mjölk*
pepper	*pehp-puhrr*	*peppar*
rice	**rrees**	*ris*
salt	**suhlt**	*salt*
shampoo	*fham*-**poo**	*schampo*
soap	**tvorl**	*tvål*
sugar	*sok*-**kehrr**	*socker*
toilet paper	**too-uh**-*leht-puhp*-**pehrr**	*toalettpapper*
toothpaste	*tuhn-krrairm*	*tandkräm*
washing powder	*tveht-mea*-**dehl**	*tvättmedel*

AT THE MARKET

Basics

bread	brrerd	*bröd*
butter	smer-rr	*smör*
cereal	*fling-er/müs*-li	*flingor/müsli*
cheese	oost	*ost*
chocolate	fhook-*lahd*	*choklad*
cooking oil	*maht-ol*-yuh	*matolja*
eggs	ehg	*ägg*
flour (plain)	*vea*-teh-*myerl*	*vetemjöl*
marmalade	muhrr-meh-*lahd*	*marmelad*
milk	myerlk	*mjölk*
pasta	*pahs-tah/ nood-lahr*	*pasta/nudlar*
rice	rrees	*ris*
sugar	*sok*-kehrr	*socker*
water	*vuht*-tehn	*vatten*
yoghurt	*yorg*-urt	*yoghurt*

Meat & Poultry

beef	*nert-chert*	*nötkött*
chicken	*chük-ling*	*kyckling/broiler*
ham	*fhing-kuh*	*skinka*
lamb	luhm	*lamm*
meat	chert	*kött*
pork	*grees-chert/*	*griskött* (lean)/
(with fat)	*flehsk*	*fläsk*
sausage/salami	ko-rrv/suh-*lah*-mi	*korv/salami*
turkey	kuhl-*koon*	*kalkon*
veal	*kuhlv-chert*	*kalvkött*

Vegetables

beans	*ber-ner*; huh-rri-koo-*vaer*	*bönor; haricot vert*
beetroot	*rrerd-beht*-ter	*rödbetor*
cabbage	*veet-korl*	*vitkål*
capsicum	*puhp*-rri-*kuh*	*paprika*

carrot	*moo-rroot*	morot
cauliflower	*bloom-korl*	blomkål
cucumber	*gurr-kuh*	gurka
lettuce	*suhl*-luhd	sallad
mushrooms	svuhmp/ fham-pin-*yoo*-nehrr	svamp/ champinjoner
onion	lerk	lök
peas	*a-rtehrr*	ärter
potato	poo-*tah*-tis	potatis
spinach	speh-*naht*	spenat
tomato	too-*maht*	tomat
vegetables	*grrern*-sahk-ehrr	grönsaker

Seafood

cod	toshk	torsk
crayfish	*krrehf-ter*	kräftor
fish	*fisk*	fisk
herring	sil	sill
lobster	*hum*-mehrr	hummer
mussels	*mus-ler*	musslor
oysters	*oost-rron*	ostron
salmon	luhks	lax

Fruit

apple	*ehp-leh*	äpple
banana	buh-*nahn*	banan
fruit	frrukt	frukt
grapes	*veen-drrü*-ver	vindruvor
lemon	sit-*rroon*	citron
orange	uh-pehl-*seen*	apelsin
peach	*pa*-shi-*kuh*	persika
pear	*pae-rron*	päron
plum	*ploo-mon*	plommon
strawberries	*yoord-gub*-buhrr	jordgubbar

Souvenirs

earrings	*er-rr-behng*-ehn	*örhängen*
glassware	glahs	*glas*
handicraft	*behm-sleyd*	*hemslöjd*
necklace	*huhls-buhnd*	*halsband*
pottery	cheh-rruh-*meek*	*keramik*
ring	*rring*	*ring*

Clothing

bathers	*bahd-drrehkt*/ *bahd-bük*-sorr	*baddräkt*/ *badbyxor* (f/m)
clothing	*klae*-dehrr	*kläder*
coat	*kuhp-puh*/rrok	*kappa*/*rock* (f/m)
dress	*klehn-ning*	*klänning*
jacket	*yak-kuh*	*jacka*
jumper (sweater)	*trrer-yuh*	*tröja*
shirt	*fhoo-rtuh*	*skjorta*
shoes	skoorr	*skor*
skirt	chool	*kjol*
trousers/pants	*bük-ser*	*byxor*

It doesn't fit.
dehn *puhs*-uhrr *in*-teh — *Den passar inte.*

It's too ...	dehn air fer-rr ...	*Den är för ...*
big/small	*stoorr/lee-tehn*	*stor/liten*
long/short	*long/kort*	*lång/kort*
loose/tight	*veed/trrong*	*vid/trång*

Materials

brass	*mehs-sing*	*mässing*
cotton	*boom-ul*	*bomull*
fabric	tüg	*tyg*
flax	leen	*lin*
gold	guld	*guld*
handmade	*huhnd-yoord*	*handgjord*
hand woven	*behm-vairvd*	*hemvävd*

leather	*lair*-dehrr	*läder*
linen	*lin-neh*	*linne*
silk	*sil-kehl see-dehn*	*silke/siden*
silver	*sil*-vehrr	*silver*
wood	trrair	*trä*
wool	*ül-leh*	*ylle*

Colours

black	svuhrt	*svart*
blue	blor	*blå*
brown	brrün	*brun*
green	grrern	*grön*
orange	o-*rruhnsh*	*orange*
pink	*rror*-suh/fhaer	*rosa/skär*
purple	*lee*-luh	*lila*
red	rrerd	*röd*
white	veet	*vit*
yellow	gül	*gul*

Toiletries

comb	kuhm	*kam*
condoms	kon-*dor*-mehrr	*kondomer*
deodorant	dea-oo-doo-*rruhnt*	*deodorant*
hairbrush	*hor-rr-bosh*-teh	*hårborste*
moisturising cream	*hüd-krrairm*	*hudkräm*
mosquito repellent	*müg-ohl*-yuh	*myggolja*
razor	*rrahk-hü*-vehl	*rakhyvel*
razor blades	*rrahk-blahd*	*rakblad*
sanitary napkins	*dahm-bin*-der	*dambindor*
shampoo	*fham*-poo	*schampo*
shaving cream	*rrahk-tvorl*	*raktvål*
soap	tvorl	*tvål*
sunblock cream	*sool-krrairm*	*solkräm*
tampons	tuhm-*pong*-ehrr	*tamponger*
tissues	*nairs-dü*-kuhrr	*näsdukar*
toilet paper	too-uh-*leht-puh*-pehrr	*toalettpapper*
toothbrush	*tuhn-bosh*-teh	*tandborste*

Stationery & Publications

envelope	ku-*vaer*	*kuvert*
map	*kah-rtuh*	*karta*
newspaper (in English)	(*ehng*-ehlsk) *tee*-ning	*(engelsk) tidning*
novels in English	*ber*-kehrr po *ehng*-ehls-kuh	*böcker på engelska*
paper	*puh-pehrr*	*papper*
pen	*pehn-nuh*	*penna*
scissors	suhks	*sax*

Photography

How much is it to process this film?

hurr mük-eht *kost*-**uhrr deh uht** *frruhm*-**kuhl-luh dehn** *haer fil*-**mehn?**	*Hur mycket kostar det att framkalla den här filmen?*

When will it be ready?

naer air dehn *klahrr?*	*När är den klar?*

I'd like a film for this camera.

yuh skool-leh vil-yuh *hah* **ehn** *film* **til dehn** *haer kahm*-**rruhn**	*Jag skulle vilja ha en film till den här kameran.*

B&W (film)	*svuhrt-veet film*	*svart-vit film*
battery	buh-teh-*rree*	*batteri*
camera	*kahm*-rruh	*kamera*
colour (film)	*farry-film*	*färgfilm*
copy	ko-*pee-uh*	*kopia*
film	film	*film*
flash	blikst	*blixt*
lens	ob-yehk-*teev*	*objektiv*
light meter	*yüs-mair*-tuh-rreh	*ljusmätare*

Smoking

A packet of cigarettes, please.

eht puh-*keat*	*Ett paket*
si-guh-*rreht*-tehrr *tuhk*	*cigarretter, tack.*

Are these cigarettes strong/mild?

air dom *haer*	*Är de här*
si-guh-*rreht*-tehrr-nuh	*cigarretterna*
stuhrr-kuh/mil-duh?	*starka/milda?*

Do you have a light?

hahrr du *ehld?*	*Har du eld?*

May I smoke here?

for-rr yuh *rrer*-kuh *haer?*	*Får jag röka här?*

cigarette papers	**si-guh-*rreht-puhp*-pehrr**	*cigarrettpapper*
cigarettes	**si-guh-*rreht*-tehrr**	*cigarretter*
filtered	***fil*-tehrr**	*filter*
lighter	***tehn*-duh-*rreh***	*tändare*
matches	***tehnd-stik*-korr**	*tändstickor*
menthol	**mehn-*torl***	*mentol*
pipe	***pee-puh***	*pipa*
tobacco (pipe)	***(peep-)too*-buhk**	*(pip)tobak*

Sizes & Comparisons

small	***lee-tehn***	*liten*
big	**stoorr**	*stor*
heavy	**tung**	*tung*
just right	***lah-gom***	*lagom*
light (not heavy)	**leht**	*lätt*
more	**mearr**	*mer*
less	***min*-drreh**	*mindre*
too much/many	**fer-rr *mük-keh/mong-uh***	*för mycket/många*
many	***mong-uh***	*många*
enough	***til-rrehk*-lit**	*tillräckligt*
also	***ok-so***	*också*
a little bit	***lee*-teh *grruhn***	*lite grand*

HEALTH

Where is the ...?	vahrr air ...?	*Var är ...?*
chemist	uh-poo-*tea*-keht	*apoteket*
dentist	*tuhnd-lair*-kuh-rrehn	*tandläkaren*
doctor	*dok*-to-rn	*doktorn*
hospital	*fhük-hü*-seht	*sjukhuset*

I'm/My friend is sick.
yuh air/min *vehn* air *fhük* — *Jag är/Min vän är sjuk.*

Could I see a female doctor?
kuhn yuh for *trrehf*-fuh ehn *kvin*-li *lair*-kuh-rreh? — *Kan jag få träffa en kvinnlig läkare?*

What's the matter?
vuh air deh fer-rr *feal* po *day?* — *Vad är det för fel på dig?*

Where does it hurt?
vahrr yer-rr deh *oont?* — *Var gör det ont?*

I have ...	yuh hahrr ...	*Jag har ...*
It hurts here.	deht yer-rr *oont haer*	*Det gör ont här.*

Parts of the Body

ankle	*vrris*-tehn	*vristen*
arm	*uhrr*-men	*armen*
back	*rrüg*-gehn	*ryggen*
chest	*brrerst*-eht	*bröstet*
ear	*er-rruht*	*örat*
eye	*er-guht*	*ögat*
finger	*fing*-rreht	*fingret*
foot	*foo*-tehn	*foten*
hand	*huhn*-dehn	*handen*
head	*hü-veht*	*huvudet*
heart	*yarr-tuht*	*hjärtat*
leg	*bea*-neht	*benet*
mouth	*mun*-nehn	*munnen*
nose	*nair-suhn*	*näsan*
ribs	*rreav-bea*-nehn	*revbenen*
skin	*hü*-dehn	*huden*

spine	*rrüg-rrah*-dehn	*ryggraden*
stomach	*mah-gehn*	*magen*
teeth	*tehn*-dehrr-nuh	*tänderna*
throat	*huhl*-sehn	*halsen*
wrist	*huhnd-lea*-dehn	*handleden*

Ailments

an allergy	ehn uh-lehrr-*gee*	*en allergi*
anaemia	*blood-brrist*	*blodbrist*
a blister	ehn *blor-suh*	*en blåsa*
a burn	eht *brrehn-sor-rr*	*ett brännsår*
a cold	ehn fer-*chül*-ning	*en förkylning*
constipation	fer-*shtop*-ning	*förstoppning*
a cough	*hoos-tuh*	*hosta*
diarrhoea	dee-uh-*rrea*	*diarré*
fever	*fea*-behrr	*feber*
glandular fever	*ker*-rtehl-*fea*-behrr	*körtelfeber*
headache	*hü*-vud-*varrk*	*huvudvärk*
hepatitis	heh-puh-*teet/gül-soot*	*hepatit/gulsot*
indigestion	*dor*-li	*dålig*
	maht-smehlt-ning	*matsmältning*
an infection	ehn in-fehk-*fhoon*	*en infektion*
influenza	in-flu-*ehn*-suh	*influensa*
lice	lers	*löss*
low/high	*lorgt/hergt*	*lågt/högt*
blood pressure	*blood-trrük*	*blodtryck*
motion sickness	*ork-fhü*-kuh	*åksjuka*
a pain	oont	*ont*
sore throat	oont i *huhl*-sehn	*ont i halsen*
sprain	*stük-ning*	*stukning*
a stomachache	oont i *mah*-gehn	*ont i magen*
sunburn	*sool-brrehn*-nuh	*solbränna*
urinary tract infection	*blors*-kuh-*tuhrr*	*blåskatarr*
venereal disease	*cherns*-fhük *-doom*	*könssjukdom*
worms	*muhsk* i *mah*-gehn	*mask i magen*

Some Useful Words & Phrases

I'm ...	yuh air ...	*Jag är ...*
asthmatic	uhst-*mah*-ti-kehrr	*astmatiker*
diabetic	dee-uh-*bea*-ti-kehrr	*diabetiker*
epileptic	eh-pi-*lehp*-ti-kehrr	*epileptiker*

I'm allergic to antibiotics/penicillin.
yuh air uh-*lehrr*-gisk moot uhn-ti-bi-*or*-ti-kuh/pehn-i-si-*leen* — *Jag är allergisk mot antibiotika/penicillin.*

I'm pregnant.
yuh air grruh-*veed* — *Jag är gravid.*

I'm on the pill.
yuh air-tehrr *pea-pil*-lehrr — *Jag äter p-piller.*

I haven't had my period for ... months.
yuh hahrr *in*-teh huhft *mehns* por ... *mor*-nuh-dehrr — *Jag har inte haft mens på ... månader.*

I have been vaccinated.
yuh air vuhk-si-*nea*-rruhd — *Jag är vaccinerad.*

I have my own syringe.
yuh hahrr min *ea*-gehn *sprrü-tuh* — *Jag har min egen spruta.*

I feel better/worse.
yuh mor-rr *behr*-rreh/*sehm*-rreh — *Jag mår bättre/sämre.*

accident	*oo-lük*-kuh	*olycka*
addiction	*mis-brrük*	*missbruk*
antiseptic	uhn-ti-*sehp*-tisk	*antiseptisk*
aspirin	mang-neh-*sül*	*magnecyl*
bandage	fer-rr-*buhnd*	*förband*
band-aid	*plos*-tehrr	*plåster*
a bite	eht *beht*	*ett bett*
blood pressure	blood-*trrük*	*blodtryck*
blood test	*blood-prroov*	*blodprov*
contraceptive	prreh-vehn-*teev-mea*-dehl	*preventivmedel*
injection	*sprrü-tuh*	*spruta*
injury	*skah-duh*	*skada*
itch	*klor-duh*	*klåda*

medicine	meh-di-*seen*	*medicin*
menstruation	mehns	*mens*
nausea	*il*-luh-*mor*-ehn-deh	*illamående*
oxygen	*sü-rreh*	*syre*
panadol	puh-noo-*deel*	*panodil*
vitamins	vi-tuh-*mee*-nehrr	*vitaminer*
wound	sor-rr	*sår*

At the Chemist

I need medication for ...
yuh beh-*her*-vehrr eht *mea*-dehl moot ... — *Jag behöver ett medel mot ...*

I have a prescription.
yuh *hahrr* eht rreh-*sehpt* — *Jag har ett recept.*

At the Dentist

I have a toothache.
yuh hahrr *tuhnd-varrk* — *Jag har tandvärk.*

I've lost a filling.
yuh hahrr *tuhp*-puht ehn *plomb* — *Jag har tappat en plomb.*

I've broken a tooth.
yuh hahrr slah-git *ahv* ehn *tuhnd* — *Jag har slagit av en tand.*

My gums hurt.
yuh hahrr *oont* i *tuhnd-cher*-teht — *Jag har ont i tandköttet.*

I don't want it extracted.
yuh vil *in*-teh hah dehn *üt-drrah*-gehn — *Jag vill inte ha den utdragen.*

Please give me an anaesthetic.
yuh vil hah be-*derv*-ning — *Jag vill ha bedövning.*

TIME & DATES

What date is it today?

vil-keht ***dah*-tum air deh i-*** ***dah?*** *Vilket datum är det idag?*

What time is it?

hürr ***mük*-keh air** ***klok-kuhn?*** *Hur mycket är klockan?*

It's ...	**hun air ...**	*Hon är ...*
in the morning (early)	**por** ***mo*-rro-*** ***nehn***	*på morgonen*
in the morning (later on)	**por** ***fer-rr-mid*-duhn**	*på förmiddagen*
in the afternoon	**por** ***ehf*-tehrr-*** ***mid*-duhn**	*på eftermiddagen*
in the evening	**por** ***kvehl*-lehn**	*på kvällen*
at night	**por** ***nuht*-tehn**	*på natten*

Days of the Week

Monday	***mon*-duh**	*måndag*
Tuesday	***tees*-duh**	*tisdag*
Wednesday	***oons*-duh**	*onsdag*
Thursday	***toosh*-rduh**	*torsdag*
Friday	***frrea*-duh**	*fredag*
Saturday	***ler*-rduh**	*lördag*
Sunday	***sern*-duh**	*söndag*

Months

January	**yuh-nu-*** ***ah*-rri**	*januari*
February	**feb-rru-*** ***ah*-rri**	*februari*
March	**muhsh**	*mars*
April	**uhp-*** ***rril***	*april*
May	**muhy**	*maj*
June	***yü*-ni**	*juni*
July	***yü*-li**	*juli*
August	**uh-*** ***gus*-ti**	*augusti*
September	**sehp-*** ***tehm*-behrr**	*september*
October	**ok-*** ***too*-behrr**	*oktober*
November	**noo-*** ***vehm*-behrr**	*november*
December	**deh-*** ***sehm*-behrr**	*december*

Seasons

summer	*som-muhrr*	*sommar*
autumn	herst	*höst*
winter	*vin*-tehrr	*vinter*
spring	vor-rr	*vår*

Present

today	i-*dah*	*idag*
this morning	i-*dah* po *mo*-rro-*nehn*	*idag på morgonen*
tonight (evening)	i-*kvehl*	*i kväll*
tonight (very late)	i-*nuht*	*i natt*
this week	dehn *haer vehk-kuhn*	*den här veckan*
this year	i *or-rr*	*i år*
now	nü	*nu*

Past

yesterday	i-*gor-rr*	*igår*
day before yesterday	i-*fer*-rr-*gor*-rr	*i förrgår*
this morning	i-*mo-sheh*	*i morse*
yesterday morning	i-gor-rr *mosh-eh*	*igår morse*
last night	i-gor-rr *kvehl*	*igår kväll*
last week	i fer-rruh *vehk*-kuhn	*förra veckan*
last year	fer-rruh *or*-rreht	*förra året*

Future

tomorrow (morning)	i-*mo-rron (bit-ti)*	*i morgon (bitti)*
day after tomorrow	i *er*-vehrr-*mo*-rron	*i övermorgon*
tomorrow	i mo-rron	*i morgon*
afternoon/ evening	*ehf*-tehrr-*mid*-duh/ *kvehl*	*eftermiddag/ kväll*
next week/year	*nehs*-tuh *veh-kuh/or-rr*	*nästa vecka/år*

WHAT TIME IS IT?

Swedes often use the 24-hour system for telling the time.

During the Day

afternoon	*ehf*-tehrr-*mid*-duh	*eftermiddag*
dawn	*grrü-ning*	*gryning*
day	dahg	*dag*
dusk	*fhüm-ning*	*skymning*
early	*tee-dit*	*tidigt*
evening	kvehl	*kväll*
late	seant	*sent*
late morning	*fer-rr-mid*-duh	*förmiddag*
midnight	*meed-nuht*	*midnatt*
morning	*mo-rron*	*morgon*
night	nuht	*natt*
noon	*mit* po *dahn;* klo-kuhn *tolv*	*mitt på dagen; klockan tolv*

NUMBERS & AMOUNTS

0	nol	*noll*
1	eht	*ett*
2	tvor	*två*
3	trrea	*tre*
4	*fü-rruh*	*fyra*
5	fehm	*fem*
6	sehx	*sex*
7	fhü	*sju*
8	*ot-tuh*	*åtta*
9	*nee-oo*	*nio*
10	*tee-oo*	*tio*
11	*ehl-vuh*	*elva*
12	tolv	*tolv*
13	*trreh-ton*	*tretton*
14	*fyoo-rton*	*fjorton*
15	*fehm-ton*	*femton*
16	*sehx-ton*	*sexton*
17	*fhu-ton*	*sjutton*
18	*ah-rton*	*arton*
19	*ni-ton*	*nitton*

20	*chü*-goo	*tjugo*
21	chü-goo-*eht*	*tjugoett*
30	*trreh*-ti	*trettio*
40	*fer*-rti	*fyrtio*
50	*fehm*-ti	*femtio*
60	*sehx*-ti	*sextio*
70	*fhu*-ti	*sjuttio*
80	*ot*-ti	*åttio*
90	*ni*-ti	*nittio*
100	eht *hun*-drruh	*ett hundra*
101	hun-drruh-*eht*	*hundraett*
1000	eht *tü*-sehn	*ett tusen*
one million	ehn mil-*yoon*	*en miljon*
one billion	ehn mil-*yahrd*	*en miljard*
1st	*fersh-rtuh*	*första*
2nd	*uhnd-rruh*	*andra*
3rd	*trread-yeh*	*tredje*
1/4	ehn *fyae*-rdeh-*deal*/ehn *kvartsh*	*en fjärdedel/en kvarts*
1/3	ehn *trrea*-dyeh-*deal*	*en tredjedel*
1/2	ehn *huhlv*	*en halv*
3/4	trrea *fyae*-rdeh-*dea*-luhrr/ trrea *kvartsh*	*tre fjärdedelar/ tre kvarts*

Some Useful Words

Enough!	deh *rrehk*-kehrr!	*Det räcker!*
a little (amount)	lee-teh *grruhn*	*lite grand*
double	*dub*-behl	*dubbel*
a dozen	eht *dus-sin*	*ett dussin*
few	nor-grruh *for*	*några få*
just right	*lah-gom*	*lagom*
less	*min*-drreh	*mindre*
many	*mong-uh*	*många*
more	*mea*-rruh	*mera*
once	*ehn gong*	*en gång*
a pair	eht *pahrr*	*ett par*

percent	prroo-*sehnt*	*procent*
some	*nor-grruh*	*några*
too much	fer-rr *mük-keh*	*för mycket*
twice	*tvor gong-ehrr*	*två gånger*

ABBREVIATIONS

AB	limited corporation
avd	department
dl	decilitre (100 ml)
e Kr/f Kr	AD/BC
EU	European Union
exkl	excluded
FN	United Nations
fr o m	from and including
Gbg	Göteborg (Gothenburg)
hg	hecto (100 grams)
Hr/Fr/Frk	Mr/Mrs/Miss
inkl	included
jvgstn	railway station
kg	kilogram
kl	at (about time)
km	kilometre
kr	kronor (Swedish currency)
M	Motorists' National Organisation
moms	VAT/GST – sales tax
N/S/Ö/V	north/south/east/west
Obs!	Important
osv	and so on
Rea	Sale
SAS	Scandinavian Airlines System
SJ	Swedish railways
STF	Swedish Tourism Organisation
Sthlm	Stockholm
T-bana	underground, metro
t o m	until and including
tr	stairs (in an address)

EMERGENCIES

Help!	*yehlp!*	*Hjälp!*
Fire!	*ehl*-dehn air *lers!*	*Elden är lös!*
Thief!	tuh *fuhst chü*-vehn!	*Ta fast tjuven!*
Call the police!	rring poo-*lee*-sehn!	*Ring polisen!*
I'm lost.	yuh hahrr got *vil-seh*	*Jag har gått vilse.*

It's an emergency!
deh air ehn *nerd*-si-tu-uh-*fhoon!*
Det är ett nödsituation!

There's been an accident!
deh hahrr *helmt* **ehn** *oo-lük*-kuh!
Det har hänt en olycka!

Call a doctor/an ambulance!
rring ehf-tehrr ehn *dok*-to-rr/ ehn uhm-boo-*luhns!*
Ring efter en doktor/ en ambulans!

I've been raped.
yuh hahrr blee-vit *vold-tah*-gehn
Jag har blivit våldtagen.

I've been robbed!
yuh hahrr blee-vit *rror-nuhd!*
Jag har blivit rånad!

Where is the police station?
vahrr air poo-*lees*-stuh-*fhoo*-nehn?
Var är polisstationen?

Go away!
fer-*shvin!*; *gor* din *vairg!*
Försvinn!; Gå din väg!

I'll call the police!
yuh *kuhl*-luhrr po poo-*lees!*
Jag kallar på polis!

I'm/My friend is ill.
yuh air/min *vehm* air *fhook*
Jag är/Min vän är sjuk.

Where are the toilets?
vahrr air too-uh-*leht*-tehn?
Var är toaletten?

Could you help me please?
kuhn du *yehl*-puh *may?*
Kan du hjälpa mig?

Could I please use the telephone?
kuhn yuh for *lor*-nuh teh-leh-*for*-nehn?
Kan jag få låna telefonen?

I'm sorry. I apologise.
fer-*lort.* yuh bearr om *ü-shehkt*
Förlåt. Jag ber om ursäkt.

I didn't realise I was doing anything wrong.

yuh fer-*shtood* in-teh uht yuh yoo-rdeh *feal*	*Jag förstod inte att jag gjorde fel.*

I didn't do it.

yuh *yoo*-rdeh deh *in-teh*	*Jag gjorde det inte.*

I wish to contact my embassy/consulate.

yuh vil kon-*tuhk*-tuh min uhm-buh-*sahd*/mit kon-su-*laht*	*Jag vill kontakta min ambassad/mitt konsulat.*

I speak English.

yuh tah-luhrr *ehng*-ehl-skuh	*Jag talar engelska.*

I have medical insurance.

yuh hahrr *fhük*-fer-*shairk*-rring	*Jag har sjukförsäkring.*

My possessions are insured.

yuh hahrr fer-*shairk*-rring	*Jag har försäkring.*

My ... was stolen.	min ... hahrr blee-vit *stü-lehn*	*Min ... har blivit stulen.*
I've lost my ...	yuh hahrr fer-*loo*-rruht ...	*Jag har förlorat ...*
bags	mee-nuh *vehs-korr*	*mina väskor*
handbag	min *huhnd-vehs*-kuh	*min handväska*
money	mee-nuh *pehng*-uhrr	*mina pengar*
travellers cheques	mee-nuh *rrea*-seh-*chehk*-kuhrr	*mina resecheckar*
passport	mit *puhs*	*mitt pass*

INDEX

DANISH 17

Abbreviations 73
Accommodation 36-40
Age 21
Ailments 67
Air Travel 30
Amounts 71
Around Town 41-46

Bank 43
Body Language 26
Body, Parts of 66
Booking
  Accommodation 36
  Restaurant 50
  Tickets 29
Breakfast 52
Bus 31

Camping 49
Car 34
Chemist 68
Civilities 19
Clothing 62
Colours 62
Comparisons 65
Country 49

Dates 69-71
Days 69
Dentist 68
Directions 28
Drinks 57

Emergencies 75
Entertainment 44-48
Etiquette 20, 21, 48

Family 22
Feelings 24
Festivals 47-48
Food 50-59
Forms of Address 20
Fruit 56, 59

Getting Around 27-35
Going Out 46
Greetings 19, 24
Groceries 61

Health 65-69
Hotel 36

Interests 44-48
Internet 42

Kids 23

Market, At the 58-59
Materials 62
Meat 53, 58
Meeting People 20
Menu Decoder 52-56
Metro 31
Months 70

Nationalities 20
Numbers 71

Occupations 21

Paperwork 27
Photography 64
Post Office 42
Problems
  Accommodation 39
  Car 34-35
  Emergencies 75-76
  Health 65-69
  Language 25
Pronouns 18
Pronunciation 13, 17, 18
Publications 63

Quick Reference 16

Religion 22
Seafood 55, 59
Seasons 70
Shopping 60-65
Sightseeing 44
Signs 26, 31, 32, 35, 38, 75
Sizes 65
Small Talk 20
Smoking 64
Souvenirs 61
Sports 46
Stationery 63

Taxi 33

Telephone 42
Tickets 29
Time 69-71
Toiletries 63
Train 32
Vegetables 55, 58
Vegetarian Meals 50
Weather 49

FAROESE 79

Abbreviations 126
Accommodation 97-100
Age 83
Ailments 120
Air Travel 93
Amounts 125-126
Around Town 101-104
Bank 104
Boat 94
Body Language 88
Body, Parts of 120
Booking
  Accommodation 98
  Restaurant 109
  Tickets 92
Breakfast 112
Bus 93
Camping 108
Car 96
Chemist 122
Civilities 81
Clothing 115
Colours 116
Comparisons 119
Country 107
Dates 122-124
Days 123
Dentist 122
Directions 90
Drinks 113
Emergencies 127-128
Entertainment 104-107
Etiquette 81, 82
Family 85
Feelings 86
Festivals 107
Food 109-113
Forms of Address 82
Fruit 111
Getting Around 90-97
Going Out 105
Greetings 81, 82
Groceries 115
Health 119-122
Hotel 98
Interests 106-107
Internet 103
Kids 86
Main Meals 112
Materials 116
Meeting People 83
Menu Decoder 112-113
Months 123
Nationalities 83
Numbers 125-126
Occupations 84
Paperwork 89
Photography 118
Post Office 102
Prepositions 89
Problems
  Accommodation 99
  Car 96-97
  Emergencies 127
  Health 119-122
  Language 88-89
Pronouns 82
Pronunciation 13, 79
Publications 117
Quick Reference 78
Religion 84
Seafood 112
Seasons 123
Shopping 114-119

Sightseeing 104
Signs 91, 97, 108, 128
Sizes 119
Small Talk 83
Smoking 118
Souvenirs 115
Sports 106
Stationery 117
Taxi 94
Telephone 103
Tickets 92
Time 122-124
Toiletries 117
Vegetables 111
Vegetarian Meals 110
Weather 107

FINNISH 131

Abbreviations 191
Accommodation 151-156
Age 137
Ailments 184
Air Travel 146
Amounts 190
Around Town 157-159
Bank 160
Body Language 141
Body, Parts of 183
Booking
  Accommodation 154
  Restaurant 166
  Tickets 145
Breakfast 167
Bus 146
Camping 165
Car 149
Chemist 186
Civilities 134
Clothing 179
Colours 180
Comparisons 182
Country 164-165
Dates 187-189
Days 187
Dentist 186
Directions 144
Drinks 173
Emergencies 192-194
Entertainment 161-163
Etiquette .. 135, 148, 156, 162, 182
Family 138
Feelings 140
Festivals 164
Food 166-175
Forms of Address 135
Fruit 169, 175
Getting Around 143-150
Going Out 162
Grammar 143
Greetings 134, 135, 182
Groceries 178
Health 183-186
Hotel 151-156
Interests 161-163
Internet 158, 159
Kids 139
Market, At the 174-175
Materials 179
Meat 168, 174
Meeting People 136
Menu Decoder 170-172
Metro 147
Months 187
Nationalities 136
Numbers 189-190
Occupations 137
Paperwork 142
Photography 181
Post Office 158
Problems
  Accommodation 154
  Car 149-150
  Emergencies 192-194
  Health 183-186
  Language 140-141

Pronouns 133
Pronunciation 13, 132-133
Publications 181
Quick Reference 130
Religion 138
Sauna 187
Seafood 168, 175
Seasons 188
Shopping 176-182
Sightseeing 161-162
Signs 134, 142, 147, 150, 153, 165, 194
Sizes 182
Small Talk 135
Smoking 182
Souvenirs 177, 178
Sports 163
Stationery 181
Taxi 148
Telephone 159
Tickets 145
Time 187-189
Toiletries 180
Train 147
Vegetables 169, 174
Vegetarian Meals 167
Weather 164

ICELANDIC 197

Abbreviations 238
Accommodation 211-214
Age 200
Ailments 233
Air Travel 209
Amounts 237
Around Town 215-217
Bank 217
Body Language 205
Body, Parts of 232
Booking
  Accommodation 212
  Restaurant 222
  Tickets 208
Breakfast 223
Bus 209
Camping 221
Car 210
Chemist 234
Civilities 199
Clothing 229
Colours 230
Comparisons 231
Country 221
Dates 235-236
Days 235-236
Dentist 234
Directions 207
Drinks 225, 227
Emergencies 239-240
Entertainment 218-220
Etiquette 199
Family 202
Feelings 203
Festivals 220
Fish 224
Food 222-227
Forms of Address 199
Fruit 224
Getting Around 206-211
Going Out 218
Greetings 199
Groceries 228
Health 232-234
Hotel 212
Interests 218-220
Internet 217
Kids 202
Materials 229
Meat 224, 226
Meeting People 200
Menu Decoder 226-227
Months 235
Nationalities 200
Numbers 237

Occupations 201
Paperwork 206
Photography 231
Post Office 216
Problems
Accommodation 213
Car 210
Emergencies 239-240
Health 232-234
Language 204
Pronouns 198
Pronunciation 13, 198
Publications 230
Quick Reference 196
Religion 201
Seasons 236
Shopping 228-231
Sightseeing 218
Signs 205, 209, 211, 215, 239
Sizes 231
Small Talk 200
Smoking 231
Souvenirs 229
Sports 219
Stationery 230
Taxi 210
Telephone 216-217
Tickets 208
Time 235
Toiletries 230
Vegetables 225
Vegetarian Meals 222
Weather 221

INTRODUCTION 9

Abbreviations 13
Consonants 14
Diphthongs 14
Gender 12
How to Use This Phrasebook 12
Map 10-11
Polite Forms 12
Pronunciation Guide 13
Consonants 14
Diphthongs 14
Semiconsonants 14
Vowels 13
Semiconsonants 14
Transliterations 12
Vowels 13

NORWEGIAN 243

Abbreviations 301
Accommodation 261-266
Age 246
Ailments 295
Air Travel 256
Amounts 299
Around Town 266-269
Bank 269
Body Language 252
Body, Parts of 294
Booking
Accommodation 262-263
Restaurant 275
Tickets 255
Breakfast 276
Bus 256
Camping 274
Car 259-260
Chemist 296
Civilities 245
Clothing 290
Colours 293
Comparisons 293
Country 273
Dates 297-299
Days 297
Directions 253
Drinks 280, 285
Emergencies 302-304

Entertainment 270-273
Etiquette 245

Family 248
Feelings 250
Festivals 272-273
Food 275-287
Forms of Address 245
Fruit 284, 287

Getting Around 253-260
Going Out 271
Greetings 245
Groceries 289

Health 294-296
Hotel 262-266

Interests 270-273
Internet 268

Kids 249

Market, At the 286-287
Materials 291
Meat 278, 281, 282, 286
Meeting People 246
Menu Decoder 277-280
Metro 258
Months 298

Nationalities 246
Numbers 299

Occupations 247

Paperwork 252
Photography 292
Post Office 267

Problems
Accommodation 264-265
Car 259-260
Emergencies 302-304
Health 294
Language 250
Pronouns 244
Pronunciation 13, 244
Publications 291

Quick Reference 242

Religion 248

Seafood 278, 281, 287
Seasons 298
Shopping 288-293
Sightseeing 270
Signs 253, 254, 256, 257, 258, 260, 262, 274
Sizes 293
Small Talk 246-250
Smoking 292
Souvenirs 290
Sports 272
Stationery 291

Taxi 258
Telephone 268
Tickets 255
Time 297-299
Toiletries 291
Train 257

Vegetables 283, 286
Vegetarian Meals 276

Weather 273

SWEDISH 307

Abbreviations 370
Accommodation 326-330
Age 312
Ailments 363
Air Travel 321
Amounts 369-370
Around Town 331-334

Bank 334
Body Language 317
Body, Parts of 362

Booking
Accommodation 326-327
Restaurant 343
Tickets 320
Breakfast 346, 349
Bus 321

Camping 340-341
Car 324
Chemist 365
Civilities 310

Clothing 358
Colours 359
Comparisons 361
Country 340
Dates 366-368
Days 366
Dentist 365
Directions 319-320
Drinks 348, 353
Emergencies 371
Entertainment 334-339
Etiquette 310
Family 313
Feelings 315
Festivals 338-339
Food 341-353, 356-357
Forms of Address 310
Fruit 345, 357
Getting Around 318-325
Going Out 336
Greetings 310
Groceries 355
Health 362-365
Hotel 326
Interests 334-339
Internet 333
Kids 314
Market, At the 356, 357
Materials 358
Meat 346, 350, 356
Meeting People 311
Menu Decoder 349
Metro 322
Months 366
Nationalities 311
Numbers 368-369
Occupations 312
Paperwork 318
Photography 360
Post Office 332
Problems
  Accommodation 328-329
  Car 325
  Emergencies 371
  Health 362
  Language 316
Pronouns 309
Pronunciation 13, 308
Publications 360
Quick Reference 306
Religion 313
Seafood 347, 351, 357
Seasons 367
Shopping 354-361
Sightseeing 334-335
Signs 317, 324, 330
Sizes 361
Small Talk 311-315
Smoking 361
Souvenirs 358
Sports 336-337
Stationery 360
Taxi 322
Telephone 332-333
Tickets 320
Time 366-368
Toiletries 359
Train 322
Vegetables 344, 352, 356
Vegetarian Meals 344
Weather 340

LONELY PLANET

Phrasebooks

Lonely Planet phrasebooks are packed with essential words and phrases to help travellers communicate with the locals. With colour tabs for quick reference, an extensive vocabulary and use of script, these handy pocket-sized language guides cover day-to-day travel situations.

- handy pocket-sized books
- easy to understand Pronunciation chapter
- clear & comprehensive Grammar chapter
- romanisation alongside script to allow ease of pronunciation
- script throughout so users can point to phrases for every situation
- full of cultural information and tips for the traveller

'...vital for a real DIY spirit and attitude in language learning'

– Backpacker

'the phrasebooks have good cultural backgrounders and offer solid advice for challenging situations in remote locations'

– San Francisco Examiner

Arabic (Egyptian) • Arabic (Moroccan) • Australian *(Australian English, Aboriginal and Torres Strait languages)* • Baltic States *(Estonian, Latvian, Lithuanian)* • Bengali • Brazilian • Burmese • British • Cantonese • Central Asia • Central Europe *(Czech, French, German, Hungarian, Italian, Slovak)* • Eastern Europe *(Bulgarian, Czech, Hungarian, Polish, Romanian, Slovak)* • Ethiopian (Amharic) • *Farsi (Persian)* • Fijian • French • German • Greek • Hebrew • Hill Tribes • Hindi/Urdu • Indonesian • Italian • Japanese • Korean • Lao • Latin American Spanish • Malay • Mandarin • Mediterranean Europe *(Albanian, Croatian, Greek, Italian, Macedonian, Maltese, Serbian, Slovene)* • Mongolian • Nepali • Papua New Guinea • Pilipino (Tagalog) • Quechua • Russian • Scandinavian Europe *(Danish, Finnish, Icelandic, Norwegian, Swedish)* • South-East Asia *(Burmese, Indonesian, Khmer, Lao, Malay, Tagalog Pilipino, Thai, Vietnamese)* • South Pacific Languages • Spanish (Castilian) *(also includes Catalan, Galician and Basque)* • Sri Lanka • Swahili • Thai • Tibetan • Turkish • Ukrainian • USA *(US English, Vernacular, Native American languages, Hawaiian)* • Vietnamese • Western Europe *(Basque, Catalan, Dutch, French, German, Greek, Irish)*

COMPLETE LIST OF LONELY PLANET BOOKS

AFRICA Africa on a shoestring • Cairo • Cairo Map • Cape Town • Cape Town Map • East Africa • Egypt • Ethiopia, Eritrea & Djibouti • The Gambia & Senegal • Healthy Travel Africa • Kenya • Malawi • Morocco • Mozambique • Read This First: Africa • South Africa, Lesotho & Swaziland • Southern Africa • Southern Africa Road Atlas • Tanzania, Zanzibar & Pemba • Trekking in East Africa • Tunisia • Watching Wildlife East Africa • Watching Wildlife Southern Africa • West Africa • World Food Morocco • Zimbabwe, Botswana & Namibia

AUSTRALIA & THE PACIFIC Auckland • Australia • Australia Road Atlas • Bushwalking in Australia • Cycling Australia • Cycling New Zealand • Fiji • Healthy Travel Australia, NZ and the Pacific • Islands of Australia's Great Barrier Reef • Melbourne • Melbourne City Map • Micronesia • New Caledonia • New South Wales & the ACT • New Zealand • Northern Territory • Outback Australia • Out to Eat – Melbourne • Out to Eat – Sydney • Papua New Guinea • Queensland • Rarotonga & the Cook Islands • Samoa • Solomon Islands • South Australia • South Pacific • Sydney • Sydney Map • Sydney Condensed • Tahiti & French Polynesia • Tasmania • Tonga • Tramping in New Zealand • Vanuatu • Victoria • Walking in Australia • Watching Wildlife Australia • Western Australia

CENTRAL AMERICA & THE CARIBBEAN Bahamas, Turks & Caicos • Baja California • Bermuda • Central America on a shoestring • Costa Rica • Cuba • Dominican Republic & Haiti • Eastern Caribbean • Guatemala • Guatemala, Belize & Yucatán: La Ruta Maya • Havana • Healthy Travel Central & South America • Jamaica • Mexico • Mexico City • Panama • Puerto Rico • Read This First: Central & South America • World Food Mexico • Yucatán

EUROPE Amsterdam • Amsterdam Map • Amsterdam Condensed • Andalucía • Austria • Barcelona • Barcelona Map • Belgium & Luxembourg • Berlin • Berlin Map • Britain • Brussels, Bruges & Antwerp • Brussels Map • Budapest • Budapest Map • Canary Islands • Central Europe • Corfu & the Ionians • Corsica • Crete • Crete Condensed • Croatia • Cycling Britain • Cycling France • Cyprus • Czech & Slovak Republics • Denmark • Dublin • Dublin Map • Eastern Europe • Edinburgh • Estonia, Latvia & Lithuania • Europe on a shoestring • Finland • Florence • France • Frankfurt Condensed • Georgia, Armenia & Azerbaijan • Germany • Greece • Greek Islands • Hungary • Iceland, Greenland & the Faroe Islands • Ireland • Istanbul • Italy • Krakow • Lisbon • The Loire • London • London Map • London Condensed • Madrid • Malta • Mediterranean Europe • Moscow • Mozambique • Munich • the Netherlands • Norway • Out to Eat – London • Paris • Paris Map • Paris Condensed • Poland • Portugal • Prague • Prague Map • Provence & the Côte d'Azur • Read This First: Europe • Romania & Moldova • Rome • Rome Map • Russia, Ukraine & Belarus • Scandinavian & Baltic Europe • Scotland • Sicily • Slovenia • South-West France • Spain • St Petersburg • St Petersburg Map • Sweden • Switzerland • Trekking in Spain • Tuscany • Venice • Vienna • Walking in Britain • Walking in France • Walking in Ireland • Walking in Italy • Walking in Spain • Walking in Switzerland • Western Europe • World Food France • World Food Ireland • World Food Italy • World Food Spain

COMPLETE LIST OF LONELY PLANET BOOKS

INDIAN SUBCONTINENT Bangladesh • Bhutan • Delhi • Goa • Healthy Travel Asia & India • India • Indian Himalaya • Karakoram Highway • Kerala • Mumbai (Bombay) • Nepal • Pakistan • Rajasthan • Read This First: Asia & India • South India • Sri Lanka • Tibet • Trekking in the Indian Himalaya • Trekking in the Karakoram & Hindukush • Trekking in the Nepal Himalaya

ISLANDS OF THE INDIAN OCEAN Madagascar & Comoros • Maldives • Mauritius, Réunion & Seychelles

MIDDLE EAST & CENTRAL ASIA Bahrain, Kuwait & Qatar • Central Asia • Dubai • Iran • Israel & the Palestinian Territories • Istanbul • Istanbul Map • Istanbul to Cairo on a shoestring • Jerusalem • Jerusalem Map • Jordan • Lebanon • Middle East • Oman & the United Arab Emirates • Syria • Turkey • World Food Turkey • Yemen

NORTH AMERICA Alaska • Boston • Boston Map • Boston Condensed • British Colombia • California & Nevada • California Condensed • Canada • Chicago • Chicago Map • Deep South • Florida • Great Lakes • Hawaii • Hiking in Alaska • Hiking in the USA • Honolulu • Las Vegas • Los Angeles • Los Angeles Map • Louisiana & The Deep South • Miami • Miami Map • Montreal • New England • New Orleans • New York City • New York City Map • New York City Condensed • New York, New Jersey & Pennsylvania • Oahu • Out to Eat – San Francisco • Pacific Northwest • Puerto Rico • Rocky Mountains • San Francisco • San Francisco Map • Seattle • Southwest • Texas • Toronto • USA • Vancouver • Virginia & the Capital Region • Washington DC • Washington, DC Map • World Food Deep South, USA • World Food New Orleans

NORTH-EAST ASIA Beijing • Beijing Map • China • Hiking in Japan • Hong Kong • Hong Kong Map • Hong Kong Condensed • Hong Kong, Macau & Guangzhou • Japan • Korea • Kyoto • Mongolia • Seoul • Shanghai • South-West China • Taiwan • Tokyo • World Food – Hong Kong

SOUTH AMERICA Argentina, Uruguay & Paraguay • Bolivia • Brazil • Buenos Aires • Chile & Easter Island • Colombia • Ecuador & the Galapagos Islands • Healthy Travel Central & South America • Peru • Read This First: Central & South America • Rio de Janeiro • Rio de Janeiro Map • Santiago • South America on a shoestring • Santiago • Trekking in the Patagonian Andes • Venezuela

SOUTH-EAST ASIA Bali & Lombok • Bangkok • BangkokMap • Cambodia • Hanoi • Healthy Travel Asia & India • Ho Chi Minh City • Indonesia • Indonesia's Eastern Islands • Jakarta • Java • Laos • Malaysia, Singapore & Brunei • Myanmar (Burma) • Philippines • Read This First: Asia & India • Singapore • Singapore Map • South-East Asia on a shoestring • Thailand • Thailand's Islands & Beaches • Thailand, Vietnam, Laos & Cambodia Road Atlas • Vietnam • World Food Thailand • World Food Vietnam

Also available; Journeys travel literature, illustrated pictorials, calendars, diaries and Lonely Planet videos. For more information on Lonely Planet products and services, visit our website at **www.lonelyplanet.com**.

439.5 Sca6
Scandinavian phrasebook
FEB 15 2002

www.lonelyplanet.com

shoestring guides	for travellers with more time than money
condensed guides	highlights the best a destination has to offer
citySync	digital city guides for Palm TM OS
outdoor guides	walking, cycling, diving and watching wildlife
phrasebooks	don't just stand there, say something!
city maps and road atlases	essential navigation tools
world food	for people who live to eat, drink and travel
out to eat	a city's best places to eat and drink
read this first	invaluable pre-departure guides
healthy travel	practical advice for staying well on the road
journeys	travel stories for armchair explorers
pictorials	lavishly illustrated pictorial books
eKno	low cost international phonecard with e-services
TV series and videos	on the road docos
web site	for chat, Upgrades and destination facts
lonely planet images	on line photo library

LONELY PLANET OFFICES

Australia
Locked Bag 1, Footscray,
Victoria 3011
☎ 03 9689 4666
fax 03 9689 6833
email: talk2us@lonelyplanet.com.au

UK
10a Spring Place,
London NW5 3BH
☎ 020 7428 4800
fax 020 7428 4828
email: go@lonelyplanet.co.uk

USA
150 Linden St, Oakland,
CA 94607
☎ 510 893 8555
TOLL FREE: 800 275 8555
fax 510 893 8572
email: info@lonelyplanet.com

France
1 rue du Dahomey,
75011 Paris
☎ 01 55 25 33 00
fax 01 55 25 33 01
email: bip@lonelyplanet.fr
website: www.lonelyplanet.fr

World Wide Web: www.lonelyplanet.com *or* AOL keyword: lp
Lonely Planet Images: lpi@lonelyplanet.com.au